Bankruptcy: An Action Plan for Renewal

By the Editors of Socrates

SOCRATES™
KNOW HOW TO DO MORE
AND SAVE

Socrates Media, LLC
227 West Monroe, Suite 500
Chicago, IL 60606
www.socrates.com

Special discounts on bulk quantities of Socrates books and products are available to corporations, professional associations and other organizations. For details, contact our Special Sales Department at 800.378.2659.

This publication is designed to provide accurate and authoritative information in regard to the subject matter covered. It is sold with the understanding that the publisher is not engaged in rendering legal, accounting or other professional service. If legal advice or other expert assistance is required, the services of a competent professional person should be sought.

From a Declaration of Principles Jointly Adopted by a Committee of the American Bar Association and a Committee of Publishers and Associations

ISBN 1-59546-246-5

This product is not intended to provide legal or financial advice or substitute for the advice of an attorney or advisor.

Printing number 10 9 8 7 6 5 4 3 2 1

Bankruptcy:
An Action Plan
for Renewal

Special acknowledgment to the following:

Katharine Norman, Managing Editor; Ann Heinz, JD, Associate Editor; Lucas Otto, JD, Editor; Chip Butzko, Encouragement Press, Production; Jeannie Staats, Product Manager; Derek Vander Laan, Cover Art; Peri Hughes, Editor; Alison Somilleda, Copy Editor; Kristen Grant, Production Associate; Edgewater Editorial Services, Inc.

Get the most out of Bankruptcy: An Action Plan for Renewal.

Take advantage of the enclosed CD and special access to Bankruptcy: An Action Plan for Renewal resource section of Socrates.com that are included with this purchase.

The CD and Bankruptcy: An Action Plan for Renewal resource section offer readers a unique opportunity both to build on the material contained in the book and to utilize tools such as forms, checklists, spreadsheets and appraisals that will save time and money. More than $100 worth of free forms and content are provided.

The CD bound into the back cover contains a read-only version of this book. Readers can access the dedicated Bankruptcy resource section by registering their purchase at Socrates.com. A special eight-digit Registration Code is provided on the CD. Once registered, a variety of free forms, checklists, appraisals, research articles, government forms and other useful tools are available at

www.socrates.com/books/bankruptcy-renewal.aspx.

From time to time, new material will be added and readers will be informed of changes in the law, as well as updates to the content of this book.

Finally, readers are offered discounts on selected Socrates products designed to help implement and manage their business and personal matters more efficiently.

Table of Contents

Section One

SOCRATES™
KNOW HOW TO DO MORE
AND SAVE

1 How This Book Can Help

Before you file for personal bankruptcy, it is very important to understand the process, and to make an informed decision. This book has up-to-date information on the significant changes that passed into American law in 2005. There is also information throughout for Canadian residents, including a specific overview of Canadian bankruptcy procedures.

You are probably reading this book because you have financial problems and are seeking a solution to them. Perhaps you have reached the point where you have built up so much debt that you just cannot see a way to pay it all off. You do not know how to cope without some help and advice. All you can think about right now is finding a way to get those creditors off your back, but you just do not know where to start.

It may be that your income has suddenly decreased unexpectedly, or your spending has spiraled out of control and you just do not know how to make things better. Whatever your reasons for considering bankruptcy, this book can help you understand the options open to you, and give you clear advice on how to proceed.

What Is in This Book?

This book provides you with comprehensive information on the two types of personal bankruptcy, Chapters 7 and 13, and explains the difference between them. Around 90 percent of bankruptcies filed fall into one of these two categories. Chapter 11—which is for individuals or corporations engaged in business—generally requires an attorney and is not within the scope of this book.

This book will help you decide which kind of personal bankruptcy best suits your situation, or whether either makes economic sense for you at this time. In addition to explaining the process of filing for bankruptcy in detail, there are chapters outlining the information you must gather, the forms you need to complete, and what will happen during and after the filing process.

Before you file for bankruptcy, you need to understand exactly what bankruptcy is and what it is not. Although everyone tends to think they know what bankruptcy is, you may be surprised to find out what it means to file for bankruptcy and how the law operates—especially in light of recent changes. This book answers many of the questions that most people ask and provides guidance on where to find more detailed information on the subject.

Finally, there are a few chapters to help you move forward after you emerge from bankruptcy. There is guidance on how to improve your credit rating after bankruptcy and where to get good financial counseling (and some tips on how to avoid the less scrupulous folks lurking out there).

Why Me?

Why do people get into debt? At first glance, the reasons for getting into insurmountable debt may seem obvious: if you spend more money than you have coming in, you will have insufficient funds to meet your bills. If you continue this trend for a long time, the debts—and the interest you must pay on them—will increase. But in a society that thrives on lending and credit, where it is common to buy now and pay later, our spending can easily get out of hand. But the problem of exceeding debt is not always as simple as out of control spending. While some people find that a habit of overspending has built up into significant debt over a number of years, many people fall suddenly into debt for reasons outside their control.

Whatever caused your debts, filing for personal bankruptcy can offer a way of paying off your debts without harassment; or it can offer a way of completely eradicating many, if not all, of your financial headaches. With a realistic understanding of how filing can help you and what the end result will be, you will be better equipped to navigate through what can be a stressful and quite demanding process. With the information and guidance in this book, as well as tips on where to look for more assistance, you will be able to make the best decision possible for your situation.

As your credit card bills mount up, and your checking account balance decreases, it is easy to despair at the state of your financial affairs. But first of all, remember that you are not alone. Also, take comfort from knowing that many people have come out of bankruptcy and built their finances up again, with great success.

Above all, to make the most of filing for bankruptcy, you need to be positive and make changes in your financial habits. Some of these changes will be tough, and for a while you may find the financial adjustments difficult to add to your daily lifestyle. There are strategies in this book to help you, as well as advice on how to improve your credit so that you can shrug off the effects of bankruptcy as quickly as possible.

Why Does Bankruptcy Happen?

It is a fact that bankruptcy filings have been extremely high in the U.S. for a number of years. Canada has also seen a big increase in the number of bankruptcy filings, beginning in the late 1980s and continuing today. So why are more and more people seeking financial relief by filing for bankruptcy? Recent studies show that, contrary to some opinion, the vast majority of personal bankruptcies are not the result of excessive consumer spending or credit card abuse. Instead, most bankruptcies are triggered by the following:

- losing a job
- a serious health problem in the family and the medical costs that go with it
- divorce or separation

Analysts also point to two other significant factors that have contributed to the rapid increase in personal bankruptcy filing:

- Changes in the law in 1978 made bankruptcy much easier and more attractive to individuals. People no longer see bankruptcy as a last resort. (However, recent changes in U.S. bankruptcy laws have made it more difficult to file for Chapter 7. See the chart on page 14 for more information on recent changes to bankruptcy law.)
- Credit card companies have made it increasingly easy for people to obtain large amounts of credit without necessarily having the income to pay it off.

Of course, not everyone who loses a job or becomes seriously ill goes bankrupt. Some people have sufficient savings to get by or manage to get a new job quickly. Others have good medical insurance that covers those unexpected bills. But for those of us with fewer resources to fall back on when times get tough, financial problems can build up very quickly.

Other Questions You May Be Asking

Many of the questions you may be asking yourself will be answered as you read this book. It is quite natural that you should be worried about what might happen as a result of filing for bankruptcy. In fact, that is a good sign: it shows that you realize that the process is a serious one that will affect your life in both positive and negative ways. Asking questions indicates that you are much more likely to work hard to maximize the benefits and will be able to plan ahead to cope with the difficulties that may arise.

Before going any further, it is probably a good idea to put your mind at rest on some basic questions you may have right off the bat.

What Happens after I Have Filed for Bankruptcy? Will Everyone Know?

Bankruptcy is a matter of public record. But nobody shouts your bankruptcy from the rooftops when you file.

- Your employer will not know, unless your wages are being garnished (then they have to know).
- Your colleagues and friends likely will not know unless you tell them.
- Your creditors will know—but that is what you want, so that they will stop taking action against you.
- Your bankruptcy will go on your credit report for some years, but this will only be available when someone does a credit check on you, with your permission.

After you file for bankruptcy, what happens next? Although bankruptcy can turn your financial life around, it can also have a negative effect on it for quite a while. Later in this book there is help and advice on how to start over after bankruptcy. This information will assist you in that important transition from becoming bankrupt to starting anew.

Will I Lose My Home?

It is a common misconception that filing for bankruptcy means you will immediately be thrown out on the street. You will not necessarily have your home taken away against your will, although you may decide to sell it. If you own a house with a mortgage that you cannot pay off, you will need to be careful to follow the appropriate filing procedures. If you have equity in your home, you may be better off filing for Chapter 13 and you will normally get to keep your home. If you file for Chapter 7, you will lose many of your assets, but your home may be exempt—meaning you can keep it.

> The comparable situation is somewhat different in some Canadian provinces. If you are in doubt you should contact an attorney to clarify the regulations in your area. Also see Chapter 18 for specific information on the Canadian filing process.
>
> See Chapter 8 for strategies to save your house, and Chapter 9 for more information on your home and filing for bankruptcy.

Will I Ever Get a Credit Card Again?

It might come as a bit of a shock to find out that you will likely receive offers for credit cards almost immediately after filing for bankruptcy! But these are usually the companies you need to avoid—they are going to charge you very high rates and find other ways to exploit your situation. You will almost certainly have difficulty getting a good deal on a credit card for some time, but after 2 years of sensible spending and repairing your credit (see Chapter 22) you will get more favorable rates.

Will Filing for Bankruptcy Erase All My Debts?

Filing for bankruptcy can certainly erase many of your debts, especially if you are able to file for Chapter 7. But you may have to face the fact that not all your financial obligations will be wiped out by bankruptcy. If you can file for Chapter 7, most of your debts will be discharged—that is, written off—but some will not. This applies especially to debts from theft or embezzlement or other criminal causes. If you file for Chapter 13, you will be seeking to continue paying off as much of your debts as you can, within a clearly defined plan.

Recent changes in bankruptcy law have made it much more difficult to file for Chapter 7. See Chapter 10 for more information on eligibility.

Will I Have to Hand over All My Most Cherished Possessions?

If you file for Chapter 7, you will likely have to liquidate all nonexempt assets. Sadly, these normally include family heirlooms and other valuables that are not essential to your trade. If you cannot bear the thought of possibly losing valuables that mean a lot to you, you should think hard about whether to file for Chapter 7. Many people simply do not realize that they may be eligible to file for Chapter 13 bankruptcy, which allows you to keep a larger portion of your possessions. There is much more on choosing which type of personal bankruptcy makes sense for you to file in Chapter 13.

Will I Lose My Job or Have Trouble Getting a New One?

If someone fires you or refuses to hire you because you filed for bankruptcy, they are unlawfully discriminating against you. But unless the employer overtly gives this reason, you can be in a difficult position. Employers increasingly perform credit checks as part of their screening process, and may look at your payment history unfavorably. But they cannot do a credit check without your permission. Most employers are more interested in having the right person for the job, and the farther you are away from your bankruptcy the less of a problem your history will pose. See Chapter 19 for more information on your rights on this subject and other matters.

Bankruptcy Is Not a Moral Judgment

Above all, remember that filing for bankruptcy does not make you a bad person. The days are long gone when people were run out of town—or not allowed to own property again—simply because they fell into debt. Today it is widely recognized that:

- most people genuinely want to meet payments on their debts and
- bankruptcy is a legal right that protects people from harassment by their creditors.

Learning the Language of Law and Finance

A short glossary is provided at the end of the book to assist in your understanding of the terms used in the book. In addition, readers are entitled to full access and use of the comprehensive Personal Law and Personal Finance Dictionaries found on the Web landing page:

www.socrates.com/books/bankruptcy-renewal.aspx

Please remember to register the first time you use this free resource. See page iv for further details.

What Is Bankruptcy?

Before you file for bankruptcy, you need to understand exactly what bankruptcy is and what it offers. For many people, choosing to file for bankruptcy is a realistic, intelligent choice. The immediate benefit of filing is that your current creditors cannot pursue further action against you, and many of your debts are likely to be written off. On the other hand, although it is easy to think of bankruptcy as a way of escaping from paying off your debts, it is actually quite a bit more complicated.

There are several types of bankruptcy, and you need to know which bankruptcy process would be best for your situation. You also need to think hard about whether filing for bankruptcy makes economic sense or if there might be other ways to get your life back on track.

Understanding Bankruptcy

According to the United States Bankruptcy Courts' Web site, the primary purposes of bankruptcy laws are:

- to give an honest debtor a fresh start in life by relieving the debtor of most debts and
- to repay creditors in an orderly manner to the extent that the debtor has property available for payment.

In general terms, bankruptcy is a process regulated by federal law which provides debtors—individuals and corporations—with a legal way of seeking relief from their creditors. If you file for bankruptcy, the court protects you from your creditors and releases you from the need to pay off many, but not all, of your debts. But the court can also decide to sell property that belongs to you and use the proceeds to pay off some of the money you owe. Selling property, or assets, to pay off debts is called liquidation. At the end of the bankruptcy process, those debts that are eligible are canceled, or discharged, meaning you no longer have any liability to pay them.

Bankruptcy is essentially a form of protection. The degree of protection it provides depends on what Chapter you file for and the type of assets you own.

Here are some things that bankruptcy is not:

- dishonest
- the coward's way out
- a way of escaping from the consequences of illegal behavior

There are several kinds of bankruptcy. Some apply to individuals, while others are more suited to businesses. The different kinds of bankruptcy are commonly referred to by citing the chapter contained in Title 11 of the U.S. Code. If you are filing as an individual or as the sole proprietor of a business, you may file for either Chapter 7 or Chapter 13. Other types of bankruptcy, Chapter 11 and Chapter 12, are more commonly used by businesses or large companies, and offer fewer advantages for individuals. In all cases, there are certain criteria you have to meet to be eligible to file for each particular type of bankruptcy. This book provides information about the most commonly used bankruptcy filings; that is, individuals filing either Chapter 7 or Chapter 13.

Note

Personal bankruptcy can also be referred to as consumer bankruptcy and this terminology is probably more common in Canada. Although Canada has the equivalent of Chapter 7 and Chapter 13 personal bankruptcy, they are referred to differently and have somewhat different requirements. The filing process is similar, and much of the information in this book is useful for anyone, but Canadian information will be flagged when it greatly differs from U.S. bankruptcy law. You should also read Chapter 18 for an overview of the Canadian system.

Filing for Bankruptcy

When you file for bankruptcy, you are actually filing a bankruptcy petition with the court. A petition is a written request, or appeal, to an authority, which asks for certain actions to be taken. A bankruptcy petition is a request to be made bankrupt and have your debts discharged (subject to certain exemptions and conditions, which will be described with greater detail in the next chapters.)

Making the Decision to File

When making your decision to file it is a good idea to start by looking carefully at your financial situation. You will need to answer honestly the following questions about your personal situation.

- What exactly has caused your financial crisis?
- What do you hope to get from filing for bankruptcy?
- What do you expect life after bankruptcy to be like?

Your answers will give you a clearer idea of whether filing for bankruptcy is likely to help you at this time, or whether you should consider filing at a later stage if things do not improve.

What Exactly Has Caused Your Financial Crisis?

If you have been spending more than you earn, you will be in debt. If you cannot find a clear reason for your financial problems, you need to take a hard look at your current spending patterns. It is essential that you are honest with yourself. If you have problems that going bankrupt will not solve—perhaps a serious drinking or drug problem, or reckless spending—you need to address those as well. Filing for bankruptcy only helps alleviate your debts, so if other serious problems exist, be prepared to ask for help elsewhere, and if necessary, seek medical help or counseling.

Signs of Financial Crisis

For many people, the difficult part of the process is knowing when they have reached a point where filing for bankruptcy is their best option. Only you can make the final decision on this matter, although you should consider professional advice to help you make up your mind if you are unsure. The following are some signs that may indicate your financial problems cannot be solved easily.

- You never have enough money to pay your regular bills on time.
- You pay bills at the last minute, or not at all.
- You have one or more credit cards with a large amount of accumulated debt.
- You are not able to meet more than the minimum payment on your credit cards.
- You use your bank overdraft to pay for regular bills, or normal expenses like food.
- You have no idea just how much you owe.
- You get calls or visits from debt collection agencies.
- You have your requests for credit denied.
- You get further into debt each month.
- You have to borrow from friends and family to pay your bills.

What Do You Hope to Get from Filing for Bankruptcy?

It is undeniable that some people choose to file for bankruptcy without much thought, and some have even been accused of using it as a rather dishonest kind of financial planning. Recent changes in bankruptcy laws have made it more difficult to escape all your debts simply by filing for bankruptcy (especially Chapter 7). In Canada, there have also been fairly recent legal changes that have made it harder to use bankruptcy inappropriately.

If you are looking to use bankruptcy as a way of starting a new life, completely stress free and without any financial issues at all, think again. Bankruptcy can affect you in many ways:

- Emotionally—the stress of dealing with it, and life afterwards, can be considerable. Marriages and relationships frequently suffer as a result of filing for bankruptcy.

- Economically—you will still have payments to make, especially if you file for Chapter 13 (more on that later). You will have to budget very carefully for the long term.

- Getting credit—for at least 2 years, and in some cases longer, you will find it hard to get good credit, and may have to pay higher interest rates. Your bankruptcy is a matter of public record and will appear on your credit report for some time.

What Do You Expect Life after Bankruptcy to Be Like?

When you are in dire financial straits, it is tempting to think no further than actually filing Chapter 7 or Chapter 13 (or the Canadian equivalents), without worrying about what will happen next. After all, surely anything is better than the stress of dealing with angry creditors or unpaid bills! Do not fall into the trap of thinking that filing for bankruptcy is going to make life wonderful. Remember that there are reasons why you reached this point, and they may still be there. So first and foremost, be realistic.

It is important to realize that the effects of becoming bankrupt are long-lasting, and can have a negative effect on your life for quite a while. While you may be relieved of many of your financial responsibilities, filing for bankruptcy does not necessarily provide a completely clean slate. You may have to survive on a smaller income than you are used to and you will find it difficult to get credit.

Considering Alternatives

Although the purpose of this book is mainly to guide you through the process of filing for bankruptcy, there are other alternatives you should consider before you take that final step.

Contact your creditors—you may be able to work out a plan with creditors to pay off some of your debt, or pay it off in smaller amounts over a longer period. Many creditors will be sympathetic to this proposal, not because they are being generous, but because they know that they are likely to get even less money if you go bankrupt.

Try and analyze where your money is going—just writing down full details of your expenditures and trying to see what is going wrong can help. Of course, if your spending is completely out of control, it is going to be difficult to isolate a particular problem. But if you are spending all your money on one thing—whether it is expensive holidays, shoes or alcohol—this might help you see the specific changes you need to make.

Seek professional advice—both before and after filing for bankruptcy, it can be helpful to consult a credit counseling service. A reputable service can help you understand your financial situation and get control over it. It can also help you negotiate a payment plan with your creditors. But beware, not all counseling services are reputable. Read Chapter 23 for more on how to recognize good counseling services from bad ones.

It is important to regard filing bankruptcy as a very serious decision, one that should only be taken if it is your best option. It is also essential to regard filing for bankruptcy as going hand in hand with making lasting changes in how you manage your finances, so that the same problems will not surface again.

> In Canada, the possibility of approaching your creditors before making the final decision to file for bankruptcy is more formalized. A way of avoiding full-out bankruptcy is to file a Personal Proposal, under the Canadian Bankruptcy and Insolvency Act (BIA).

> A Personal Proposal is an agreement between you and your creditors, in which you agree to pay off a part of the money you owe. In some ways it is similar to Chapter 13 bankruptcy. See Chapter 18 for a full description.

It is also important to understand the difference between unsecured and secured credit, described more fully in Chapter 3. Secured debts (for instance, a mortgage where the terms require you to hand over your house if you do not meet the payments) are not normally discharged by bankruptcy.

Communicating with Others

Filing for Chapter 7 or Chapter 13 bankruptcy is something you can do alone or with your spouse or partner. In many cases it will be most beneficial to file as a couple, so that both of you are protected from creditors. The reasons for doing this are described in the next part of the book.

But remember, even if you are filing as an individual, others are sure to be affected by your decision to file for bankruptcy. Your family may feel betrayed or shocked at how bad things are, especially if you have hidden the true extent of your financial problems from them. Relatives and friends may be dismayed, embarrassed or angry, especially if you have borrowed money from them or called on them for financial help. You need to be prepared to explain your decision to them, and why it is the best course of action to take. Just remember:

- do not feel guilty and
- make sure to communicate.

A surprising number of people conceal their financial difficulties from even their closest family members, often because they do not want to cause distress to the people they care about, or they realize that they have a problem that has spun out of control and cannot explain how this has happened. It is not uncommon to feel that eventually you will be able to pay off all those bills, meet those loan payments, and/or clear that credit card, so nobody needs to know. But there comes a time when you realize you are in over your head and actually hiding the truth from yourself and there is no way you can cope alone. Filing a petition for bankruptcy with the court may be the assistance you need to get your finances back on track.

The following chart provides details on recent changes to bankruptcy law. Read on for more information on bankruptcy.

Law before Bankruptcy Abuse Prevention and Consumer Protection Act of 2005	Bankruptcy Law after October 17, 2005
There was no income or expense test to determine if someone could file for Chapter 7 bankruptcy.	A means test is applied to determine if people can file for Chapter 7. More people must go into repayment plans under Chapter 13 and cannot file under Chapter 7 because their incomes are too high. Debts that used to be wiped clean under Chapter 7 are instead repaid according to a different formula over a 5-year time frame.
Consumers did not have to contact a credit counselor before filing for bankruptcy, and after filing, did not have to finish a financial management course.	Before consumers file, they must receive a briefing from a credit counseling agency that is approved by the bankruptcy court. After filing for bankruptcy, consumers must complete a financial management class that is supposed to help them identify and correct what led to bankruptcy in the first place.
It was easier for consumers to file a bankruptcy themselves or to use nonattorney petition-preparers.	The bankruptcy reform law requires close regulation of nonattorney bankruptcy petition preparers and attorneys, both of whom are required to give consumers detailed contracts about what they will do and charge. Fees for services cost more than before.
Consumers who filed Chapter 7 had to wait 6 years before filing another Chapter 7 case. Consumers could file any number of Chapter 13 cases as long as they filed in "good faith," even if they had filed for Chapter 7 the day before.	Consumers who file after the reform law's effective date have to wait 8 years between filings. Consumers cannot file for Chapter 13 for 4 years if they received a discharge under Chapter 7, 11 or 12 during the past 4 years, or for 2 years if they received a discharge under Chapter 13.
Filers in some states could take advantage of what is called the homestead exemption, no matter what the homes cost.	The new bankruptcy law limits the state homestead exemption to $125,000 for property acquired during the 1,215-day period before filing for bankruptcy (roughly, during the past 3 years and 4 months).
Giving written or even verbal notice to a creditor was enough to stop the creditor from trying to collect.	Verbal notice or written notice without information like the address and account number used by the creditor may not be enough to stop collection attempts.
Income tax returns for the current year, and maybe the year before, were reviewed by a bankruptcy trustee but were not filed with the court.	Filers must file any tax returns for the past 3–4 years that are due. The returns (along with any that become due while the bankruptcy is pending) must be filed with both the tax authorities and the court. If they are not, the bankruptcy case will be dismissed.
The standard for having student loans discharged in bankruptcy was to establish that repayment would constitute an undue hardship on the debtor.	The types of educational loans that may not be discharged are broadened and the hardship standard for discharging a student loan in bankruptcy is preserved.

3 Secured & Unsecured Debts

Probably the last thing you feel like doing right now is thinking about all your debts. But, before you file for bankruptcy, it is very important to understand the different kinds of credit you have, and the different kinds of debts you may have incurred as a result of that credit. Some kinds of debt may not be removed simply by filing for bankruptcy (either Chapter 7 or Chapter 13), so it is essential to have a clear understanding of where you stand.

You will find a checklist on the Web landing page www.socrates.com/books/ bankruptcy-renewal.aspx that compares which debts are discharged for each different Chapter of personal bankruptcy filed. Use this as a guide. The chapters on different filing processes provide more information on what debts are exempt and which are not when you file for bankruptcy.

> **Note**
>
> The list of debts that are wiped out, or discharged, through bankruptcy is now shorter than before due to recent changes to bankruptcy laws—meaning the rules are even more stringent. One glaring change is that you can no longer discharge any debts created from taking out loans to pay off other debts that would not have been dischargeable under Chapter 7. For instance, if you take out a loan to pay off a debt accumulated from unpaid child support, the new loan would not be considered a dischargeable debt.

Even the simple act of gathering together information about what you owe will give you a much clearer idea of the extent of your debt. The answer may not be one you want to hear, but you will need to realize it in order to commence filing. On the positive side, coming to grips with what you owe may reveal that things are not quite as bad as you thought. You may even decide that it is better to use this information to help set up a payment plan, rather than filing for bankruptcy at this stage.

This chapter explains the kinds of credit commonly available. When you fail to meet the payments required on a debt, the creditor has various means of redress, depending on the terms of the credit they extended. Actions that a creditor may take are also described.

Lenders and Creditors

If you take out a loan, the person or company who lends to you is also the person you owe money, the creditor. The two terms lender and creditor are often used interchangeably; however, creditor is used more often when it comes to discussing unpaid loans.

Much of this information will also be extremely valuable to you after your bankruptcy has been discharged (that is, completed) and you are beginning anew. With a better understanding of how credit operates, you will be able to recognize possible pitfalls and avoid deals that are obviously bad, or even illegal. Chapter 23 has more information on how to avoid some of the nastier financial scams.

Secured Loans

A secured loan is one where the loan is linked to property that you own. You have been lent the money on condition that, if you default on the payments, the lender has the right to claim your property in lieu of payment. You have secured the loan with this tangible property, which is referred to as collateral. The collateral must be specified—the lender cannot just take anything. A secured creditor is someone you owe money to through a secured loan.

Sometimes the collateral is the property that you have bought with the loan. The most common example of this is a house. Other examples are your car, a computer or furniture.

Example

Loans for vehicles are normally secured in this way. If you buy a truck with a loan, and then fail to meet the payments, the company who sold it to you will claim it back.

Other times the collateral is something you already own, that has sufficient monetary value. For instance, you may be able to borrow cash on conditions that pledge your home or some other significant item.

Secured personal loans from finance companies work in this way. If you fail to meet payments, they will collect the property you pledged as security.

Pawnbrokers are another example of a rather straightforward secured loan. You ask to borrow some money and leave an item of comparable value behind as security. If you return with the money you owe (with the included interest), you can claim back your property.

Liens and Foreclosures

The creditor's legal right to claim your property if you do not pay is known as a lien. If you own property that has a lien against it, you cannot sell or transfer the property until the debt is fully paid. For instance, if you take out a loan to buy a car, and the car is the security, you cannot sell the car to someone else until the loan is paid.

Consensual and Nonconsensual Liens

A mortgage is a secured loan where you agree to a lien and your house is collateral against the loan. This is an example of a consensual lien. If you do not meet your mortgage payments, the mortgage company will have the right to claim the house and sell it to pay off your mortgage. This is known as a foreclosure.

> If you are behind with your mortgage payments and have not communicated with your mortgage company, do so right away! Mortgage companies are often willing to negotiate smaller payments or allow you to miss some payments during times of financial hardship. But it is essential that you talk to them—do your absolute best to try and contact your mortgage company before you fall into arrears. Even if that is not possible, do not ignore letters or calls concerning your mortgage. See the Web landing page www.socrates.com/books/bankruptcy-renewal.aspx that comes with this book for examples of letters to send to creditors and mortgage companies.

A nonconsensual lien is one where you have not agreed to a lien, but a creditor has (legally) created it because of nonpayment—an example is a lien placed on your property by the IRS as a result of your nonpayment of taxes.

Consensual Liens

(Also known as voluntary security interests) include:

- mortgages to buy or refinance some real estate;
- home equity loans (a second mortgage);
- loans for cars or other motor vehicles;
- personal secured loans from banks or other finance companies; and
- store charges with a security agreement (Although most purchases bought with a credit card are unsecured, big stores sometimes overprint your receipt to state they retain a security interest in goods you have bought—usually in the case of white goods like dishwashers or stoves.)

Nonconsensual Liens

These fall into three main categories:

1. **Judicial liens**—imposed on your property after someone sues you and wins. This usually affects your real estate, but in some states can affect other personal property (these states include Alabama, Connecticut, Florida, Georgia, Maine, Massachusetts, Mississippi, New Hampshire and Rhode Island).

2. **Statutory liens**—liens created automatically by law. For instance, if you hire someone to roof your house, and then do not pay, the contractor may put a lien on your house. Statutory liens affect your real estate.

3. **Tax liens**—if you owe taxes, the IRS or other taxing authority can issue a tax lien against your property. This affects your real estate or, in the case of IRS liens, can affect your retirement or bank accounts.

Important

A Chapter 7 bankruptcy discharge does not actually eradicate liens. If you owe $5,000 on a car loan, the obligation to pay the debt is discharged at the end of your Chapter 7 bankruptcy, but the loan company can still repossess the car. However, if you owe them $5,000 and the car is now only worth $3,000, they cannot go after you for the difference.

Unsecured Loans

An unsecured loan has no collateral against it. Although you have been lent money (or have had credit extended to you, which is simply another form of loan) you were not required to pledge any property as security.

Common examples of unsecured loans or credit are credit cards, cash advances on a cash or charge card and store cards.

Note

Not all credit and store cards are unsecured. If you were required to sign a security agreement when you obtained the card, read it carefully. The card will be secured and your property will be collateral.

Other loans that are generally unsecured include:

- student loans, alimony and child support
- loans from friends or parents
- payment for rent and/or utilities
- union dues
- payments to church or synagogue
- health club subscriptions
- medical and dental bills
- fees to lawyers and accountants

Some General Advice

Make sure to read the paperwork that accompanies your loans—and do not forget credit and charge cards. It may be too late to change the fact that you took out a secured loan that has a deadline you cannot meet, at an exorbitant interest rate that you cannot afford. At this stage, when considering filing bankruptcy, you need to understand how each loan operates, what the exact terms are, and how much you owe. If you decide to file for bankruptcy, you will need to list all your debts, secured and unsecured, and have all the details at hand. This is especially important if you are filing for Chapter 13 bankruptcy, because you will be working out how much to pay each of your creditors. (See Chapter 14 for more on this.)

Remember that day-to-day bills are also forms of credit. Your utility bills, for instance, are requests for payment for services you have already received up front.

A Word to the Wise…

In the future, never take out a secured loan without being knowledgeable and comfortable with the loan terms. While it is easy to think, "I will not have any problems paying off this loan," problems may arise unexpectedly. What if you suddenly lose your job or go out of business? Always imagine the worst-case scenario and decide whether you can live with that possibility.

Actions Creditors May Take

If you have reached a point of financial crisis—meaning you are seriously considering filing for either Chapter 7 or Chapter 13 bankruptcy—you have probably already been approached by creditors.

- In some states, creditors do not have to contact you at all before taking property that you have put up as collateral against a secured loan.
- In many states, creditors are required by law to inform you of their intention to take the property, which is called their Right To Cure the loan.
- Some states require a creditor to get a court order before they can take property. This also applies in some Native American tribes.

In reality, creditors rarely take this action until they have to. If they do, they will probably go after your vehicle, since this property is easiest for them to repossess, and is likely to provide the most value. There is more information on dealing with debt collection agencies and how to avoid harassment from them in Chapter 19.

Tip

Even if you do owe money, you are entitled, by law, to ask creditors not to contact you at your place of work or to telephone you. Send your creditors a letter asking them to cease contacting you (there is an example on the Web landing page www.socrates.com/books/bankruptcy-renewal.aspx).

Without any collateral from you, the company or person extending you unsecured credit is in a far more precarious situation. In the case of unsecured loans, one of the first things creditors may consider doing is suing you. But all is not equal in the world of unsecured loans: creditors have more aggressive means of collecting student loans and unpaid child support or alimony.

For example, the government can use strong-arm tactics: If you do not pay off your student loan, you cannot get another one in the future. Also, the government can charge high collection fees to get the money you owe, keep any income tax refunds you may have, and also take part of your wages—all without getting a court order. This is called wage garnishing.

A Note about Wage Garnishment

Whether or not creditors can garnish your wages depends on your state's laws. Each state has its own rules regarding the types of property that can and cannot be seized by creditors. There are a few states that do not allow any wage garnishment.

It is important to remember that even if you live in a state that prohibits wage garnishment, the law typically does not prevent state or federal governments from garnishing your wages if you owe them money. This means that if you do not repay a student loan or are behind on child support payments, you can still have your wages garnished.

In addition to state laws, federal legislation also regulates wage garnishments. Title III of the Consumer Credit Protection Act limits the amount of an employee's earnings that may be garnished, and prohibits employers from firing employees who have had wages garnished for a single debt.

Again, communication is key. It is far better to work out a payment plan with the lender, if possible, or to arrange postponing the payments that are due, rather than ignore the fact that your student loan is in arrears.

In summary, here are a few of the actions that creditors may legally be able to take when you fail to meet your debt(s) and do not show any indication of being able to pay them in the near future:

- The creditor can and probably will sue you.
- Bank setoff—a bank may take money from your deposit account to cover money you owe them. There are quite a few rules as to when and how a bank can do this and these rules vary from state to state.
- Wage garnishment—money will be taken directly from your paycheck.
- Collection of unsecured debts from third parties—someone who holds some of your property (for example, a bank where you have a deposit account, or a landlord to whom you paid a security deposit) may be sued to get at your money.
- Interception of your tax refund—the government may grab this if you owe it money.
- Loss of insurance coverage—if your policy lapses because of nonpayment, your coverage may also lapse.
- Loss of utility services—your service will be cut off. Note that this cannot be done without providing you a warning—if the company is publicly owned.

Will It End in Jail?

Take some comfort from the fact that, though it may seem as if you owe the whole world money, it is unlikely you will go to jail simply for failing to pay a debt. Some states still have debtors' prisons, but even in those states, if you have no money to pay your debts, you are unlikely to be kept in jail.

This does not apply, of course, if your behavior was criminal or willfully fraudulent. Also, you can be prosecuted if you violate a court order (for instance, by not paying child support), or for willfully refusing to pay your taxes. You should consult an attorney specializing in your state's regulations if you have any doubts about your situation.

Going Ahead

Bankruptcy may be your best option if:

- your debts run into the thousands of dollars and far exceed your ability to pay them;
- negotiations with creditors have failed; and/or
- creditors have started repossession or foreclosure on your property.

The next chapters explain Chapter 7 and Chapter 13 in detail. Make sure to read about both. Although Chapter 7 can release you from liability for many debts, it really is a last resort—and you have to be eligible to file for it. Chapter 13 offers a chance to repay at least some of your debts, while releasing you from the full burden of payment.

Section Two

SOCRATES™
KNOW HOW TO DO MORE
AND SAVE

4 The Automatic Stay

This chapter explains how the automatic stay can protect you, and in some instances, where it will not.

What Is the Automatic Stay?

When you file for bankruptcy an automatic stay is put into action. This applies to both Chapter 7 and Chapter 13 bankruptcy (and also to other kinds) and in Canadian bankruptcy. The automatic stay is like a court injunction: It immediately stops virtually all actions against your property and income by creditors. Any lawsuits that have been filed against you are temporarily halted, as well as any actions filed by creditors (including the government and collection agencies acting on behalf of creditors).

The purpose of an automatic stay is not to solve your financial problems per se, but to provide you some breathing space while your situation is assessed and your bankruptcy case moves forward. An automatic stay immediately takes a lot of the pressure off, and puts a temporary hold on some actions that creditors may be pursuing, including foreclosure on your home. It is important to understand that the hold is not permanent, and it is also important to understand that the stay does not halt some actions—recent changes in bankruptcy laws have not negated the fact that landlords are still able to pursue eviction, for instance. And in some cases, creditors can succeed in lifting the stay—allowing them to resume action against you. This chapter explains all these possibilities in detail.

What Happens Once You Have Filed an Automatic Stay?

- The automatic stay goes into effect as soon as you file for bankruptcy.
- The court sends a letter to all your creditors. This notice orders them to refrain from any further action against you.
- If any of your creditors deliberately violates this order, they may be held in contempt of court.

What Is Not Halted by the Automatic Stay?

- Criminal proceedings will go forward even if an automatic stay has been granted.
- Any attempts to collect alimony, maintenance or support from exempt property or property that you acquired after filing the case will not be halted. (See Chapter 6 for information on exempt property and the Appendix to this book for a list of exemptions in your state or province.)

The Automatic Stay and Co-Signers

The automatic stay does not protect a friend or relative who has co-signed a loan for you if you file Chapter 7. Creditors can still come after him or her for the entire sum you owe.

However, if you file Chapter 13, your co-signers may be protected if:

- the debt is a consumer debt;
- the debt cannot be incurred in the ordinary course of business; and
- the co-signer cannot benefit from the debt proceeds.

If these conditions are met, your co-signer will generally be protected and will not be liable for your debt.

How Long Does It Last?

The automatic stay remains in effect until one of the following occurs:

- the bankruptcy case is canceled or dismissed;
- the bankruptcy case is finished—that is, discharged; or
- the bankruptcy court grants an order for Relief from Stay.

> **Note**
>
> If you are filing Chapter 7 or 13 within 1 year of having a previous bankruptcy proceeding dismissed, the automatic stay will terminate 30 days after your new case is filed. However, the stay can remain in effect if the court finds that you have brought the present case in good faith.

If you had two or more previous bankruptcy cases pending during the year before your present case, the automatic stay does not go into effect. Again, however, the court may allow the stay if it finds that your present case was brought in good faith.

What Is a Relief from Stay?

Although the automatic stay goes into effect when you file for bankruptcy and protects you from your creditors, a creditor may choose to file an action that requests an exception in their case. To do this they have to file a Motion for Relief from Stay.

Relief from Stay in Chapter 7

The following are situations in which creditors will take this option:

- When the property your debt is secured against is at risk. For instance, your car is the collateral against the loan they provided, but you have failed to insure it.
- When the property is depreciating in value rapidly and the creditor has reason to believe you will not give it back to them promptly. Again, motor vehicles are high on the list.
- When there is a consensual lien (one that you have agreed to) on your home, and you are unable to meet mortgage payments to pay off the debt.

Important

Until quite recently, landlords could not pursue evictions without asking for relief from the stay. But recent changes to the law indicate that landlords can now pursue evictions more easily, and the stay will not protect you. However, debts from nonpayment of rent remain subject to the automatic stay.

But a creditor with whom you have a secured debt (for instance a vehicle purchase loan or mortgage) is likely to try to find other ways of getting payment from you. These may include reaffirming the debt (see Chapter 11 and the glossary for more information) or an agreement that you will continue to make payments on the debt, even though you have declared bankruptcy.

Relief from Stay in Chapter 13

A relief from stay is probably more common in Chapter 13 bankruptcy, where the creditor is more likely to regard it as worthwhile (that is, they think you have some way of paying the money owed). For example, as part of a Chapter 13 bankruptcy, you are protected from foreclosure by the automatic stay. But you may also have agreed to continue paying mortgage payments as part of your Chapter 13 repayment plan (see Chapter 16). However, if you stop paying the mortgage payments you agreed to, the bank or mortgage company will likely apply for a relief from the stay in order to foreclose on your home.

Objecting to an Application for Relief from Stay

If a creditor applies for a relief from stay, you can object and attempt to stop them. You will need to file a written objection within a given period of time. If you do not object, the relief is quite likely to be granted. If you do file an objection, the procedure differs from state to state. Normally there will be a hearing at which you or your attorney can explain why you have been unable to meet the previously agreed payments. You should contact the court trustee dealing with your bankruptcy case if the need to do this arises.

The Automatic Stay as an Emergency Protection and Its Limitations

As a form of temporary protection, the automatic stay can be a good reason to file for bankruptcy. This is particularly true if you face the risk of foreclosure or having your utilities cut off. Below is more detailed information on how the automatic stay affects common emergency situations:

Utility Disconnections

An automatic stay will protect you from disconnection for at least 20 days, but not forever. This means that utility companies cannot threaten you with disconnection during this time. If your bankruptcy is successfully discharged, you are unlikely to have to pay the bills you owe on utilities. However, it is not a good idea to file bankruptcy simply because your utility company is going to cut you off. In this situation, it is far better to approach them directly to see if you can work out a repayment plan or other solution.

Eviction

The automatic stay offers little protection from eviction. This is because your landlord can proceed with an eviction action if he or she follows court-defined procedures. From the court's point of view, your eviction is not going to affect your bankruptcy. Your alternatives are to try and fight the eviction in a state court (if you have a good reason) or to move.

In summary, recent bankruptcy law amendments mean that an eviction can continue if you:

- as tenant, had filed bankruptcy in the previous 24 months and had failed to pay rent;
- are being evicted for endangerment to property or person or for the use of illegal drugs; and/or
- failed to make even one payment after the filing of the bankruptcy.

This last condition is important to understand. It means that you can owe rent before you filed for bankruptcy, but must have kept up rental payments since filing for bankruptcy. The past rent that you owe would be treated as a debt, protected under the automatic stay. But if you fail to pay rent after filing, the landlord can continue with eviction proceedings.

Remember, you are still under the protection of the landlord tenant laws of your state, which are entirely separate from bankruptcy laws. Filing for bankruptcy does not affect your rights as a tenant.

Foreclosure

If the mortgage company has set foreclosure proceedings into action, the automatic stay will stop them temporarily—but only for a while. Eventually the lender will probably be able to proceed with foreclosure to recover their secured debt. Although there are ways of minimizing the likelihood of this happening, keeping the house may not be an option if you file for Chapter 7. You should consider filing Chapter 13 instead, where you are far more likely to be successful in retaining your house.

Public Benefit Overpayments

If you have been overpaid for public benefits you receive, like Medicaid or unemployment benefits, the particular government agency can normally grab that overpayment back if you owe them money. In effect, they will reduce your benefits. But if you file for bankruptcy, the automatic stay will stop them. Normally, debts you have incurred through overpayment of public benefits are dischargeable. This means the debt(s) will be canceled at the conclusion of the bankruptcy process.

Loss of Driver's License because of Liability for Damages

If you are unable to pay the damages arising from a court judgment resulting from a vehicle accident that you were involved in, your driver's license may be suspended. Although this is not true in all states, an automatic stay may prevent this suspension.

Note
Recent changes in the law indicate that in most cases the stay no longer halts actions to withhold or suspend a driver's license.

Wage Garnishments

If you file for bankruptcy, wage garnishments will be stopped immediately. The result is that you receive your full salary almost at once. The debt that originally led to wage garnishment might therefore be discharged by bankruptcy.

Your Rights as an Employee

If you have only one wage garnishment, your employer cannot fire you because of it; federal law protects you. But where there are multiple garnishments, your employer may be able to fire you. Most people think that wage garnishment can only be implemented by government agencies like the IRS, but in fact any company that goes to court and wins a case against you may be able to garnish your wages. Employers dislike dealing with wage garnishment because it means complicated calculations for them. For more information on how wage garnishment operates in your state, consult the Department of Labor Web site at www.dol.gov. There is also more information in Chapter 19.

Child Support

Beware! The situation regarding child support and alimony payments deducted from your wages is different from other kinds of wage garnishment.

- If your current child support and alimony payments are being deducted from your wages, this will continue, despite the stay.
- But if you are having support arrearages deducted (money you owe because of previous nonpayment) these will be halted.
- BUT—and this one's an important one to consider if support issues are your reason for filing—your support arrearages are not going to be wiped out, or discharged, by bankruptcy.

Recent Changes in the Law and Their Effect on the Automatic Stay

Recent changes in bankruptcy legislation mean that the automatic stay offers far less protection to people who file for bankruptcy than it used to.

In most cases the stay no longer halts, or postpones, the following:

- lawsuits regarding paternity, child custody or child support
- divorce proceedings
- interception of tax refunds
- suspension of driver's, professional, occupational and recreational licenses
- lawsuits regarding domestic violence

Under Canadian bankruptcy law, there are similar restrictions in the protection offered by the automatic stay. You are still liable for secured debts, and have less protection against creditors who want to repossess or claim the property you put up as collateral. Similarly, your driving license suspension may not be protected, and even temporary protection from eviction or foreclosure is not guaranteed.

Above all, remember that not all of your debts are protected by your decision to file for bankruptcy. You need to look at what is protected by the stay and see if filing makes sense for you.

The Automatic Stay as an Emergency Procedure

Filing for bankruptcy involves completing and submitting quite a few forms, which we will talk about in more detail later. But what if your house is about to be repossessed, or the electricity is being turned off and debt collectors are knocking on your door? There are two courses of action you can take.

1. File for bankruptcy, and also send immediate written notice of the filing and the automatic stay that results from it to the creditors involved. That way, a creditor cannot claim that they were not informed of the automatic stay. This is worth doing if one or two particular creditors are making your life miserable. You can ask an attorney to send a more formal letter on your behalf if a creditor ignores your letter or you think they may. There is an example on the Web landing page www.socrates.com/books/bankruptcy-renewal.aspx that you can use as a model.

2. The court recognizes that the automatic stay is something you may need to put in place very quickly. For this reason, you do not have to file all your bankruptcy papers at once. In order to get the automatic stay, simply file the two-page petition and include a mailing list of all your creditors. See the chapters on filing for Chapter 7 and Chapter 13 for more information.

If you only file the two-page petition and list of creditors, you will be protected quickly. But remember that you will not have completed the bankruptcy filing process. You must file the rest of the papers and forms required within 15 days or your bankruptcy case will probably be dismissed. If your case is dismissed, you are prevented from filing again for another 180 days.

For Further Information

Be sure to visit the Web landing page www.socrates.com/books/bankruptcy-renewal.aspx to keep up-to-date on how the recent reforms to bankruptcy law affect the nature of the automatic stay.

5 Change Your Bankruptcy Estate

This chapter explains:

- What is included in your bankruptcy estate.
- How property is defined.

When you file for bankruptcy—either Chapter 7 or Chapter 13—you will need to take an inventory of the property you own, including its value. You can use this chapter as a way of gathering this information. Be sure to read the next two chapters as well; they will show you which property is exempt from liquidation (particularly important if filing for Chapter 7) and also how to collect the required information on property value. There are strategies in these chapters to maximize your chances of keeping property that is important to you, and there are others to help you minimize the effect of bankruptcy on your estate.

Most of this information applies to Chapter 7 bankruptcy (or, in Canada, straight bankruptcy), since your assets are not normally liquidated if you file for Chapter 13.

But knowing how much property you own, and its current value is important when filing for both Chapter 7 and Chapter 13. Even in Chapter 13 you must pay your unsecured creditors as much, or more, than they would have received if you had filed for Chapter 7. To do this, you need to know the exact value of your property.

What Is Your Bankruptcy Estate?

When you file for Chapter 7 nearly everything you own becomes subject to the court's authority. Your bankruptcy estate includes all of the property you own at the time of filing for bankruptcy, with the exception of items that you are able to claim as exempt. The court-appointed trustee liquidates the balance of the estate—everything remaining after exemptions have been agreed to—and the money is used to pay creditors and to pay for the bankruptcy proceedings.

The liquidated bankruptcy estate is rarely enough to cover more than a portion of the debts that you owe, so creditors are paid according to priority. High on the list are creditors with whom you have secured debts, since you are likely to lose the most if they are not paid. Lower down on the list are all the unsecured debts you may have. Some creditors will receive very little, or nothing at all. You can see why credit card companies, which usually extend unsecured credit, are unhappy about the situation.

Many of the recent changes in bankruptcy law were the result of increased pressure from the credit card industry, which loses huge amounts of money from unpaid credit cards every year. Some argue that the credit card industry's tendency to hand out credit to almost anyone is part of the problem. Whatever the reason, these changes provide more protection to the creditor and put more restrictions on the person who owes them money.

Property Defined

The definition of property under bankruptcy law is quite broad. We tend to think of property as tangible items we own—a stereo system, our car, jewelry, etc. But to the bankruptcy courts, property is defined as all legal and equitable interests of the debtor, and can include stocks and shares, savings and other cash.

The property that you own falls into different categories:

Property That You Own and Possess

This type of property is straightforward. If something belongs entirely to you, it is your property. Examples include your clothing, computers, stereo, car, real estate, and stock certificates—in short, anything that is entirely your property.

Do not forget that in some cases property that feels as if it is yours does not entirely belong to you. For instance, you do not fully own a car that you are still making payments on, even if you are up-to-date on the payments. You are only entitled to possess it.

Property That You Own but Do Not Possess

If you own a car but gave it to your son to use while he is at school, it still belongs to you, even though it is not in your possession. If you paid your landlord a security deposit in order to move into your apartment, the security deposit belongs to you and is simply in your landlord's possession while you are living there. In both cases, the property forms part of your bankruptcy estate.

If you were thinking of giving everything you own to someone else to look after, remember: Simply moving property or money that is yours into someone else's possession will not remove it from your bankruptcy estate.

Property That You Have Recently Given Away (or Had Taken Away)

It might be tempting to consider giving your valuable possessions to a family member or friend as a way of hiding them from the courts. However, you must include property that you have recently given away on the list of property that makes up your bankruptcy estate.

Willfully signing over property to someone else to conceal your ownership from the courts is dishonest. If you do not report a transfer of property of this kind as part of your bankruptcy paperwork you are liable to lose it; the bankruptcy trustee can liquidate it, and probably will do so. You might also be prosecuted for perjury, and your bankruptcy case may even be dismissed. This applies whether you sold or gifted the property concerned.

> **Note**
>
> Even though it may seem like a good idea, do not pay off a creditor shortly before filing for bankruptcy. If you show preference to a particular creditor, the bankruptcy trustee may have the right to sue them for the amount you paid them—making that amount part of your estate. As a guideline, your action will be seen as preferential if you pay or transfer property worth more than $600 within 90 days. If the creditor is a friend or relative, or a business that you own, the period is extended to 1 year.

Property You Are Entitled to, but Do Not Possess When Filing

Broadly speaking, this means money owed to you, or other property that you are due to receive at, or after, the time of filing for bankruptcy. This includes an inheritance where the person has already died (but not if you are mentioned in the will of someone who is still living). It also includes any vacation or severance pay you are due, compensation payments you are owed (for instance if you were hit by a car) and money payable to you for services you provided. This last one is particularly hard to accept, since nonpayment of invoices by others may be the very reason you are considering filing for bankruptcy.

Other property in this category includes:

- royalties
- rent from commercial or residential property
- dividends on stocks (in most cases)
- tax refunds
- tax attributes (such as loss carry forwards)

> **Note**
>
> If you have a trust fund from which you are receiving payments but are not yet entitled to all of the principal and interest, the full amount of the trust will become part of your bankruptcy estate. Do not try and hide it, although there are ways that you can legally make it more difficult for the bankruptcy trustee to have access to it. You should consult an attorney to discuss the specific terms of your trust fund.

Proceeds from Property Included in Your Bankruptcy Estate

If property that you have included as part of your bankruptcy estate is making money, then that money is also part of the bankruptcy estate. For instance, if you own a commercial property, any rent collected from it becomes part of the estate. This continues even after you have filed.

Another example is any proceeds that you are likely to receive after filing for bankruptcy. For instance, if you receive a check from a profit-sharing plan at your place of work, it may become part of your estate.

Property Acquired Within 180 Days of Filing

You must report certain kinds of property you acquire within 180 days of filing (in other words, for 6 months). The court-appointed trustee will decide whether or not to include it in your bankruptcy estate. The property involved includes:

- inherited property;
- death benefits or life insurance policy proceeds that became owed to you during this time; and
- property from a property settlement or divorce settlement that goes into effect during this period. (This does not include alimony.)

The court is quite tough on this subject, and you have to report these items, even if your bankruptcy has ended.

Your Share of Marital Property

The division of property here depends on whether you file alone or with your spouse, and also depends on the laws in your state. If you file jointly, all marital property that falls into any of the categories above will become part of your bankruptcy estate. But if you file alone, some of the property you jointly own may not be part of your bankruptcy estate. This depends on what kind of ownership you have, which is often defined by the state you live in.

Here is a brief description of the different kinds of ownership and how they affect your bankruptcy estate if you file alone, but own property jointly with your spouse.

Joint tenancy: This is when two or more people own equal shares in a property. Each person is a joint tenant and has an undivided right to possess the whole property, and a proportionate right of equal ownership interest. If one tenant dies, his or her share is distributed automatically amongst the remaining tenants. Not all states permit this kind of ownership. If you file alone, the bankruptcy trustee cannot take the proportion of the property belonging to others.

Tenancy in the entirety: Many states have this special form of joint tenancy where the tenants are husband and wife. Neither spouse can sell the property without the permission of the other. In general, if you file alone for bankruptcy, any property you jointly own with your spouse under these terms does not become part of the bankruptcy estate. However, this has been challenged successfully by some bankruptcy courts, and around half the states have abolished this kind of tenancy.

Common law property: If your state is not a community property state or a tenancy by the entirety state, it generally falls into this category. Under this term, if you file alone, all your property plus half of your jointly owned property becomes part of the bankruptcy state. Normally, property is only deemed to be jointly owned if it was purchased or received as a gift by both parties.

Community property: This type of ownership is only available to married couples, and relates to assets jointly purchased by them during their marriage. Both partners are deemed to have an equal right to possess the property during their marriage. The property cannot be transferred without both people's permission. This type of property ownership currently applies in Arizona, California, Idaho, Louisiana, Nevada, New Mexico, Texas, Washington and Wisconsin.

Note

Even if you file alone for bankruptcy, the whole of any community property that you own jointly with your spouse is considered part of the bankruptcy estate.

A Final Note on Property

Remember that joint property does not refer only to tangible items like houses or cars, but also to any assets—even lottery winnings. However, the most common jointly owned property is the family home. Since your home is also protected by some degree of exemption (see Chapters 8 and 10) it is unlikely to become part of the bankruptcy estate in its entirety.

Real Property and Personal Property

If you own or part-own your own home, or any other real estate, you are considered to own some real property. All other property you own is referred to as personal property. It is important to understand this distinction when listing what property you own.

Pensions

You may be relieved to find out that almost all money held in retirement plans does not count as part of the bankruptcy estate. Under the new bankruptcy law, all tax-exempt retirement accounts, including IRAs, are protected. However, there is a $1 million cap on IRAs, which means that creditors can collect any IRA money that exceeds this amount.

Retirement Plans in Canada

In Canada some retirement plans count as part of the bankruptcy estate while others are protected. Registered Pension Plans (RPPs) are generally not considered property, but Registered Retirement Savings Plans (RRSPs) usually are.

The next chapter explains what exemptions apply to your property, and also provides some strategies on how to maximize the benefit of claiming exemptions.

6 The Property Exemption System

If you file for Chapter 7 bankruptcy, much of your property will be liquidated, and the proceeds used to pay off at least part of your debts to unsecured creditors. But you will be able to keep property deemed to be exempt. This chapter explains what is meant by exempt and nonexempt property, and how this will affect you when filing for bankruptcy. The next chapter will guide you through a worksheet where you can list your property, add up its value, and decide what exemptions you are able to claim. This will help you maximize your exemptions, and have a better chance of keeping property that you cannot bear to lose.

Obviously you want to claim as much property exempt as possible. There are various kinds of exemptions. Some allow you to keep property outright, while others allow you to keep property up to a certain dollar amount.

- Exempt property is property that you can keep both during and after your bankruptcy. It does not become liquidated as part of your bankruptcy estate.
- Nonexempt property is property that the bankruptcy trustee can liquidate to pay your creditors.

Why Exemptions Are Still Important If You File for Chapter 13

If you file for Chapter 13 bankruptcy, you normally get to keep all your property, provided you fulfill the requirements of your repayment plan (see Chapter 16 for more information). But even if you file for Chapter 13, it is still important to know about exemptions; when you file you are still required to list all your property and specify which property you are claiming as exempt.

The Purpose of Property Exemption

The property exemption system is designed to help you continue with your life and carry on your employment. The bankruptcy court wants you to be able to continue earning money, which you will need to avoid government support and also to pay taxes. Your savings and retirement funds are also protected to an extent because savings are another way in which people remain independent of support. Finally, the court recognizes that many items you hold dear are not of significant monetary value, or may be difficult to sell. As a result, there is no point in making them subject to liquidation.

Claiming Exemptions

You are legally entitled to keep certain property when you file for Chapter 7. But it is your responsibility to claim these property exemptions. Because it is not an automatic process, it is particularly important to understand exactly what property you own and what exemptions you are eligible to claim. This can be quite confusing since there are both federal exemptions and state exemptions. In Canada there are provincial exemptions that function in a very similar manner to state exemptions. But once you understand how exemptions work, the procedure is not that complex.

The appendices at the end of this book provide a list of exemptions in the various states and provinces. You can also view them online at:

www.bankruptcyaction.com/bankruptcyexemptions.htm

www.banruptcycycanada.com/bankruptcyexemptions.htm

Federal and State Exemptions

Not all states permit you to use the federal exemptions. But some will allow you to choose between using the federal and state exemptions. At this time the states that permit you to choose are:

Arkansas	New Mexico
Connecticut	Pennsylvania
Hawaii	Rhode Island
Massachusetts	South Carolina
Michigan	Texas
Minnesota	Vermont
New Hampshire	Washington
New Jersey	Wisconsin

When you file for bankruptcy, you must choose whether you are going to use federal or state exemptions—you cannot combine them. But you can change your decision later by amending your paperwork accordingly.

California and Exemptions

California is a special case because it has adopted a unique exemption system. In California you cannot use the federal exemptions, but there are two sets of state exemptions that you can choose between. One of these is actually very similar to the federal exemption list.

Nonbankruptcy or Supplemental Exemptions

Although you must choose which system to use, some state exemption systems allow you to use supplemental federal exemptions as well, which are called Nonbankruptcy Exemptions. This applies in all states, including California. These are not the same as the main list of federal exemptions—you can only use these supplemental federal exemptions if you are using the state exemptions for your other exemptions.

Nonbankruptcy exemptions are mostly military and federal benefits, specific types of pensions, and up to 75 percent of earned but unpaid wages. See appendices for a full list.

Types of Exemptions

Exemptions fall broadly into three categories:

1. family exemptions

2. head-of-household exemptions

3. specific property exemptions

Family Exemptions

Many states have family exemptions that you are only eligible for if you are married. They are designed to protect a family that has a single debtor as the head-of-household, sometimes called a Family Debtor. Usually it means that you are able to keep more unsecured property. All states have measures that prevent all unsecured property from being taken and protect a family from becoming completely destitute.

Head-of-Household Exemptions

Even if you are not married, you may have a legal or moral obligation to support people living with you. Under the head-of-household exemption, you must be responsible for providing over 50 percent of the support for at least one member of the household. Essentially, this is a way of accounting for unmarried partners or households with elderly relatives or young children where the person filing brings in most of the income.

In this situation, you are usually allowed more exemptions than a single person because of the detrimental effect the loss of property would have on your dependents.

Specific-Property Exemptions

Certain property is exempt from liquidation. You may choose to exempt specific property, normally up to a defined dollar amount. See the state and federal exemption lists in the appendices for full information.

Normally, you are allowed to choose exactly what property you wish to exempt within the terms of the exemption system you are using. Some states are very precise about what is included, while others offer more flexibility.

> **Example**
>
> In Colorado, state exemptions for personal property include the following—pictures and books to $1,500; burial place; clothing to $1,500; food and fuel to $600; household goods to $3,000; jewelry to $1,000 total; motor vehicle if used in occupation to $3,000 or if owned by disabled or elderly person and used to obtain medical care to $6,000; personal injury recoveries, unless debt related to injury; proceeds for damaged exempt property; health aids; security deposit; full amount of federal or state earned income tax credit refund.

The federal exemption system is also very specific about the types of household goods that you can keep. The new bankruptcy law contains a much more restrictive definition of household goods that includes one radio, one television, one VCR, and one personal computer (if used for a minor child's education or entertainment), among other things.

Claiming Exemptions with Your Spouse

If you are filing according to the federal exemption system, you and your spouse may each claim the full exemption value—that is, you simply double the amount allowed. But many state exemption systems will not let you do this, or will only allow it in relation to certain kinds of property. The situation is different from state to state; in some states the courts have ruled that doubling is not allowed, in others the legislature has not addressed the issue either way (in which case doubling is probably allowed).

Choosing between Federal and State Exemption Systems

Making the best choice will maximize the value of your nonexempt property. Most states exempt the same kinds of property as the federal system, but the dollar amounts permitted can vary considerably. In general, there are two ways to make your choice:

1. **Look at the homestead exemption.** Even if your house was purchased with a mortgage that you are still paying (or having trouble paying), you will still own part of it. The exemption applying to equity in your home is called the Homestead Exemption. If you have equity in your home, the way the exemption system treats it will probably dictate your decision.

   If you have the option of choosing between federal and state exemption systems, compare the federal amount to the homestead exemption for your state. If the equity value of your home is much more than the homestead exemption, the property may need to be sold. But in some states, the homestead exemption is significantly more than the federal equivalent.

Important

If you own your home, read Chapter 10 for more detailed information on the subject. Before passage of the new bankruptcy law, many debtors were able to keep their home regardless of its value if they lived in a state with an unlimited homestead exemption. However, under the new bankruptcy law, debtors can no longer take an unlimited homestead exemption. Instead, the exemption is now limited to $100,000/$125,000.

2. Consider property of value. Identify valuable property that you own and compare the exemptions relating to it in state and federal lists.

Example

Jane lives in Texas, and does not own her home. But she does own a valuable horse worth $10,000. Texas state exemptions allow her to include two horses in her list of exempt personal property, up to a total value of personal property of $60,000 for a family debtor ($30,000 for a nonfamily debtor).

Wildcard Exemptions

You can use a wildcard exemption as an add on to the exemption limit for one or more exemption categories. Many states have a wildcard value, and it can be very useful when you face the risk of losing important property.

Example

John owns his car outright, and it is worth $4,000. His state only allows a $1,500 exemption on cars, so he will either have to hand it over or find another $3,500 to give the bankruptcy trustee instead. But his state also allows a $5,000 wildcard exemption. John can therefore set $3,500 of his wildcard amount against his car in order to exempt his car completely. And he still has $1,500 of his wildcard exemption to use against something else.

You can also use a wildcard exemption to exempt items that are not exempted at all in any other category. This gives you the chance to keep items that are important to you.

Wildcard exemption values vary from state to state, and some states do not have them.

Exemption Limits

Any equity above the exemption limit for a property is nonexempt. For example, if your house is worth $150,000 and your equity in it is $50,000, not all the equity is covered by the homestead exemption limit. In this case you need to pay the balance—the difference between the equity you have and the exemption limit—in order to hang on to that property.

Keeping Nonexempt Property

There is an element of bartering involved in the process, which can be useful if you really want to hang onto a particular item of property that is nonexempt.

- You may be able to keep property that is nonexempt if you can provide the bankruptcy trustee with the equivalent value in exempt cash or other property.

- In addition, you get to keep any nonexempt property that the trustee regards as too difficult to sell (usually where the value of the property does not warrant the effort of trying to sell it). This property is rejected or abandoned by the bankruptcy trustee.

Claiming Your Exemptions

This chapter has explained why the bankruptcy court allows exemptions, what kinds there are and how they differ from one state to another. The next chapter helps you fill in a worksheet that will enable you to list your property, value it and decide which exemptions to claim. The next chapter also provides strategies for maximizing your exemptions so you can exempt as much of your property as possible and avoid liquidation. When you are ready to fill in your official paperwork, this list will be the basis for your exemption claims.

7 Completing the Personal Property Worksheet

This chapter helps you complete a property worksheet that you will need when you are ready to start the official paperwork for filing your bankruptcy petition. Once you have listed all your property, there are some strategies on how to turn as much of it as possible into exempt property. There are many things you can do to maximize the effect of your exemptions. This worksheet does not include information on real estate, which is discussed separately in the next chapter.

Again, this procedure is relevant to both Chapter 7 and Chapter 13 bankruptcy, although you are more likely to need to claim your exemptions if you are filing for Chapter 7.

How to Complete the Personal Property Worksheet

The attached property worksheet is laid out under various headings, corresponding to those in the list of property exemptions. Information on these categories is described briefly below.

Fill in each category with as much information as you can. List absolutely everything you own—it will take some time and will involve some calculation. Allow yourself an appropriate amount of time, and seek assistance where necessary. Remember, this is not a legal document; it is a way for you to organize the information you are going to need.

- Keep track of the statutory number(s), which authorizes each exemption. This information is listed with the exemption categories for each state (or province) or with the federal exemptions list. Make notes along the way that will help you or to point out where you need to find more information. You are going to need this information when you file.

- Remember, this worksheet is not an official document, and you will not be submitting it when you file. But it will become the basis for your official paperwork, so it should be as complete as possible.

Overview of Categories

Under each category, list items individually with a note about the value of the property and to whom it belongs. If you are not sure whether property is owned jointly or as common property, seek advice.

- **Cash in hand**—includes money in your home, wallet, etc. All actual cash you have in your place of residence.
- **Checking/savings account, etc.**—list how much money you have in all your accounts, CDs, savings and loans accounts. In short, any account you hold. This includes savings in a safe deposit box.
- **Security deposits**—money you paid as a deposit to electric, gas, heating or telephone companies. Also include rental deposits on a residence, furniture or equipment.
- **Household goods, etc.**—you can list everything in your house that qualifies as household goods or furniture—from your antique dresser to your microwave oven. Do not forget garden equipment. The total value of food in your house should be included too. If in doubt, write it on the list. (It helps to do this room by room with someone aiding you.)

Note

When it comes to filling in the bankruptcy filing papers, the amount and type of property that you can claim as household goods is somewhat restricted—even more so since the recent amendments to the bankruptcy law.

- **Books, records, etc.**—include any art works, figurines or portraits. Do not forget to include videotapes and DVDs. This category is for goods that are not ordinary household items.
- **Clothing**—everything in the closet and what you are wearing too.
- **Furs and jewelry**—do not forget the things you are wearing, which might include wedding and engagement rings and watches.
- **Sports equipment, etc.**—as well as the obvious, include musical instruments, weapons, exercise machinery and board games.
- **Insurance policies**—put down the refund value of any insurance you have. Include health, disability, travel, homeowner or renter's life insurance and credit insurance.
- **Annuities**—the amount of any income from investment.
- **Interests in pensions, etc.**—IRA, Keogh, pension or retirement plan, 401(k) plan.
- **Stocks**—list any you have.
- **Interests in partnerships**—limited and general partnership interests.
- **Bonds**—corporate, municipal, promissory notes, U.S. Savings Bonds.
- **Accounts receivable**—money due from business and commissions you have already earned but not yet received.

How to Decide the Value of Property

It is important to provide as accurate an estimate as you can for your property. When it comes to submitting your paperwork, any willful attempt to mislead the court is regarded seriously. Bankruptcy trustees have a very good idea of the value of different kinds of property—they have a great deal of experience. Although, if you do not know the value of an item, or get it genuinely wrong, you will not be penalized.

When it comes to listing cash, accounts, investments, etc., it is quite easy to list the exact value. The approximate value of other financial property can be more difficult to estimate.

- For insurance polices, call your insurance agent to get the information.
- In the case of annuities, pensions and other business interests, you might benefit from getting some expert financial help.
- For stocks and bonds, look at listings in the newspaper or take the amount provided in your last statement.

Other property, like household items or furnishings, is generally valued as the amount you would get for it in a garage sale or through the classifieds. Do not put down the as new value. If you have older goods and have no idea of their value, have a look at flea market prices or secondhand stores. This is especially useful if you are trying to value items that depreciate very quickly; a computer that you bought new 3 years ago may be worth very little on today's market.

Valuables should be appraised professionally, especially in the case of antiques and jewelry.

Allocating Exemptions

Look at the list of exemptions under the system you have chosen and make a note of the exemption limit for each type of property. If you have not chosen between state and federal yet (and have that option), make a note of the limit for each. Seeing how the figures balance out may help you make your decision. Alternatively, you might prefer to fill out two copies of the worksheet, one for each situation.

If you are not sure if a property is exempt, it is worth assuming that it is. You will not be penalized if you have made a genuine mistake, but you will need to claim everything you can at the time of filing.

At the end, add up the value of your property in each category, and compare the total against the exemption limit for that category. Remember, you cannot mix and match state and federal exemption limits!

Strategies for Maximizing Your Exemptions

Prioritize Property That Means a Lot to You

You will probably have more property than your exemptions cover. You are going to have to choose which property you would prefer to claim as exempt. Rather than become overwhelmed by the different items that are exempt, start with a list of property you really cannot bear to part with.

- Prioritize which items you want to keep. Check your state's exemptions for these items.
- If they are not exempt, or the limit is low, check for a wildcard exemption amount that you can apply.
- If you can use federal bankruptcy exemptions (or the alternatives in California) see if you are better off with these.
- If not, see if the federal wildcard exemption would be best.

Note

If you are filing jointly with your spouse, you may be able to double your exemption(s). Also remember that your pension may already be exempt (see the information on retirement plans and IRAs in Chapter 5.)

Sell Nonexempt Property before You File

If you decide to sell your property rather than hand it over for liquidation you must be careful. It is certainly not illegal in all cases, but you should consult a lawyer to see what is permissible in your locality.

Turn Nonexempt Property into Exempt Property

Here is where you can do quite a bit to keep your property. You can sell items, which are nonexempt—either because they are not listed as possible exemptions or they come in over the limit in an exemption category.

- You can sell a nonexempt asset and use the money to buy a completely exempt item. For example, you could sell a book collection that is not exempt and buy clothing instead.
- You can sell an asset that comes in over your exemption limit and buy something similar, but in a cheaper model that is entirely exempt. For instance, sell your expensive stereo system and buy a more modest one that is within the exemption limit.
- You can buy an exempt item with cash (which is not usually exempt).
- You can sell a nonexempt asset and buy one that is exempt up to the amount you receive from selling the nonexempt asset. For instance, sell your book collection for $1,300 and buy a car that is exempt up to $1,300 in value.

Pay off Debts

You need to be very careful if you decide to pay off some debts. It is important not to be seen as favoring a creditor. But also remember that many of your debts are likely to be discharged by bankruptcy, so there is no real point in paying off many debts now. However, if a friend or relative has co-signed a loan, paying off the debt would be a way of protecting them from having to pay off the loan on your behalf.

Think Hard about Choosing to Pay off Secured Debts

However much your creditors are hassling you about paying off secured debts, and however much you want to be honest, sometimes paying off the debt at this point will not help you. If the collateral for the debt is not exempt, the trustee will take it anyway when you file for bankruptcy. But if it is exempt, you will not lose it.

Pay Your Bills

You can keep paying your regular bills until you file for bankruptcy. This way you can minimize the amount of cash in your checking account and avoid having your utilities disconnected.

A Warning: Do Not Undertake Fraudulent Transactions

As already mentioned, you must not deliberately try to hide property from the court by transferring it to friends or relatives or failing to report its existence. Although it may seem tempting, the bankruptcy court looks unfavorably on evidence of fraudulent transactions.

- **Reporting transactions**—you are required to report all transactions on Form 7, the Statement of Financial Affairs. Be open about any legal transactions you have made to maximize your exemptions. Do not lie or conceal information or your bankruptcy may be dismissed.

- **Selling and buying property**—if you sell an item, you should sell it at its market value, or as near to it as possible. For instance, do not sell your expensive TV to your sister for $50; the bankruptcy trustee is likely to challenge this. Similarly, buy items at a reasonable price—if you buy a used TV for $2,000 the trustee will suspect this is not a genuine sale. It will appear more likely that you did it in order to offload cash that you will get back later.

- **Do not make last minute transfers**—judges frequently rule that last minute transfers are an attempt to defraud creditors, even if they might not be. An exception exists when there is clear proof that you have openly arranged and planned to sell or buy property, and the final transfer took place shortly before you filed for bankruptcy.

- **Moving to a state with better exemptions**—it may seem unfair that your state has very ungenerous exemption limitations, while the state next door offers higher homestead exemptions. But beware of moving simply to take advantage of better situations. Recent changes in the law mean that people can no longer get away with moving to a state with more favorable homestead exemptions shortly before filing. Read the next chapter for further information on your home and homestead exemptions.

- **Changing the form of ownership**—do not move nonexempt property into joint ownership simply so that it becomes exempt (for instance, a house). This would probably be regarded as fraudulent and the bankruptcy court would take the property.

- **Taking out loans to pay off dischargeable debts**—some debts are not canceled, or discharged, by bankruptcy. One of the most common is a student loan. You might be tempted to take out another loan to pay off your student loan, and then have this new loan treated as dischargeable. However, the court is likely to penalize you by not allowing this new loan to be discharged.

Play Safe

Before you sell off or transfer any nonexempt property, find out how your local bankruptcy court regards this action. You can get information on all the U.S. bankruptcy courts at www.uscourts.gov/bankruptcycourts.html. If you are in Canada you should consult a Trustee in Bankruptcy.

Learning the Language of Law and Finance

A short glossary is provided at the end of the book to assist in your understanding of the terms used in the book. In addition, readers are entitled to full access and use of the comprehensive Personal Law and Personal Finance Dictionaries found on the Web landing page:

www.socrates.com/books/bankruptcy-renewal.aspx

Please remember to register the first time you use this free resource. See page iv for further details.

Section Three

8 Keeping the House

If you do not own your home, or any other real estate, this chapter will not apply to you. But if you do own real property, that is, real estate, you will want to protect it from repossession, if possible. If you are considering bankruptcy because you are behind on your mortgage payments and cannot meet them, read this chapter before you decide to file. There may be alternatives that can help you keep your home.

This chapter outlines why and how people run into trouble with their mortgage payments, often for reasons that are beyond their control. It offers various strategies to avoid reaching the stage where filing for Chapter 7 bankruptcy is your only choice. If losing your home is likely, you should do everything you can to avoid declaring Chapter 7 bankruptcy, even if you are eligible to do so. Many people file Chapter 13 to avoid foreclosure. By filing for Chapter 13 they are able to continue paying their mortgage and face less risk of losing the property. They may still surrender the house, as collateral against a secured loan, if they choose to.

If you do face the inevitable and have to file for Chapter 7, you need to understand exactly what might happen and what you may be able to do to prevent it. The next chapter concentrates on how your home is treated as part of your bankruptcy estate, what exemptions you can claim, and how bankruptcy affects other real estate you may own or part-own. Remember that this only applies if you own your home, not if you are renting.

Much of the information here is more relevant to Chapter 7 bankruptcy and pre-bankruptcy situations where you are not able to meet your mortgage payments. If you are filing for Chapter 13, you are probably employed and are continuing to pay your mortgage. (If you are not able to pay your mortgage or to negotiate more flexible repayment terms, you should be considering converting your case to Chapter 7 if eligible.)

> **Note**
>
> If you are filing for Chapter 13, you should still read this chapter because you will need to declare the value of your home and claim the exemptions you are entitled to.

Can You Afford Your House?

You risk losing your house (or other property) if you cannot afford to pay your mortgage payments and fall behind; at this point your mortgage loan is considered in default. It may not be simply your mortgage payments that are causing your financial problems. Sit down and work out how much it costs to own your house. Consider the following expenses:

- monthly mortgage payment
- homeowner's/condo association fees
- utilities
- landscaping/yard work
- homeowner's insurance
- property tax
- home repair/maintenance fees

If the total of these items comes to more than 40 percent of your monthly income (combined income if you share with a spouse or partner), you are probably living beyond your means.

Your Mortgage and the Lien on Your Home

A mortgage is a specific kind of lien—the mortgage itself is an agreement, or deed of trust that places a lien on a piece of real estate as a pledge against the loan that has been provided, in order to purchase the property. For mortgage companies, the security provided by your home is a way of protection for them against severe loss. You must keep making payments on your mortgage. If you stop making payments the lender has the right to foreclose on your mortgage. That is, they will sell your home in order to recoup the money you owe them.

Other Liens and How Bankruptcy Affects Them

If you have taken out other secured loans with your home as the collateral, each loan of this kind will place a lien on your home. This is in addition to any mortgage you may have. Perhaps you took out a second mortgage or maybe a creditor has placed a nonconsensual lien on your home.

Bankruptcy will not eradicate liens that were made with your consent (consensual liens, like a second mortgage). It also will not remove some non consensual liens—perhaps the most common is a tax lien, placed by the IRS for nonpayment of taxes.

Some Liens That Can Be Removed by Bankruptcy

Some nonconsensual liens are eliminated by bankruptcy. In certain circumstances you may be able to have your bankruptcy eliminate judgment liens—liens placed as a result of a creditor successfully suing you. To do this, you can file a motion to avoid a judicial lien, or file a separate lawsuit to remove the lien. Normally, a judicial lien can be removed if it is considered to impair an exemption (see Chapter 6 on exemptions)—that is, it prevents the debtor from retaining property (or equity in his or her home) that would otherwise be considered exempt property.

Keeping Your Home: Consider the Alternatives to Bankruptcy

Before immediately filing for bankruptcy, consider some of the alternatives. If you are faced with foreclosure or can see it on the horizon, consider the following strategies before filing for Chapter 7 or Chapter 13.

Get advice. Consult a lawyer who specializes in foreclosures. See if together you can find a way of saving your home. Alternatively, seek counseling from a specialist, but beware of scams (see Chapter 23 for some warning signs). The U.S. Department of Housing has a list of approved counseling agencies. Also, your lender may be able to give you information on counseling options.

See if you can get financial help. If you are 65 or over, or blind or disabled, you may qualify for Supplementary Security Income (SSI). Contact your local Social Security office.

Contact your lender; do not keep them in the dark. If you cannot meet payments, go into your bank or write to your mortgage company. Be completely honest about your situation. Most lenders do not want the hassle of having to foreclose; they would rather work out an alternative plan with you. It is your responsibility to explain your situation and to ask for help. Keep a record of all communications that you write or receive.

Do not ignore letters or calls from your mortgage holder. Technically, your lender can begin foreclosure proceedings the day after your payment should have been due—at the close of the business day on which your payment was due, your mortgage may be deemed to be in default. Most lenders will normally contact you after your payment is 16 days late to try and work out a way to help you make the payments. After 30 days the lender's efforts will become more strenuous, and you will start incurring late payment fees and other costs.

A Positive Note

The secondary mortgage market associations—Fannie Mae, Freddie Mac and the Federal Housing Administration (FHA)—require their mortgage companies to work with borrowers to avoid foreclosure. (See Glossary for definitions.)

Do not leave. The worst thing you can do is simply stop paying the mortgage and leave the home. This will almost certainly spur your mortgage company into foreclosing on your loan and selling your home.

Pay your mortgage. Even if you are heavily in debt, it may be best to pay your mortgage and leave other debts for the moment.

More on Mortgage Payment Workouts

Your mortgage lender may be able to offer various temporary ways to help make the payment process easier for you. But you must work these out with your lender, and they will require evidence of your financial problems. The following points illustrate possible payment adjustments.

- Skipping a payment.
- Allowing a longer grace period for late payments.
- Restructuring—permanently changing the terms of the loan. Usually this means rolling the delinquent payments (those you have missed) into the rest of the loan and spreading them out over the remaining duration. It can also involve lowering the interest rate temporarily.
- Mortgage modification—for instance, extending your remaining mortgage over a longer period or refinancing the equity you hold in your home.

Even if your payment attempts do not work out, the fact that you have shown a genuine desire to communicate with the lender will likely assist you in dealing with your mortgage company if you do decide to file for bankruptcy.

When Foreclosure Seems Inevitable

If none of the above payment adjustments are possible, you will probably have to consider selling your home or letting the mortgage lender sell it to foreclose on the loan. Even so, if this is your main financial problem, you may not need to file bankruptcy. In fact, it may be that bankruptcy would not solve much and would only result in a ruined credit record and other problems you can avoid.

After Foreclosure Proceedings Have Begun

It is still not too late to take action. Foreclosure can take several months—anywhere from 3 to 18—depending on what kind of loan you have and where you live. Consider some of these possible options.

Get another loan—Depending on the state of your current mortgage, you may be able to get an additional loan to pay off the mortgage payments you have missed, along with other costs and interest relating to your current mortgage. You still face the burden of paying off your mortgage regularly, in addition to payments on this new loan. If you select this option, you will often have to pay high fees and interest rates. Some companies try to hide this fact from you, so be careful.

File for Chapter 13—This might be the best option if you can afford to keep paying your mortgage and can also pay off the missed payments over time. Many people file Chapter 13 in order to avoid foreclosure.

Partial claim—If you have a HUD/FHA loan you may be able to claim a one-time payment from the FHA-insurance fund. This payment will be in the amount needed to bring your mortgage payments up-to-date. In exchange for this you are required to sign a promissory note, (which is legally binding) promising to repay the loaned amount. Until you pay off this loan there will be a lien on your home. But, on the plus side, the payment is interest-free and only due when you pay off the mortgage or sell the property.

Sell the house—It may be possible for you to sell the house, pay off the mortgage and move on. A Short Sale may be acceptable to your lender: in this scenario you sell the house quickly, but for less than you owe. Your mortgage company accepts this amount and forgives (releases you from) the rest of the loan.

You may qualify for a Pre-Foreclosure Sale if you can meet the following criteria:

- your mortgage is 2 months delinquent or more;
- you are able to sell your home within 3 to 5 months; and
- a new appraisal from your lender shows that your home's value meets HUD program guidelines.

You may opt for what is known as a Friendly Foreclosure, or a Deed in Lieu Foreclosure. Actually, this is the least attractive possibility. It involves handing the deed over to the lender, who then sells it to meet their costs. In doing this, you lose all equity you might have had in the house, plus many of your rights towards the mortgage lender. Do not choose this option unless there is no alternative.

Do Not Get Scammed—Equity Skimming

Equity skimming is a common scam when it comes to mortgage payment difficulties. You are in a vulnerable position and should watch out for the following scenario:

Someone—a company or financial specialist of some kind—approaches you and offers to help you out with your difficulties. They offer to pay off your mortgage, or give you a sum of money when the property is sold. They may suggest that you legally sign over the property to them and move out. Far from helping you out, this buyer is simply taking advantage of your desperation. Rather than sell the property, they will rent it out and keep the rent. But they will not make the mortgage payments on your property, and the mortgage will still be in your name. As a result, your mortgage lender will foreclose on the property and you may still be responsible for the outstanding debt.

Stopping Foreclosure

You may have a defense to foreclosure, which will enable you to delay, or even stop the foreclosure. If you think this is the case, you should contact a lawyer to investigate this for you. Below are some defenses to foreclosure.

- **Failure to follow foreclosure procedures**—Each state has requirements that lenders have to follow, which give you certain rights. For instance, there is usually a period of notice that lenders are required to provide to you before they commence foreclosure.

- **Interest rates that violate state or federal law**—Lenders are not allowed by federal law to make deceptive or false representations about the loan or the costs you may have to pay. Some states limit how much interest you can be charged on a loan.

- **Home improvement fraud**—If you took out an additional mortgage to have some work done on your home and the contractor ripped you off or did shoddy work, you may be able to cancel this loan.

- **Violations of the Truth in Lending Law**—This federal law requires loan companies to provide you with certain information before you sign the loan papers so that you are fully aware of the terms of the loan. If they did not, you may be able to cancel the loan. Note that this usually does not apply when you take out a loan to purchase your home.

A Note on Foreclosure in Canada

In Canada, the situation is very similar: There are two ways that a lender can recover a mortgage debt by forcing the sale of your home. These are by Judicial Sale or Power of Sale. Judicial Sale requires court involvement, and the lender must apply to the court. Power of Sale has virtually no court involvement; provincial legislation and the mortgage document provide all the power needed for the lender to sell.

Judicial Sale is used in British Columbia, Alberta, Saskatchewan, Manitoba and Quebec.

Power of Sale is more common in Newfoundland, New Brunswick, Prince Edward Island and Ontario. In Nova Scotia, there is a different process, also involving court approval, called Mortgage Foreclosure and Sale.

In order to gain access to free forms, dictionaries, checklists and updates, readers must register their book purchase at Socrates.com. An eight digit Registration Code is provided on the enclosed CD. See page iv for further details.

9 Your Home & the Homestead Exemption

If paying the mortgage is just one of many serious financial troubles you have, filing for bankruptcy may be your only realistic option. In this case, you are likely to be filing for Chapter 7, if you can, since in Chapter 13 you would normally be expected to continue paying off your mortgage. The information in this chapter explains more about the property exemption relating to your home. Anyone considering bankruptcy should read this chapter for information that will help in completing the filing paperwork.

This chapter also explains how to calculate the equity in your home, and the special kind of exemption you can apply against it—called the Homestead Exemption. In many cases, this exemption alone is insufficient to protect you from losing your home, so you need to consider additional strategies for keeping it. Finally, although you may have to face losing your home, you might also consider other possible strategies.

As already mentioned, real estate you own is termed real property and includes not only your home—your primary residence—but also any other real estate property you own or have a share of ownership in. When you file for bankruptcy, your home is considered part of your bankruptcy estate along with your other property. But, as with other property, there are exemptions you can claim. How likely you are to lose your home depends on how you balance the equity you have in your home against the amount of exemptions you can claim.

The Equity in Your Home

The equity in your home is based on the value of the portion of the property that you actually own. Some people own their home outright; in this case the equity is the value of the home. But most people have a mortgage; we are gradually paying off a loan that helped us to buy our home. In this case, the equity is the difference between the value of the property and the amount you owe on the mortgage.

For instance, if you own a house that is now worth $120,000 and took out a mortgage of $100,000 to buy it, then the equity you have in the house is $20,000. That is, if you sold the house at the market value today, and then paid off your mortgage, you would have $20,000 in your pocket.

But remember that this example is more straightforward than most situations. In reality, you may have paid off some of the mortgage already, so your equity may be more.

Another Important Note on Equity

Make sure you are aware of how your state's bankruptcy courts regard equity. Some courts divide equity into encumbered equity—the value of your home, less the amount of the mortgage—and unencumbered equity—your home's value, less the amount of the mortgage and any other liens on it. State homestead exemptions (see below) vary in how much of them you can apply to liens other than your mortgage.

The Homestead Exemption

> A homestead exemption may allow you to protect the equity in your home, up to a certain amount. But the effect this will have depends on the amount of equity you have in your home.

The federal exemption system has a specific exemption that you can apply against your home, called the homestead exemption. Many state exemption systems also have a homestead exemption, sometimes more generous than the federal system's. Some states do not have any homestead exemption, while some have an unlimited homestead exemption. (This unlimited exemption has been limited by the new bankruptcy law.)

You may have to brace for the fact that keeping your house (or apartment, mobile home or other real estate that you call home) is not an option. If you have a large amount of nonexempt equity in your home, it is likely that you will lose your home if you file for Chapter 7 bankruptcy. With this realistic possibility in mind, there are factors that can protect your home.

The amount allowed as a homestead exemption in the federal exemption system is currently defined as:

Real property, including co-op or mobile home to $18,450; unused portion of homestead to $9,250 may be applied to any property.

Example

If you own a house worth $90,000 and have an $80,000 mortgage (and no other liens on your home) you can put $10,000 of the exemption against the $10,000 equity you have in your house. Your house is then safe, and you have $8,450 left over from the homestead exemption, all of which can be used to protect other property you own.

Be sure to look at your state exemption system to see if their homestead exemption is more generous. If you own your home, the exemption system you choose is likely to be dictated by the homestead exemption terms.

However, if you have significant equity in your home, it is unlikely to be covered by the homestead exemption. In the following example, the equity in the home is significantly more than the homestead exemption:

Jack lives in Texas and owns his home. He cannot meet the payments on his mortgage now and is filing for Chapter 7 bankruptcy.

At current prices his home is now worth $250,000. But he still owes $150,000 to the mortgage company. He also has a separate lien on the house for a loan of $70,000. His home equity is $250,000 minus $150,000 minus $70,000, and equals $30,000.

The federal exemption system allows him to claim $18,450, but that still leaves the balance of his equity as nonexempt ($30,000 minus $18,450 equals $11,550). As it stands, he would need to find $11,550 from other sources that are not part of his bankruptcy estate—for instance his current earnings since filing for bankruptcy—or his house will be sold to pay his creditors.

If the cost of the sale would be more than the equity that is nonexempt, the bankruptcy trustee will probably not decide to sell your house.

Some states require you to file a declaration of homestead before you file for bankruptcy—this essentially involves declaring which is your primary residence or home, in the situation where you own two or more properties. If in doubt, do it anyway, since some creditors require it also. States that may require a declaration are Alabama, Idaho, Massachusetts, Montana, Nevada, Texas, Utah, Virginia and Washington.

Is Your Equity Protected by the Homestead Exemption?

If you have some home equity, you need to check if it qualifies for the exemption.

These state exemption systems have no homestead exemption:

• Delaware	• Maryland
• New Jersey	• Pennsylvania

Certain kinds of dwellings are not protected by the homestead exemption. Check your state's exemption to determine if the following are covered:

• mobile home	• co-op or condominium building
• apartments	

Some state exemption lists specifically mention the above as being included in the homestead exemption. Others say that the homestead exemption can be applied to any real or personal property used as a residence. This usually means that any kind of property is fine, including a trailer, mobile home or even a houseboat. If you live in a trailer and the homestead exemption for your state will not cover it, you may be able to claim it as a motor vehicle. If you are at all unsure, consult a lawyer or do some investigating of your own to get clarification.

What Is Your Homestead Exemption Based on?

In many cases, your homestead exemption is simply based on the equity value of your home, as described above. But in some states it is based on the lot size of your home, while in others it is based on a combination of lot size and equity.

- Five states and the District of Columbia (D.C.) have unlimited homestead exemptions that allow debtors who file for bankruptcy to shelter their homes from creditors. These five states include Florida, Iowa, Kansas, South Dakota and Texas.
- In states with unlimited homestead exemptions, the lot size of the property is considered, although this is rarely a significant factor. Lot size exemption means that the state has an upper limit of lot size that is considered exempt. If your property's acreage is equal to or less than that limit, it is exempt. You will not lose your home. If your property exceeds the maximum acreage that is allowed, the trustee will sell the excess acreage—if you have equity in it.
- Lot size and equity: In this case, if your property's lot size is within the allowable limit, your equity in the property is considered. If your property's lot size is larger than the allowable lot size, the trustee will sell the excess acreage—if you have equity in it. Currently, Alabama, Hawaii, Louisiana, Michigan, Minnesota, Mississippi, Nebraska and Oregon use this system.
- All other states with homestead exemptions consider only the amount of equity in your home.

It is important to understand that recent amendments to the federal bankruptcy law limit the state homestead exemption to $125,000 if the individual filing bankruptcy bought the residence at least 3 years and 4 months before filing. Also, the length of time that you must live in a state in order to claim that state's exemptions has been increased from 180 days to 730 days. This prevents people from moving into an unlimited state in order to evade creditors shortly before filing. The limit on the homestead exemption also applies if the person filing is convicted of criminal acts—some specific felonies of willful or reckless misconduct—in the 5 years preceding filing.

You may be eligible for a higher homestead exemption if there are special circumstances, particularly if you are a medically distressed debtor (see Glossary).

Strategies for Keeping Your House after Filing for Bankruptcy

Reduce your equity in the house—You may be able to do this if done at least 1 year before filing for bankruptcy.

Borrow against the equity—This will not reduce your debt (quite the opposite), but will mean that you have less equity and therefore less chance of having to hand over your house to the bankruptcy trustee.

Sell some of your equity—If you sell half your house to someone else, for instance a friend or relative, this will reduce both your equity and some of your financial burden.

A word of caution: some bankruptcy courts have ruled unfavorably against people who have followed these strategies, in particular where the sale has been for an unrealistic price.

Offer Cash Instead of Equity

If the equity in your home exceeds any exemption you can claim, you face the prospect of losing the home, and this means that the bankruptcy trustee can obtain the nonexempt equity. The trustee may be willing to accept cash for an equivalent or lesser amount, in the alternative. You may be able to raise cash by selling exempt property or by saving money from your wages that you earn after filing for bankruptcy. The trustee may also accept other exempt property up to the value of the equity that is nonexempt.

For instance, you may have claimed a valuable book collection as exempt. You can sell that book collection and give the proceeds to the bankruptcy trustee in lieu of the nonexempt amount of equity in your home. You will lose the book collection but keep the house.

The bankruptcy trustee may forgive some of the loan if the difference between what you can raise and the equity in your home is less than the cost of actually selling the house. In general, bankruptcy trustees try to be accommodating for quite practical reasons: Selling a home is an expensive and time consuming business.

Use Those Wildcard Exemptions

Do not forget that in many states there are wildcard exemptions that you can use to boost the exemption limit on certain kinds of property, or to create exemptions for property that would otherwise be nonexempt. Some states have wildcard exemptions that can be applied to real estate (in addition to your homestead exemption). Check the terms of the wildcard exemptions for your state. (Remember, you can only use state exemptions if you have chosen that system.)

File for Chapter 13 or Convert from Chapter 7 to Chapter 13

It is important to understand the distinction between Chapter 7 and Chapter 13 when it comes to your home.

- In Chapter 7 bankruptcy, the court appointed bankruptcy trustee could demand any nonexempt equity in your home to pay off creditors. This means selling your home or finding an alternative.

- In Chapter 13 bankruptcy you get to keep your home, even if you have nonexempt equity in it. You still need to work out the value of your home and the amount of equity is nonexempt. Chapter 13 can halt foreclosure on your home, and also allows you to pay off the fees and missed payments over time. If you have a continual income, even if it is not high, you may be able to negotiate when you can pay and how much in fees you can afford.

> If you live in Canada you should also consider the possibility of filing a Personal Proposal, if you are eligible. See Chapter 18 for more information on how the Canadian process works.

Losing Your Home: Making the Most of It

If there is no alternative to foreclosure, you can at least try to get the most you can out of it. The following strategy may have negative consequences, but can offer you a way to avoid handing the equity in your home over to the bankruptcy trustee. (However, although it will let you hang onto more cash, it probably will not help you to keep your home.)

- You have fallen way behind on your mortgage payments, and cannot figure out a way to get caught up. Because of this, your mortgage company wants to foreclose. You can and do file for Chapter 7. This immediately halts the foreclosure temporarily.
- Now you are living in your home basically for free. You are not paying the mortgage and your bankruptcy case is in progress.
- It might take up to a year or so for the bankruptcy case to end. During this time you are saving the payments that would have gone to your mortgage company. For instance, if your payments are $2,000 a month, you have saved $24,000 over a year.
- Your state homestead exemption is very low. But you have very little equity in your home anyway, so the exemption will cover it and the bankruptcy trustee cannot sell your house.
- By not paying your mortgage, you are not improving your equity in the home (essentially you are removing equity from your home.)

At the end of your bankruptcy case you will have to face tax liabilities and the fact that your credit report will note the existence of the foreclosure; this will obviously make it harder for you to get another mortgage.

Foreclosure vs. Bankruptcy Sale

It is important to know the difference between these two kinds of forced sale. Foreclosure is when your lender (usually your mortgage company) takes action to force the sale of your home, which is called a foreclosure sale. A bankruptcy sale is when the bankruptcy trustee supervises the sale—or liquidation—of your house because you are unable to protect all the equity in it from becoming part of your bankruptcy estate.

- In foreclosure, the mortgage company is not interested in selling your home for a good price. Basically, they are just interested in recovering the amount of the loan they gave you.

- In a bankruptcy sale, the bankruptcy trustee wants to get as much for your home as possible. This will enable them to pay off more of your unsecured creditors.

- The more your house is sold for, the more likely you are to retain some of the equity, (which will be protected by your homestead exemption).

Get a Valuation

It is worth getting a realtor to value your home so that you know how much it is likely to go for on the market. You can also get a rough valuation of your property at various Web sites such as www.domania.com and www.homegain.com.

In Canada, home prices can be checked at www.priceahomeonline.ca.

As a final note, remember that the bankruptcy trustee may decide not to sell your home—even if you have nonexempt equity in it. Reasons for not selling can include the cost of selling the home or the amount of equity in comparison to the amount of debt to unsecured creditors. But this does mean that the trustee can hand authority over to the mortgage company, so foreclosure is still a likely possibility.

With the information in this Chapter and the previous Chapter, you should have a good understanding of what you can do to prevent your home from being sold in a forced sale. Also, if losing your home seems very likely given your personal financial situation, you have the information necessary to maximize your exemptions.

10 Determining Eligibility & Advisability of Filing Chapter 7

Here we will discuss, in general terms, what Chapter 7 bankruptcy involves. Later in Chapter 11 we will explain further how the process works, and what forms and papers you will need. That chapter will also provide you with a summary of the schedule of events. Be sure to read this chapter first to find out if Chapter 7 is appropriate for you.

Although there are, technically, two forms of personal bankruptcy open to individuals, there are several circumstances where you may be ineligible to apply—or reapply—for Chapter 7. These circumstances are explained in full, along with some additional reasons why it may be ill advised to apply for Chapter 7 bankruptcy, even if you are eligible. Finally, this chapter discusses whether, in light of all that is involved, Chapter 7 makes economic sense for you.

After this introduction to Chapter 7, there are several more chapters explaining the way debts are treated when filing Chapter 7, the process of actually filing for Chapter 7 and then going to court and what is involved afterwards. It may help you to refer to them while reading this chapter.

> While most of this information is very relevant for people filing in Canada, there is also a separate chapter giving an overview of the Canadian filing procedure, as well as extra pointers along the way.

An Overview of Chapter 7 Bankruptcy

Chapter 7 bankruptcy allows debtors to eliminate most unsecured debts, like credit card debts. (See Chapter 3 for an explanation of different kinds of debts.) In order to do this, the debtor hands over much of the property he or she owns in a court-supervised procedure. This property is sold—or liquidated—to cover at least part of the debts involved.

This kind of bankruptcy gets its name from being Chapter 7 of Title 11 of the U.S. Code, entitled Liquidation. It is the most drastic kind of personal bankruptcy and not everyone is eligible to file it.

> In Canada, bankruptcy is subject to the Bankruptcy and Insolvency Act, or BIA. The equivalent to Chapter 7 is most often referred to as pure bankruptcy. The same general principles apply, although there are different requirements and levels of protection.

Are You Eligible to File for Chapter 7?

Recent changes in the law have made it more difficult to file for Chapter 7 bankruptcy. These changes are designed to ensure that the opportunity to file for Chapter 7 bankruptcy is not abused by people who could, but do not want to, file under Chapter 13. Those people with very low or no income and insurmountable debts are still able to file for Chapter 7.

The Means Test

Under recent bankruptcy reforms, people whose income exceeds their state's median income level and who can pay at least $6,000 over 5 years now have to file under Chapter 13 and cannot generally file for Chapter 7.

- There are some exceptions for active-duty members of the military, low income veterans and people with serious medical conditions.
- Also, certain kinds of income are excluded from consideration. This income includes Social Security benefits, payments to victims of war crimes or crimes against humanity, and payments to victims of international terrorism.

You can find out your state's median income level by going to the U.S. Census Web site at www.census.gov. Each state is listed with the median income for a four person family.

Note

You may be penalized if you intentionally file for Chapter 7 although you should have filed for Chapter 13. It may also be more difficult for you to file a Chapter 7 bankruptcy if you have previously filed another Chapter 7 bankruptcy. Under the new law, you must wait at least 8 years before filing another Chapter 7 case.

Many people will not be significantly affected by the means test since their income falls far below the local median level. In this case they would normally be eligible for Chapter 7.

What Happens?

When you file for Chapter 7, an automatic stay is put on your debts almost immediately. As soon as you file you become protected and cannot be approached by creditors. This prevents you from harassment and temporarily halts any action against you. See Chapter 4 for a full explanation of what is involved in the automatic stay.

At the end of your bankruptcy many of your debts are canceled and you are no longer liable to pay them. But some will still remain.

On the downside, Chapter 7 involves handing over much of your property to the courts, whose appointed trustee will sell, or liquidate it. Your property—also called your assets—is used as a way to raise at least some cash to pay, or partly pay, some of your creditors. Although there are some assets that you can keep, you could lose many items that mean a lot to you. It is possible that you may lose your house and car.

However, certain items are exempt from liquidation, and these include necessities like equipment or tools that you need in your job. In fact, there is quite a wide variety of property that you can keep because it is considered exempt. The rules on exemption differ from state to state (in Canada from one province to another). There is far more information on these exemptions in the next chapter, including measures you can take to retain certain property or offer alternative property to be liquidated. A full list of exemptions in each state, or province, is provided as an Appendix to this book.

In the majority of cases you will receive a discharge at the end of the bankruptcy process. This means that you are no longer liable for any of the debts that have been discharged. But you will remain liable for certain debts, including child support and most unpaid taxes.

A Note on Tax Debts in Chapter 7

Your tax debts (federal or state income taxes) can only be discharged (that is wiped out at the end of the bankruptcy) if ALL of the following hold true at the time of filing:

- the taxes are income taxes;
- you did not commit fraud or willful evasion—that is, you did not file a fraudulent return or, for instance, give a wrong Social Security number;
- you pass the 3-year rule—the tax debt concerned relates to unpaid taxes that are more than 3 years past due;
- you pass the 2-year rule—you actually filed the tax return that relates to these unpaid taxes at least 2 years before filing for bankruptcy; and
- you pass the 240-day rule—the income tax debt was assessed at least 240 days before you file or has not yet been assessed.

After you receive your bankruptcy discharge you are under no obligation to the court, except if you come into money through an inheritance, insurance policy or divorce within 180 days of your discharge. If that happens you must inform the court and some of the money will be used to further pay off your debts.

Situations Where Filing for Chapter 7 Is Not Possible or Advisable

Although filing for Chapter 7 may seem on its face the best way to get out of all your money troubles, there are many circumstances where it is inappropriate or legally impossible. The following are some specific instances where you are barred from filing for Chapter 7, followed by an explanation of why.

• You Previously Received a Bankruptcy Discharge

Remember, you have to wait 8 years from the date of your previous Chapter 7 or Chapter 13 filing before you can refile. (This has recently changed from 6 years.) But there may be special circumstances that nullify that 8-year rule. For instance, if you filed previously for Chapter 13 in good faith after paying off at least 70 percent of your unsecured debts.

Note

Remember that the 8-year period runs from the date at which the earlier bankruptcy was filed, not the date at which your debts were discharged. For obvious reasons, people tend to remember their discharge date more clearly than the date they filed!

• A Previous Bankruptcy Was Dismissed within the Previous 180 Days

There are two circumstances when you cannot file after a bankruptcy case has been canceled or dismissed.

1. If this happened because you violated a court order.

2. If you asked for the bankruptcy to be dismissed because a creditor had asked for relief from the automatic stay. That is, the creditor is requesting that you should not be protected from paying the debt you owe them.

• A Friend or Relative Co-signed a Loan

Perhaps you took out a loan that had to be co-signed because your credit was not good, or the lender had other concerns about your ability to meet the payments. If a friend or relative co-signed the loan for you, they are normally agreeing to be wholly responsible for the loan if you cannot pay. If you file for Chapter 7, you will no longer be obligated to make the payments, but the co-signer will become responsible for it all.

The only way you can protect the co-signer from complete liability is to consider a payment plan as an alternative to filing for Chapter 7 bankruptcy. By choosing this alternative you can negotiate with your creditors to pay off the loan in smaller increments, or to pay it partly, rather than causing your friend or relative any trouble.

In addition to the reasons why you might be ineligible to apply for Chapter 7 in the first place, there are several circumstances where your application for Chapter 7 bankruptcy may be dismissed. When these involve deliberate fraud or illegal behavior on your part, you may be prosecuted, and possibly even jailed. You will not be jailed if your behavior stems from confusion or lack of understanding, though you may still lose your filing fee.

Deliberate abuse of Chapter 7 is regarded seriously by the courts since the process is intended as a last ditch decision, and one which will cause financial loss to a number of creditors. Creditors, especially credit card companies, are increasingly challenging bankruptcy cases where they perceive the debtor's actions fraudulent.

Note

Credit card companies lose huge amounts of money from people who deliberately overspend on their credit cards and then try to declare bankruptcy in order to avoid the obligation to pay. Recent changes to the bankruptcy law have made it far more difficult for people to do this by making it harder to qualify for Chapter 7, and by increasing the number of debts that are nondischargeable.

In Canada, the bankruptcy law already holds debtors liable for many debts, including credit card debts.

• You Are Better Qualified to File for Chapter 13

Although Chapter 7 bankruptcy may in some ways seem the easiest way out of financial trouble, it is not necessarily the best choice for everyone. In some cases the court may not even allow you to apply for it. This is true if the court finds that you are qualified to file for Chapter 13. In this situation the court may regard your attempt to file for Chapter 7 as an abuse of the bankruptcy laws and will dismiss it.

The following circumstances present situations where a judge will tend to look unfavorably on an attempt to file for Chapter 7:

- if you are not eligible to do so;
- if you appear to have enough income to pay off your debts within 3 to 5 years;
- if your monthly income exceeds your monthly expenditures; and
- if you have enough savings, or a high enough salary, to pay off 50 percent or more of your debts.

Some states are more flexible than others concerning the dismissal of Chapter 7 bankruptcy cases in this category. In some states you will be offered the chance to convert your case to Chapter 13, in some you will be forced to. If you convert your case you will at least save the filing fee. In general, judges do not look favorably on any attempt to get out of paying debts that you have the means to pay since this is an abuse of the spirit of Chapter 7. Chapter 7 is designed to help honest debtors who genuinely want to solve their financial problems by alleviating their financial obligations.

• You Defrauded Your Creditors

If you have the means to pay off your debts, but try to hide this fact, you are guilty of defrauding your creditors.

For Instance:

- if you try to hide assets that might be used in liquidation by signing them over to friends and relatives;
- if you run up debts for luxuries—non-necessities and other things that someone in debt should really not be spending money on— despite having no money;
- if you are in the midst of divorce proceedings and try to hide your assets—money or property—from your spouse.

The court will also look on you unfavorably if you run up huge bills for luxury items, holidays or other nonessentials shortly before you declare bankruptcy. Last minute debts of this kind are generally not discharged. For example, if you purchase luxury goods within 90 days of filing, you can only discharge $500 of such debts. Similarly, if you take a cash advance under an open-end credit plan within 70 days of filing, only $750 may be discharged.

- **You Are Attempting to Defraud the Court**
  When you sign your bankruptcy papers you are required to do so under penalty of perjury. This means that you are swearing—in legally binding terms—that everything you have declared in your papers is, to your knowledge, true. If you are dishonest and are found to have deliberately misled or blatantly lied to the court, you can be prosecuted for fraud. The penalties for this can be severe and involve going to jail.

Does It Make Sense for You to File for Chapter 7?

Even assuming that you would be eligible for Chapter 7, you should consider whether this type of bankruptcy makes economic sense for you.

What Do You Own?

Do you have property or earnings that could be taken from you if you do not file? If you have no income and do not own significant property, there is not much you have to lose if creditors do make a judgment against you and demand your property. So, no matter how much you owe, there is not much your creditors can do about it.

Of course, that is not to say you should regard yourself as free of all obligations. Because even if you do not own much property, rest assured that creditors and debt collection agencies will make persistent attempts to get the money you owe.

How Much Will You Lose?

When you start considering whether to file, you should immediately work out what exemptions apply to you and what you can do to hang on to property that you treasure or desperately want to keep. The next Chapter explains these exemptions in more detail.

If it turns out that you would not be able to avoid handing over nearly everything, you may want to consider other options. There are many strategies to help you make the most of your exemptions and hang on to as much as possible, but in some cases you will have no choice.

Will Bankruptcy Get Rid of the Debts That Are Causing the Problem?

Remember, not all debts are discharged by bankruptcy. If most of the debts you have are the kind not wiped out by bankruptcy, there is not much point in going through the process.

> If you are in Canada, you should also read the chapter that relates specifically to Canadian bankruptcy for an overview of circumstances that relate to you.

> Debts that can be canceled out by bankruptcy are termed dischargeable debts; those that cannot be are nondischargeable.

Free Forms and Checklists

Registered readers can visit www.socrates.com/books/bankruptcy-renewal.aspx for free forms, letters and checklists. See page iv for details on how to register. Among the many items available are:

Request for Free Credit Report

Request for Removal of Outdated Information

Demand for Corrected Credit Report

Debt Consolidation Schedule

Analysis of Cash Available for Debt Repayment

Monthly Expenses (Worksheet)

Examples of Credit Reports (TransUnion & Experian)

Loan Worksheet

And more . . .

Section Four

SOCRATES™
KNOW HOW TO DO MORE
AND SAVE

11 Filing for Chapter 7

This chapter summarizes the process of filing for Chapter 7 bankruptcy. It explains the fees and the forms that you will need to complete. In addition, it provides information on how to find the right court, how to file and the effect of filing.

It is assumed that you are eligible to file for Chapter 7. If you are not sure, read Chapter 10 of this book and, if your situation is complicated, seek professional advice. If you are sure that you would be better off filing for Chapter 13, you do not need to read this chapter, although you may find it useful. If you are in Canada, you should read the chapter on the Canadian filing procedure, although, quite a bit of this information is very useful in general terms.

Decide When to File

Before you start, think about whether this is the best time for you to file. You should aim to file Chapter 7 as a way of discharging—essentially eradicating—as much of your debt as you can. If, for example, your bankruptcy has been brought on by huge medical costs for an illness you are currently suffering, it may be a good move to wait until all your major medical costs have been incurred. Then they will all be included in your bankruptcy filing.

A General Overview of the Process

The following sequence of events takes place when filing for Chapter 7 bankruptcy. Although a creditor can ask the court to make an order declaring that you are bankrupt, usually bankruptcy is a voluntary process.

Remember, you will find a checklist on www.socrates.com/books/bankruptcy-renewal.aspx that compares which debts are discharged in personal bankruptcy. Use this as a guide.

1. Mandatory Credit Counseling

Recent amendments to the bankruptcy law mean you must receive credit counseling during the 6 months prior to filing Chapter 7 bankruptcy or, in special cases, within 30 days of filing. If you do not receive credit counseling and file proof of compliance, your case could be automatically dismissed. If not approved, counseling services are available in your district. This requirement may be waived—but you cannot decide to do this on your own.

> (Mandatory credit counseling is already part of the Canadian system—see Chapter 18 for more information.)

Many people fall into debt when they do not fully understand how to deal with their finances, and also when their overspending gets out of hand—in particular, the misuse of credit cards. Mandatory counseling is a means to address this problem and offer people a way to pinpoint the root of their financial difficulties. For those people whose debts arise from medical expenses or unexpected employment, the cause of their bankruptcy may be apparent. Nevertheless, counseling is compulsory for almost anyone who files for bankruptcy, unless the option is not available or they are refused counseling.

After completing the counseling, you will receive a certificate of compliance from the counselor, who must be on a list of approved agents. You must then file the certificate with the court, along with a copy of the payment plan created with the counselor. There is general information on credit counseling and how to choose a good counselor in Chapter 23.

2. You File a Petition

You file a petition, along with information about your financial circumstances, to the bankruptcy court. You are required to surrender all property of the bankruptcy estate to the court-appointed trustee. The process of filing triggers the automatic stay, which stops your creditors from approaching you or taking your money outside of the bankruptcy proceedings. See Chapter 4 for a detailed explanation of the automatic stay.

> **Tip**
>
> You can also notify problem creditors of your bankruptcy filing at the same time so that they will stop approaching you.

3. 1-2 Weeks after Filing: The Court-appointed Trustee Takes over

A court-appointed trustee takes over your financial affairs. The trustee's role is to examine your papers and manage your property. The court sets a date for your creditors' meeting and notifies your creditors.

> In Canada, the process is quite similar, but the bankruptcy is administered by a Trustee in Bankruptcy, rather than by a court-appointed trustee.

4. 20-40 Days after Filing*: You Attend a Meeting of Creditors

(Sometimes Called the 341 Meeting)

About a month later, you attend a very short meeting with the trustee and your creditors. (Often creditors do not attend in person.) This meeting is a chance for your creditors to ask questions about your financial situation. You are required to attend this meeting and respond to all of the questions in good faith. It is not a trial, and there is no judge (just the trustee and other people like you); it usually lasts approximately 5 minutes.

> This meeting is not always required in Canada, although you are required to respond to requests from the trustee, and to fill in certain forms provided. See the chapter on filing in Canada.

* In many districts the meetings are much more likely to be within 45-90 days of filing.

Note

The new bankruptcy law requires you to give the bankruptcy trustee a copy of your tax return for the latest tax period, prior to filing. If this is not provided within 7 days before the initial meeting with creditors, your bankruptcy case will be dismissed.

5. After Creditor's Meeting: Your Eligibility for Chapter 7 is Confirmed

At this point the bankruptcy trustee looks at your assets and income, and your other paperwork. The court decides whether you are eligible to file for Chapter 7 or if it is more appropriate for you to file Chapter 13. The court determines this by comparing your family's gross income to the median family income in your state. If your income exceeds the state's median gross income and you can afford to pay as little as $100 per month to creditors, you may be forced to file for Chapter 13. To determine whether you have the means to repay your creditors, the court looks at allowable expenses, which are determined by IRS-approved cost figures for living expenses you would be expected to incur.

6. After Creditors' Meeting: Nonexempt Property is Sold

The trustee may collect nonexempt property and sell it. The money raised will be divided among your creditors and used to pay the costs of your case.

Tip

You may be able to keep nonexempt property if you provide the court with exempt property of the same value or can provide cash equal to the market value of the property concerned. See Chapter 6 for further information on exempt and nonexempt property.

7. Within 45 Days of the Date You File Your Statement of Intention (Usually from the Date of Initial Filing): You Deal with Secured Property

This is described later on in this chapter. Essentially you hand over any property that was put up as collateral on a secured loan, subject to the terms of the Statement of Intention.

8. You are Required to Attend a Personal Financial Management Course

One of the recent changes in the law indicates that you are now required to receive some instruction on how to better manage your financial affairs in the future. This is currently a pilot project and may not apply in the district that you file in.

9. Three to 6 Months after Filing: There Is a Final Hearing

You may not be required to attend court, in which case you will be mailed a formal notice informing you that your discharge is granted.

10. Up to a Few Weeks after the Discharge: Your Case is Closed

The trustee distributes any remaining property to your creditors. After this takes place, you are no longer legally liable to your creditors and they cannot continue to try and collect on discharged debts. However, you will still be liable for some specific payments.

> In Canada, your bankruptcy will be discharged after 9 months, but during this time, you are required to receive counseling, which can be with the trustee. If you have filed for bankruptcy before the discharge process, it is not automatic and will be heard before a judge.

Starting the Process

The rest of this chapter describes the paperwork that you will need to file and provides some further information on the process. The next chapter explains the meeting of creditors and the court processes and provides some advice on common situations.

Take Heart

If you have read the previous chapters on property and exemptions, you should have a great deal of information at your fingertips already. Even so, the process of filling in the paperwork is probably going to be quite daunting and will take some time. Filing for Chapter 7 is, for the vast majority of people, a process that coincides with a time of severe emotional stress. Do not let it take over your life: if possible, seek help or support (either professional, or a friend or relative) to help you get through this. Take comfort from knowing that the procedure you are beginning will be tough but will immediately bring relief from many of your creditors.

Get Started

The Socrates Bankruptcy Kit contains all the forms you need for Chapter 7, 13 or 11 bankruptcy and also clear instructions on how to fill them in. Visit this book's Web landing page www.socrates.com/books/bankruptcy-renewal.aspx to find out more about these and other Socrates materials that can help you.

Bankruptcy Forms Checklist:

- Form 1—Voluntary Petition
  This is the form in which you ask the court to discharge your debts.

- Form 3—Application to Pay the Filing Fee in Installments
  You only need to fill this in if you are applying to pay this way. See below for more information.

- Form 6—Schedules
  The schedules are a collection of forms as follows:

- Schedule A—Real property

- Schedule B—Personal property
- Schedule C—Property claimed as exempt
- Schedule D—Creditors holding secured claims
- Schedule E—Creditors holding unsecured priority claims
- Schedule F—Creditors holding unsecured nonpriority claims
- Schedule G—Executory contracts and unexpired leases
- Schedule H—Co-debtors
- Schedule I—Current income of individual debtors
- Schedule J—Current expenditures of individual debtors
- Summary of Schedules

(In case you are wondering, Forms 2, 4, and 5 are not required for Chapter 7 filings.)

• Declaration Concerning Debtors Schedule
With this form you will declare that the information in the schedules is true and correct. You declare this under penalty of perjury (meaning you can be prosecuted if you are shown to have been willfully misleading or have lied).

• Form 7—Statement of Financial Affairs
This statement provides information on your financial circumstances over the past few years, and you will also be subject to the penalty of perjury if you lie or mislead.

• Form 8—Chapter 7—Individual Debtor's Statement of Intention
You tell the court what you intend to do with property you own that has been put up as collateral against a loan (for instance, a car that is collateral against the car lease loan). This form is important, so here is a little more detail on what is involved: If you have secured debts, you need to explain how you are going to deal with the collateral. Creditors may take property that is considered collateral to a debt, and this applies even if the property concerned is exempt. You have some choices regarding secured debts. You can:

- **Reaffirm the Debt**—this means that you will agree to repay it, even though you are bankrupt. Bankruptcy courts generally do not prefer this choice, because it means you will still be obligated to a lender after your case is closed. You have the right to cancel a reaffirmation before your bankruptcy discharge or within 60 days of filing the reaffirmation (whichever is sooner).

- **Voluntarily Surrender the Collateral**—give the property to the lender in lieu of payment.

- **Redeem the Property**—buy the collateral at its fair market value (agreed between you and the creditor or, if you cannot agree, by the bankruptcy court). It is likely you will need an attorney in most cases, in case of disputes later.

- **Get Rid of the Debt but Retain the collateral**—in some states you can keep the property by keeping your payments current while in bankruptcy.

If you have significant collateral, you should seek advice on the best course of action. You should also have been in communication with the lender.

> **Note**
>
> If you are married and filing jointly, only complete one form for this (ignore the word individual).

- **Mailing Matrix**

  This form is essentially a list of your creditors and their addresses. It is important that you provide accurate and complete details here since the court will use it to prepare mailing labels and notices to send to your creditors.

You also have to pay a fee, and there may be additional forms that apply to you. At the time of this writing, the filing fee is $200 for a Chapter 7 case. You should verify the fee with the bankruptcy court you are using.

Emergency Filing

To stop creditors quickly, file the Voluntary Petition and the Mailing Matrix. This starts the automatic stay and the filing process. Check with your local court regarding any other cover letter or form that may be required. You still need to file the rest of the papers within 15 days.

Can Someone Else Fill in the Forms?

The answer is Yes. If you hire an attorney to file and oversee your case, then filling in the forms will be their job, not yours. But many bankruptcy cases are straightforward enough that an attorney (and their fees) is not really necessary. You might consider hiring a Bankruptcy Petition Preparer (BPP) to help you; they will fill in the forms but cannot provide you with legal advice. If you want to save money and your case is very straightforward, you may be better off filing yourself. More information and forms can be downloaded from the U.S. courts Web site (www.uscourts.gov) as well as from the individual bankruptcy court sites.

Fees—Paying by Installments

- In general, you must pay the fees, although you may apply to pay in installments if you cannot provide the full amount when you file.
- You can pay the filing fee in up to four installments over 120 days. You must fill in the form Application and Order to Pay Filing Fee in Installments before you file your petition.
- You cannot pay the fee by installments if you have hired an attorney or BPP.
- The court may waive a part of the fee if you fall below the national poverty level (this is a set level, which is very low, established by the Office of Management and Budget). You may have to appear at court to establish that you do in fact fall below the national poverty level.

Finding Your Local Bankruptcy Court

Bankruptcy is governed by federal law, so it is not possible to file for bankruptcy in a state court. Instead, you must file in a federal bankruptcy court. If you are filing for bankruptcy, you will file in a federal bankruptcy court in your court district, which is usually located in the nearest major city near the place where you have lived for 180 days or more. If you run a business, you may file in the district the business is located. Bankruptcy courts are listed online at www.uscourts.gov. You can also look in your white pages or simply call directory assistance.

Information You Need to Get from Your Local Court

Ask the court for any information you need. Sometimes courts will not respond to letters or phone calls, so you may have to visit in person. Do not forget that the U.S. bankruptcy courts are online, and there is a lot of information at individual court Web sites. There is often a Frequently Asked Questions (FAQ) page that may answer your queries.

Confirm Fees

Verify the fee with your local court and inquire about paying by installments if you need to.

Number of Copies

Check how many copies of your paperwork you need to submit. Often, four copies must be filed; one of which is returned to you and stamped with the date you filed, your case number and the date of your creditors' meeting (though this date may change).

Order of Papers and other Details

Courts usually have very meticulous requirements concerning the particular order the completed papers are to be placed in, and whether you can staple them together or how they must be attached. Usually it is not the end of the world if you get it wrong, but occasionally someone can decide to return your forms if you have not done it right. You can usually visit the court to see a sample filing, which shows exactly what they want you to do. You can also try writing to the court to get this information as well as visiting the Web landing page www.socrates.com/books/bankruptcy-renewal.aspx for a Letter to Bankruptcy Court example.

Filing the Papers (and Fee)

You can do this by mail; simply enclose the papers in a large self-addressed envelope. You can also take your papers directly to the court; if you do this, you may be able to correct small errors immediately with the help of the bankruptcy court clerk. Electronic filing is rarely available for individuals.

Should You File Jointly?

There is no set rule for this, but in general, married couples are often better off filing jointly. Exceptions apply if you are recently married or do not own any valuable property jointly. Even if you are separated, it may be beneficial to file jointly, although it may be difficult to get your spouse to agree to this. If you are in a state where you and your spouse own property as tenants by the entirety, you should consider the advantages of filing alone. If you have doubts or queries, consider consulting an attorney.

Common Law Marriages

In the following states you may be considered legally married if you have lived together for a period of time as husband and wife.

Alabama	New Hampshire*	South Carolina
Colorado	Oklahoma	Texas
Iowa	Pennsylvania	Utah
Kansas	Rhode Island	District of Columbia
Montana		

*(inheritance purposes only)

If You Own a Business

If you own a small business that is formed or incorporated as a limited liability company, you will have to decide whether to file personally for bankruptcy, or to take your business through bankruptcy. If you file for personal bankruptcy you (or you and your spouse) will have to declare your business assets as nonexempt property. If you decide to file as a business, on the other hand, it is essential that you have followed all the procedures for operating a business (e.g., holding and taking minutes at meetings, issuing stock, conducting board meetings, etc.). Business bankruptcy filing is not within the scope of this book.

Effect of Filing

It is important to understand that by filing for Chapter 7 you have handed your property over to the supervision of the bankruptcy court. As a result, you cannot throw away, sell or give away property without the authorization of the bankruptcy trustee. This applies to both exempt and nonexempt property. However, it is acceptable to buy day-to-day food, clothing and other necessities from earnings you receive after filing.

Before your case commences, the clerk of the bankruptcy court must provide you with written notice containing:

- a brief description of Chapter 7, 11, 12 and 13 bankruptcy proceedings, explaining the purpose of each and the related costs;
- a description of the types of services available from credit counseling agencies; and
- a statement specifying that:
  - a person who knowingly and fraudulently conceals assets or makes a false oath or statement under penalty of perjury in connection with a bankruptcy case is subject to fine, imprisonment or both; and
  - all information supplied by a debtor in connection with a bankruptcy case is subject to examination by the attorney general.

12 Going to Court

This chapter describes the Meeting of Creditors more fully, and explains problematic situations that might arise. There is also information on how to deal with other special problems that can arise during a bankruptcy case—often as a result of creditors disputing something in your case. In addition, this chapter has information on how to make any necessary amendments to your bankruptcy papers.

The Meeting of Creditors

As you found out in the last chapter, this initial meeting is short. Actually, you are not even really going to court, since there is no judge involved. It is simply a fact finding meeting—but if the facts (or lack of them) turn up problems, action may ensue at a later stage. You may hear it referred to as a 341 Meeting, named after the section of the U.S. Bankruptcy Code that describes it.

In Chapter 7 cases, usually the meeting is almost over before it has begun. But you are required to attend—as must your spouse, if you are filing jointly—so prepare yourself, because it can be a bit nerve wracking to be asked questions about your debts.

> If you have a legitimate reason for being unable to attend, you should contact the trustee for advice. In unusual circumstances, such as disability, a telephone interview may be a possible alternative.

Prepare

If you are acting without a lawyer, call the trustee before the meeting (their name and number will be on the notice you received).

- Ask what you need to bring, in addition to copies of all your bankruptcy filing paperwork (these include stamped copies that will have been sent back to you by the court).

- You may need to bring copies of contracts, licenses and other financial information, like tax returns, statements or checkbooks.

- Go through all your bankruptcy papers and note any mistakes you may have made. Mistakes do happen, and can be amended (see more about this later on in this Chapter).

- Sit down the night before and go through any questions the trustee might ask.

- Take a photo ID with you (ideally, your driver's license or passport). If you have neither, contact the court to see what is an acceptable alternative.

- Get there on time. You will need time to park, to go through security, and to have a couple of minutes to clear your head and look through the papers you have brought with you.

Remember, if you have been honest and straightforward in completing your paperwork, you really have no need to feel nervous. If you are concerned that you were not honest in your paperwork, consult an attorney before the meeting.

Note

You are ultimately responsible for the accuracy of the information in your forms, even if somebody else completed them for you.

Questions the Trustee May Ask

At the Meeting of Creditors you will be called forward for identification when it is your turn. The trustee will review your papers and will ask a number of required questions like those below.

- Did you read all the paperwork you submitted before signing it?

- Have you listed all your assets?

- Have you listed all your debts?

- Are the schedules accurate?

- Do you want to make any corrections to the schedules?

- Are your motor vehicles insured?

- Have you destroyed all your credit cards?

An exception: If you have credit cards that you have never used, or owe no money on, there is a possibility that you will be able to use them after bankruptcy.

If there are any unusual assets, the trustee might ask how you determined their value. If more information is needed, the meeting can be continued at a later date.

The trustee will typically ask some other questions as well, like those below.

- Are there any tax refunds due to you?

- Are there any reasons for any perceived inconsistencies in your paperwork (often simply where you have obviously answered wrongly because of a misunderstanding, but also if you appear to have been deliberately misleading)?

- Do you have any possible right to sue someone because of a business loss or accident?

- Have you made any recent large payments to creditors or family members?

- Are you due any inheritances or insurance payments?

You can see that if you are prepared, these questions are simple to answer. But if your answers differ from your submitted paperwork, you will need to explain why, and this can get very difficult. So make sure your papers are completely in order.

What Creditors are Allowed to Ask

After you have spoken with the trustee, any creditors present may ask you questions under oath. Normally, they only have a minute or so to speak. Often, none will show up. But you should be prepared to answer questions, particularly those regarding secured loans and the related collateral.

A Note on Creditors

Creditors involved in your bankruptcy case must file a proof of claim within 90 days of the first date set for the creditors' meeting. If they do not file this claim in time, they may miss out on participating in the bankruptcy proceedings. (They have no excuse in any delay because they will have received written notice of your bankruptcy case.)

But if there are funds left over at the end of the case, after all claims by creditors have been paid, then other creditors may be permitted to file a claim later. (In other words, the 90-day period is extended by the court to let them make additional claims.)

Problem Questions

If a creditor does ask questions, they may be trying to prove that you ran up your debt with them willfully, with no intention of paying the bill. Or they may be trying to show that you willfully lied on your application for credit. If they can show that either of these is the case, they will be able to make the debt survive bankruptcy. That is, you will still be liable to pay that particular debt after your bankruptcy is over.

If you know that you did not act dishonestly or in a deliberately misleading manner, you have nothing to fear. Simply be firm and calm in responding to their questions.

What Happens Next

In a normal meeting you will be finished within 5 minutes or less.

If there are no objections or disagreements from creditors or trustees, the trustee will normally collect any nonexempt property and will liquidate it (have it sold) to pay off your creditors, in part or full.

Remember, if you can find the money from earnings or friends and relatives, you may be able to provide cash, or other exempt property, in lieu of nonexempt property that you are anxious to keep. The trustee is concerned with the money available to creditors and has no interest in grabbing your property out of spite.

Your bankruptcy case will be closed in due course, probably around 6 months after your filing date. You may have to attend a short discharge hearing, at which the judge will discharge your debts and probably give you some advice about staying out of debt. In any case, once your case is closed, you will receive a copy of your discharge order shortly after. Keep this order safe and make copies.

Problems That Can Arise as Your Case Progresses

Creditor Objections to Your Right to a Discharge

After the Meeting of Creditors, all creditors and the bankruptcy trustee have a 60-day period in which they may formally challenge your right to a discharge or your right to have a particular debt discharged. They need not have been at the meeting to do this.

If a creditor contests the discharge of your debt to them, this does not affect your other debts or slow your case down.

But note that a creditor may object to the discharging of a specific debt at any time if it falls into the following categories:

- a debt for tax or customs duty;
- a government fine or penalty;
- a government issued student loan (these loans are not dischargeable by bankruptcy, except in some cases of proven hardship);
- a debt related to alimony or child support payments; and
- a debt that you failed to list in the schedules you filed.

And a creditor may contest, within a 60-day period, the discharging of debts that are:

- the result of fraud;
- consumer debts (e.g., credit card expenditure) made close to the date of filing for bankruptcy; and
- a result of willful and malicious injury to another person or property.

What You Need to Do

If a creditor objects formally to the discharge of a debt, they must give you and the trustee a copy of the complaint. You have to defend yourself with a written response, within a given time. You may also have to go to court. If this situation arises, you would be wise to obtain legal advice, although you can represent yourself in court.

Credit card companies are becoming more aggressive about challenging large credit card debts that appear to be willful or fraudulent.

A Note of Caution

If a credit card company sees that you paid for lawyers' fees on your card, they will look at the date. If the date is before the date you filed for bankruptcy, they may claim that you already knew that you were in trouble and you should not have used your card from that point on.

Creditors or Trustee Disputing a Claimed Exemption

Either creditors or the trustee may look at your list of exemptions and raise an objection. After the Meeting of Creditors, they have a set period of 30 days during which they raise an objection (although exceptions can arise).

Reasons for the objection usually fall into one of these areas:

- you appear to have sold nonexempt property and replaced it with exempt property very shortly before you filed for bankruptcy;
- the property you claim as exempt is not exempt under the law;
- property you claim as exempt is worth much more than stated on the form; and
- you have doubled an exemption (when filing jointly) in a situation where it is not permitted. (For example, in some states you cannot double the exemption value for a jointly owned car.)

What You Need to Do

In this situation, the court will arrange a hearing. The onus is on the creditor or trustee to prove that the property you claimed as exempt does not qualify. You can file a response, or go in person to explain your side. If you do not show up, the court will probably rule in favor of the creditors or trustee.

Creditor Requests to Lift the Automatic Stay

A creditor cannot take any action against you without the court's permission while the automatic stay is in place. And, as you know, the automatic stay comes into effect shortly after you file for bankruptcy. But a creditor may file a request for the stay to be lifted. They have to do this in writing through a Motion to Lift Stay. You will get written notice of a court hearing, and should attend it to make your views known (if you do not, it is quite likely that the stay will be lifted, as the decision is made immediately in court). The court will only lift the stay if the creditor shows cause for granting relief from the stay.

Usually, this kind of request comes from a creditor that wants the ability to foreclose on your home, to repossess your car or to disconnect utilities. If you have no equity in your home or if your car is not insured, the relief from stay is likely to be granted.

Other circumstances include action that is of no interest to the bankruptcy court because it will not change your financial circumstances. For instance, a child custody hearing would be allowed to proceed.

What You Need to Do

In most cases, legal advice would be advisable at this point. You need to convince the court that the stay is necessary to protect your bankruptcy estate, (which in turn protects the creditors who will benefit from it) or your exempt property. You also need to convince the court that the creditor's property will be protected by the stay and the creditor will not lose out by waiting. This type of convincing is a fine art. In particular, landlords make frequent requests to have a stay lifted to enable an eviction and are often successful.

In general, if you reach the point where creditors are formally objecting to aspects of your filing, you should consider obtaining further advice. Unless you are able to put your response forward in quite a firm and articulate manner at a hearing (and in writing), you run the risk of losing at the hearing. But remember, many straightforward Chapter 7 filings do not run into these problems.

Amending Your Paperwork

During the course of your bankruptcy case you may need to add information to your papers or change details. Note that there are formal procedures that you need to follow. Some judges will not allow you to make changes after the 60-day deadline, because a creditor's ability to object to exemptions has passed. If that happens to you, consult a bankruptcy lawyer.

Usually, you will not have to pay to amend your papers unless the court has to send information to your creditors.

Here are some common amendments that you can make:

- change of address;
- amend the list of creditors (you will need to amend the appropriate Schedule and the Mailing Matrix);
- add or delete exempt property on Schedule C (your list of exemptions);
- add or delete property on Schedule A or B (for instance, to add inherited property, death benefits, other property that you have received within 180 days of filing); and
- change your Individual Debtor's Statement of Intention (if you want to change your plans regarding secured property).

These and other amendments must be made by filling out an Amendment Cover Sheet (available from the court) and by changing the relevant forms within your bankruptcy filing paperwork. Some courts allow you to amend the forms; others ask you to fill out a new version of the form. You must check with your bankruptcy court and ask what is required.

If the amendments are significant and your Meeting of Creditors is over, another Meeting of Creditors may be scheduled.

You Want to Dismiss the Case

After your case has been filed, you may have several reasons for wanting to cancel it.

- You realize that bankruptcy is not going to help that much because many of your debts will not be dischargeable anyway. All you will have is a great big black mark on your credit record and the same amount of debt.

- You come into some money and can pay off your debts.

- You realize that some property that you thought was exempt is not and you do not want to lose it.

Or perhaps things are becoming complicated, and you realize it would be better to start again with a bankruptcy lawyer's assistance. But right now you cannot afford an attorney. Sometimes people want to cancel bankruptcy proceedings simply because the stress is too much for them. This is nothing to be ashamed of, but think hard—perhaps you can get more support from friends or family.

Unfortunately, canceling—or dismissing—your case can be difficult in some states, especially if your estate includes assets that will be sold. To dismiss your case, you must file a request with the court. Contact the court you are dealing with to find out how to do this. You need to prepare what is called a Petition for Voluntary Dismissal, and in this petition you will give the reasons why you want your case dismissed. If your petition is accepted, the court should advise you on whether you, or they, will inform your creditors that your case has been dismissed.

The next chapter explains what happens after your Chapter 7 case is over and provides some strategies for dealing with potential problems.

Learning the Language of Law and Finance

A short glossary is provided at the end of the book to assist in your understanding of the terms used in the book. In addition, readers are entitled to full access and use of the comprehensive Personal Law and Personal Finance Dictionaries found on the Web landing page:

www.socrates.com/books/bankruptcy-renewal.aspx

Please remember to register the first time you use this free resource. See page iv for further details.

13 Making the Decision: Chapter 13 or Chapter 7

This chapter describes what is generally involved in filing for Chapter 13 bankruptcy. Since you are most likely considering which of the two common forms of personal bankruptcy is available to you—and which best meet your needs—this chapter will compare the two.

If you have already read the information on Chapter 7 bankruptcy, you probably have a good idea of whether you are eligible to file it and whether it would be the appropriate chapter to file to deal with your financial circumstances. In some cases, you may find you could file for either type of bankruptcy: Chapter 13 may be more difficult but could—if you are eligible—provide you with a better chance of keeping valuable property, like your home.

After this introductory chapter there are several more chapters explaining the process of filing under Chapter 13 and what a Chapter 13 repayment plan entails; it may help to refer to them while reading this chapter.

> Remember that while most of this information is relevant for people filing in Canada, there is also a separate chapter giving an overview of the Canadian filing procedure.

An Overview of Chapter 13 Bankruptcy

Chapter 13 is powerful: You can use Chapter 13 to stop the bank from foreclosing on your home and as a way of catching up with payments you have missed. You can also use it to pay off back taxes, and to stop interest from being added to the tax debts you have. In a way it buys you time—but in return, you need to follow a repayment plan that takes quite a bit of self-discipline.

In order to file for Chapter 13 bankruptcy you need to have some income. Chapter 13 is more commonly referred to as Wage Earner Bankruptcy—even though the income does not have to come from wages. This type of bankruptcy is far less drastic than Chapter 7.

If you file for Chapter 13 bankruptcy, you arrange to pay off your debts within 3 to 5 years, in accordance with a repayment plan that is worked out with the bankruptcy trustee. Although you are required to file information about your property, its value, and what property is exempt and nonexempt—you will not lose your property if you fulfill the terms of your plan. Your plan must be approved. While the plan is in effect you are protected from lawsuits, garnishments and other creditor action (see Chapter 4 on the Automatic Stay). You will also need to go to court, at least twice, for brief hearings that usually only take a few minutes. At the end of your repayment plan the bankruptcy is discharged.

> In Canada, bankruptcy is subject to the Bankruptcy and Insolvency Act, or BIA. There is no exact equivalent to Chapter 13 bankruptcy, although the legally binding Consumer Proposal—not technically a form of bankruptcy—comes closest. In certain provinces you may apply for what is called a consolidation order, while in Quebec you may apply for a voluntary deposit scheme. See Chapter 18 for an explanation of your options.

Eligibility to File for Chapter 13

1. You Must Have a Steady Income and a Suitable Level of Disposable Income

To file for Chapter 13, you have to convince the court that your income is sufficient and frequent enough to make regular payments to the bankruptcy court over a 3- to 5-year period. Usually this means that you need to be in permanent employment or self-employment or with another proven regular income. Recent amendments to bankruptcy law mean that you are now far more likely to be filing for Chapter 13 bankruptcy unless you meet the stricter eligibility requirements for Chapter 7.

Your unsecured debts must not exceed $290,525. Again, this amount increases every three years. Unsecured debts include things like credit cards, medical and legal bills, utility bills and student loans.

Note

Be sure to read Your Living Expenses in Chapter 14 of this book—it concerns how the courts determine living expenses. You should also read the section on The Means Test in Chapter 10, which explains how eligibility for Chapter 7 is decided. Both of these topics play an important role in determining which type of bankruptcy you can file.

2. Your Debts Must Be within Proscribed Limits

At the time of writing, your secured debts must not exceed $871,550 (as of 2004). This amount increases every 3 years. Remember, these are debts that are secured by property (your house or car).

Your unsecured debts must not exceed $290,525. Again, this amount increases every 3 years. Unsecured debts include things like credit cards, medical and legal bills, utility bills and student loans.

> **Take Note**
>
> The difference between secured and unsecured debts is discussed in Chapter 3, and you will also find in that chapter information on how to calculate the amount of your debt.

> ### 3. You Cannot Be a Business
>
> You cannot file for Chapter 13 as a business—even if you are the sole proprietor of the business. You can file as an individual, but not in the name of your business. For instance, you could file as Mary Smith but not as Mary Smith Accountancy Services.
>
> But if you file as an individual, you can include business-related debts that you are personally liable for.

> **An Exception**
>
> Stockbrokers and commodities brokers cannot file for Chapter 13 bankruptcy as individuals.

Does It Make Sense for You to File for Chapter 13?

In the following scenarios, filing for Chapter 13 (rather than Chapter 7) might be the best course of action to take. In all cases, it is assumed you have fulfilled the eligibility criteria described above.

- You are way behind on paying your mortgage or car loan. You do not want to lose either, but you can only pay the arrears (late payments) spread out over time if you are to also keep up on current payments.

- You owe tax. Tax debts often cannot be discharged in Chapter 7, so there may be no point in filing for it unless you have significant debts that can be discharged. Tax debts in Chapter 13 are assessed according to certain categories (read the other Chapters concerning Chapter 13 for further information).

- You have a sincere and honest desire to pay off all your debts over a specified time, but need some protection from the bankruptcy court to let you do this without harassment.

- Filing for Chapter 7 is likely to occur at a later date, as you can see yourself falling into more debt. But right now you want to pay off some debts, and leave the door open to file Chapter 7 later (because you would not be able to file for Chapter 7 twice in quick succession).

- You want to make use of the Superdischarge of Debts that comes with Chapter 13, although this has been greatly reduced under the new bankruptcy law (more information below).

Discharging Debts and the Chapter 13 Superdischarge

If you have already read the relevant chapters, you know that the process of filing for Chapter 7 bankruptcy, or liquidation, results in your eligible debts being discharged completely at the end of your case. You are no longer required to pay them. However, not all debts are eligible for Chapter 7 discharge.

In Chapter 13, the treatment of debts is different. Although you are required to pay off your debts in installments under the terms of your repayment plan, you will not necessarily pay off all your debts in full. After successful completion of the repayment plan, you receive a Superdischarge. Before the new bankruptcy law was enacted, the terms of this discharge were much broader than the Chapter 7 discharge, and included debts that were not eligible in Chapter 7—such as those incurred through willful and malicious injury to another's property, or larceny and embezzlement. However, the list of debts that can now be discharged under Chapter 13 has been significantly curtailed.

Is Chapter 13 Best for You? A Comparison of Chapter 13 and Chapter 7

Simply comparing how different kinds of debts and other situations are treated by both Chapter 13 and Chapter 7 may help you to make a decision. This table compares just a few important factors (and assumes that you would be eligible to file for Chapter 13):

Situation	Chapter 7	Chapter 13
You are way behind with the mortgage payments on your home.	You will probably have to give your home back to the bank, or arrange to pay the value of the nonexempt equity to the bankruptcy trustee from money you have coming in since filing.	You can repay what you owe over 3 to 5 years, and keep your current mortgage payments on time as well. You will keep the home.
You filed for bankruptcy previously, and received a discharge within the previous 8 years. (Note: recent changes in the law have increased this from 6 years.)	You cannot file Chapter 7 at this time unless the previous bankruptcy was a Chapter 13 case AND you paid at least 70 percent of your debts off during the repayment period.	This may not prevent you from filing Chapter 13, depending on when you re-file. Under the new bankruptcy law, you must wait at least 5 years between filing bankruptcy cases.
You owe debts for: • student loans (but note there may be exceptions if repayment would cause hardship); • court-ordered fines or penalties; • child support or alimony; • taxes that are less than 3 years past due, filed less than 2 years ago, or were assessed less than 240 days before filing.	Normally these (and some other) debts are not discharged by Chapter 7.	These types of debts must be paid in full by the end of your Chapter 13 repayment plan. If they are not, you are still eligible to pay the balance at the end of your bankruptcy.

Situation	Chapter 7	Chapter 13
You have enough disposable income to successfully go through Chapter 13.	The bankruptcy court may not let you file for Chapter 7 or could dismiss (cancel) your case.	
You have valuable property that would not be exempt from your bankruptcy estate.	You may lose the property unless you can: • arrange to swap it with exempt property of a similar value; and/or • pay the bankruptcy trustee the fair market value of the nonexempt property.	You do not lose your property in a Chapter 13 case—provided you comply with your repayment plan.
You owe back taxes to the IRS.	If you owe back taxes to the IRS you cannot file for Chapter 7.	See "Does it Make Sense for You to File for Chapter 13?" in the earlier part of this chapter. Also note that recent changes mean that the dischargeability of tax debts in Chapter 13 is more limited.
You have debts due to larceny, breach of trust, embezzlement, fraud, or willful and malicious injury to another or his or her property.	These kinds of debts are not dischargeable in all cases.	These kinds of debts are no longer dischargeable under the Chapter 13 superdischarge.

Alternatives to Filing for Chapter 13

Before you decide to file for Chapter 13, consider the alternatives. There may be other ways of meeting your debts, especially if you have a steady and reliable income.

Negotiate with Creditors

Creditors are generally interested in getting as much money back from the debt you owe them as possible. If you communicate with your creditors, explaining your situation and your genuine willingness to pay off what you owe them, they may be willing to arrange a longer repayment period. They may also agree to let you pay them back less than you actually owe them—a compromise is better than nothing. If creditors are willing to do this, make sure that you receive written confirmation of the terms and that the payment will be regarded as a complete settlement of your debts.

Mortgage companies are generally anxious to avoid the aggravation—and expense—of initiating foreclosure proceedings. In fact, if your mortgage was issued by Fannie Mae or Freddie Mac (see Glossary), the lender is required to try and work out a solution with you. See Chapter 8 and Chapter 9 for more information on Mortgage Workouts.

Get Help to Work out Your Own Repayment Plan

If you have many different debts, you may be able to work out a way of negotiating payments that will satisfy all your creditors. You may also be able to take out another loan to pay off all your debts, and then concentrate on paying off that one big debt. This is sometimes called debt consolidation. If you take this route you will not file for bankruptcy, but you will essentially follow a payment procedure similar to the repayment plan in Chapter 13.

It is required now to get qualified assistance in the form of credit counseling before filing for bankruptcy. See Chapter 23 on how to find good support in this area, and also for tips on avoiding the many unscrupulous lenders and counseling services that may try to take advantage of your situation.

A good counseling agency, accredited by the National Council for Consumer Credit, may be able to guide you to a repayment solution that is preferable to filing for Chapter 13.

Do Nothing

Although doing nothing may seem a rather strange choice, sometimes it is the best one. You may owe money to creditors, but if the creditors feel they have nothing to gain from suing you for the debt, they probably will not bother. Instead, they will just write it off. Creditors choose this option when they think you have very little property (not just physical property but also cash, benefits or eligible wages).

If you live a very simple lifestyle and have very little personal property, you may find it very effective to just sit tight. But do not take this option if you are likely to come into more money later.

Converting from Chapter 7 to Chapter 13

You can do this if you determine that it makes more sense for you to file under Chapter 13. This might apply if, for instance, you discover that your tax debt would not be discharged under Chapter 7. Instead, you can arrange to pay it off over the course of your Chapter 13 repayment plan.

To convert your bankruptcy case, you need to make a written request to the court and send a copy to all your creditors. You also need an order from the court. For more information, consult your local bankruptcy court.

Section Five

SOCRATES™
KNOW HOW TO DO MORE
AND SAVE

14 Determining Eligibility for Chapter 13

This chapter explains what preparatory work you will need to do to confirm your eligibility to file for Chapter 13. It assumes that you have read the previous chapters in this book about property, your bankruptcy estate and property exemption. All are relevant, although your property is unlikely to be taken from you unless you fail to fulfill the terms of your repayment plan. If it turns out that you are eligible for Chapter 7, your work in this chapter will not have been wasted. Some of the contents of this chapter will also be relevant to a Chapter 7 filing.

If you are thinking of filing for Chapter 13 it is important to add up your debts, look at what kind they are, and see if you are in fact eligible. You then need to make an estimate of how much you will be required to repay through a Chapter 13 repayment plan. You also need to calculate your average monthly income based on the 6-month period before filing, and how much of it is disposable (not spent on day-to-day living expenses). In broad terms, you must have sufficient disposable income in order to meet your payment plan and be eligible to file for Chapter 13 bankruptcy.

Although the court defines how much you are expected to live on (a recent change to the bankruptcy law in 2005), it is also important that you calculate on your own how much you are actually spending on living expenses each month. If it is impossible for you to survive on the court decided figure, you will have to consider lowering your actual living expenses or not filing for bankruptcy at this time. In reality, if you are living a modest lifestyle, you are probably likely to find that the court figures and yours are more or less in agreement.

Add Up Your Debts

You need to divide your debts into secured and unsecured debts (see Chapter 3 for a reminder of what that means and for more information).

Make a List

Make a list of all your consensual liens, including joint debts taken out with a spouse, partner or child (list the whole amount). Include the information that corresponds to the statements below on your list.

- The debt and the name of the creditor.

- Find out exactly how much you owe on each debt. If in doubt, ask the lender (for instance, call your mortgage company to determine the amount outstanding).

- Note your monthly payment for that debt.

- Work out the total arrears—multiply the monthly payment by the number of months you are behind. Do not forget to add any late payment fees that may be due.

- Work out the value of the property that is collateral to the debt. (Use the information you have put together in the personal property worksheet from Chapter 7 of this book.)

- If there are debts where you are disputing the amount the creditor claims you owe, list the amount they claim. Once you have filed for Chapter 13, you can file papers with the court so that they can establish what you actually owe (you should really consider engaging a lawyer if this situation arises). This can be quite advantageous since it avoids the hassle of going to another court to resolve the dispute.

The way in which nonconsensual liens affect your property varies from state to state and is beyond the scope of this book. If in doubt, consult your local authorities and seek legal advice.

Make a similar list of all nonconsensual liens, if you have any. Here you may need more information on how nonconsensual liens operate in your state. But for now, simply note the same information as above.

Transfer Unsecured Liens

Two examples of undersecured liens:

1. If a creditor files a lien against your car for $12,000, but your car is actually only worth $10,000 on today's market, the lien is undersecured by $2,000.

2. The IRS places a lien on your house of $20,000, while another creditor puts a judgment lien on your house for $30,000, and your house is worth $200,000—but you still owe $170,000 on your mortgage. If you add up the mortgage and the two liens, it comes to $220,000—this is $20,000 more than your house is worth, so the latest lien to be taken out is undersecured by $20,000.

In both cases, the undersecured portion is an unsecured lien, because there is no property to set it against. Add up those amounts and make a note of each. Then transfer them over to your list of unsecured debts.

Add It All Up

When you are sure you have listed every single debt that is secured by any property you own, add up the total amount you owe as of today. The result is the total amount you owe in secured debts. This amount must be under $922,975 in order for you to qualify to file for Chapter 13 bankruptcy. (Note that this amount is subject to change. Consult your local court for updated information.)

Unsecured Debts

Make a List

- List all unsecured debts, noting the creditors' names and the amount you owe each of them. Make a note of your monthly payments and the amount you are in arrears (as described above).

- Include those debts where you do not yet know how much you are liable for. You will not be able to include an amount in your total, but you will need to file them to have each considered.

- List debts that may arise in the future (for example, if you are the co-signer on a loan for someone else or if the outcome of a lawsuit may or may not result in incurring a debt).

Add up the amount you owe each creditor to get the total of your unsecured debts.

If you have unsecured debts as a result of undersecured, nonconsensual liens (see above), add them to this total. The result is the total amount you own in unsecured debts. This amount must currently be under $307,675 in order for you to qualify and be able to file for Chapter 13 bankruptcy. (Keep in mind that this amount is subject to change.)

Strategies for Maximizing Your Debt Limit

If your unsecured debts are above the limit, but your secured debts are below the limit, you can transfer unsecured debts to the secured debts list. You can only do this if you are able to secure them against property that is not otherwise pledged as collateral to other secured debts. But if you do this, you will have to pay off the debt in full as part of your repayment plan—this is the case with all secured debts (if you want to keep the property).

Work out How Much You Will Have to Repay Through Your Plan

At this point, work out a rough estimate of the minimum you will have to repay. In the next chapter there is much more information on your repayment plan if you decide to proceed.

Work out the value of your nonexempt property (see Chapters 7 and 8). This amount will cover a proportion of your unsecured debts (the rest will be written off).	$_____
Add the amount for any missed payments owed to secured creditors (e.g., mortgage payments).	$_____
Add 10 percent of that amount as a rough guide to the interest you may have to pay to creditors.	$_____
Add any extra amounts to account for paying off creditors earlier (if you are not sure, estimate).	$_____
Add these lines up.	$_____
Add 10 percent as an estimate of the trustee's fees.	$_____
Total the amount.	$_____

The figure you arrive at is merely a rough estimate (and only that) of the minimum amount your plan will have to cover.

Determine Your Disposable Income

Working out your disposable income is really quite straightforward. Essentially you are looking at the difference between how much money you have coming in and how much is going out for normal day-to-day living expenses. To start the process, the court will determine your monthly income, based on your average income during the 6-month period before filing.

Calculate Your Monthly Income for the Prior 6 Months

List all income you earn. Include not only wages but any other regular payments. If you have more than one job, list each job. For wages, list your gross income and then subtract deductions (use the Monthly Income Worksheet to assist you).

The following are common sources of regular income:

- wages
- alimony or child support
- pension or other retirement income
- interest or dividends from investments
- benefits (e.g., disability payments, veterans' benefits and unemployment benefits)

List any and all income you have. Subtract deductions (look at your pay slip) and then add them all up.

> **Note**
>
> If you have income that is not monthly, make a note of its frequency (e.g., annually or every other week). Work out the equivalent monthly payment and put this in the list you will add up. For instance, if you get $100 every other week from a part-time job, that is $50 a week.

Irregular Income

If you plan to use irregular income to meet or contribute to the requirements of your payment plan in Chapter 13, you may need to convince the judge that you are very likely to receive the income. You will need to provide receipts from previous similar work, or evidence of receiving proceeds from sales or royalties. For many people, life is a series of irregular payments, and the courts will usually take this into account. However, a court is unlikely to allow you to proceed with a Chapter 13 repayment plan if you rely entirely on irregular or temporary work.

The following are examples of irregular income for which you will need evidence:

- Income from seasonal or temporary work.
- Sales (if, for instance, you are a professional artist with a good record of selling work, you may have little difficulty convincing the court).
- Alimony or child support.
- Payments from friends or relatives (e.g., if your adult son lives in your home and pays rent informally).

There are, of course, many other forms of irregular income. The main factor is to have evidence of receiving it, and also the ability to convince the court that this kind of income is likely to continue for the duration of your payment plan. The court's decision is likely to rest on whether the irregular income is a significant component of your repayment plan.

As a rough estimate, work out the irregular income you will receive over a year, and divide by 12 to get a rough monthly estimate. Add this to the monthly regular income total.

Deduct Income That Is Excluded from Consideration by the Court

Remember, recent amendments to the bankruptcy law mean that your disposable income, for court purposes, does not include certain items. These items include Social Security benefits, payments to victims of war crimes or crimes against humanity, and payments to victims of international terrorism.

Your Living Expenses

In the past, your living expenses were determined by comparing your income against your actual day-to-day living expenses (calculated by adding your expenses and regular bills). Recent bankruptcy law changes have revised this formula: The court now decides what your allowable living expenses are, using figures calculated to reflect living expenses in your locality and allowances set by the IRS on a national basis for food, clothing, personal care and entertainment. As a result, even though you are still required to submit a list of your living expenses, your actual expenses for many items may now be irrelevant; you are only allowed to claim a certain amount for expenses, even if your actual costs are much higher.

The figures the court uses to decide the amount you need for living expenses are taken from the National Collection Standards published by the Internal Revenue Service (IRS). These standards take into account the cost of clothing, food and housing and other items. You can view this information at www.irs.gov/businesses/small/article/0,,id=104627,00.html (or visit www.irs.gov and search for National Standards for Allowable Living Expenses).

The court also lets you deduct other expenses, including:

- up to $1,500 in expenses annually for grade school and high school (per each minor child);
- expenses of caring for elderly, chronically ill, or disabled household family members, including children and grandchildren;
- a domestic support obligation that first becomes payable after the petition is filed;
- charitable contributions of up to 15 percent of your gross income; and
- payment of expenditures needed to continue, preserve and operate a business.

The court will provide a figure that you are expected to live on. By subtracting this figure from your income, the court will also decide how much you can—in their view—afford to contribute to a Chapter 13 repayment plan each month. And this will normally be the amount the court requires you to repay each month.

Determine Your Actual Living Expenses

For many people, when they add up their actual living expenses they may find that their expenses are considerably higher than the figure the IRS calculated for their area. It is realistic and sensible to work out your actual living expenses on your own, and to then compare them with the IRS figures that the court will require you to follow. By doing this, you may find it to be hard or even impossible to lower your expenses accordingly. But on the flip side, you may find ways of decreasing your present living expenses to the figure that the court defines.

Having tallied your monthly income, you need to subtract your monthly living expenses. Use the Monthly Expenses form found on the Web landing page www.socrates.com/books/bankruptcy-renewal.aspx to help you. It is very easy to forget some expenses and to get others wrong; try to be as accurate as possible by looking thoroughly at your bills and receipts. Be prepared to take some time to do this, and do not become overwhelmed by trying to add up the minutiae of your life.

Broadly speaking, your expenditures will fall into the following categories:

- cost of your home (rent or mortgage, and associated expenses)

  If you are going to meet your current mortgage payments as part of your Chapter 13 repayment plan, do not list them here. Remember, now they will not be part of your day-to-day expenses, but will instead be a debt that you will be paying off over time.

- utilities (take a monthly average)• food
- clothing
- medical costs
- transport (car and public transport)
- education
- charitable contributions
- insurance
- personal expenses—toiletries, etc.

Calculating Your Actual Disposable Income

Before you make it to the final step, double-check that everything is present and correct; if you make mistakes, the figure you get will be misleading, and may be questioned if you use the information as part of your filing paperwork.

- To calculate your actual monthly disposable income, subtract your monthly expenses from your monthly income. This is how much money you can currently afford to contribute to your repayment plan each month.
- To calculate the disposable income the court will view as possible, subtract the IRS monthly living expenses amount for your state or district from your monthly income. What you have left is how much money the court may expect you to pay towards your debts each month.

Remember that it is the second calculation that you will be expected to abide by. So, if the comparison does not look good, you will have to cut your living expenses considerably, or consider not filing.

Can Chapter 13 Be Done?

Do the figures balance up? If your disposable income over 5 years is significantly lower than the amount your plan would have to cover, things are not looking good. Remember, a Chapter 13 repayment plan must be 5 years in duration if your income (determined by looking at your average income during the previous 6 months) is greater than the median income in your state. Otherwise, your repayment plan will be 3 years in length.

If you still do not think that you will have enough income to cover your expected payments (under a 3- or 5-year repayment plan, whichever applies to your case), look at your expenses and see what can be cut. Also, triple-check your income data, and get financial advice from a professional, if necessary. Always remember that you are working on estimates at the moment—if the figures are close, you are probably going to benefit from Chapter 13 bankruptcy. If they are still way off, it may be time to consider Chapter 7.

15 Filing for Chapter 13

This chapter summarizes the process of filing for Chapter 13 bankruptcy. It explains the fees and provides information on the forms that you will need to complete in order to file for Chapter 13. In addition, there is information on how to find the right court, how to actually file and the effect of filing.

If you are sure that you would be better off filing for Chapter 7, you do not need to read this chapter. If you are in Canada, you should read the chapter on the Canadian filing procedure (although quite a bit of the information in this chapter is useful in general terms).

Remember, you will find a checklist on the Web landing page www.socrates. com/books/bankruptcy-renewal.aspx that compares which debts are discharged in personal bankruptcy. Use this checklist as a guide.

A General Overview of the Process

The following sequence of events takes place when filing for Chapter 13 bankruptcy. Although a creditor can ask the court to hand down an order that you are bankrupt, usually bankruptcy is a voluntary process.

1. Mandatory Credit Counseling
As with filing under Chapter 7, you must receive credit counseling during the 6 months prior to filing Chapter 13 bankruptcy or, in special cases, within 30 days of filing. If you do not receive credit counseling and file proof of compliance, your case could be automatically dismissed. If no approved counseling services are available in your district, this requirement may be waived.

After completing the credit counseling, you will receive a certificate of compliance from the counselor, who must be on a list of approved counselors. You must then file this with the court, along with a copy of the payment plan created with the counselor.

2. You File a Petition
You file a petition, along with information about your financial circumstances,

with the bankruptcy court. This petition includes your schedule of assets and liabilities, and a statement of your financial affairs. You also file a Chapter 13 repayment plan (see Chapter 16 for much more on this subject).

The process of filing triggers the automatic stay, which stops your creditors from approaching you or taking your money outside of the bankruptcy proceedings. See Chapter 4 for a detailed explanation of the automatic stay. The court then issues a Notice of Chapter 13 Bankruptcy, Meeting of Creditors, and Deadlines, which will be sent to your creditors, to you and—if you have engaged one—your attorney.

> **Tip**
>
> You can also notify problem creditors of your bankruptcy filing to put them on notice that they must stop approaching you. An example is included on the Web landing page www.socrates.com/books/bankruptcy-renewal.aspx.

3. One to 2 Weeks after Filing: The Court-Appointed Trustee Takes over

A court-appointed trustee is appointed to receive payments. During your repayment period you will pay installments to the trustee, who will distribute them to your creditors. In Chapter 13, the trustee does not take possession of your property (either exempt or nonexempt).

> In Canada the process is quite similar, but the bankruptcy is administered by a Trustee in Bankruptcy, rather than by a court-appointed trustee. The order of events is somewhat different—see Chapter 18 for further information.

4. 20-40 Days after Filing: You Attend a Meeting of Creditors*

About a month later, you will attend a very short meeting with the trustee and your creditors. (Often creditors do not attend in person.) You are required to attend this meeting—with your spouse if you have filed jointly—and to respond to all the questions in good faith. Creditors are not allowed to decide whether your repayment plan is suitable—that is up to the court—but they can object to it formally. It is not a trial, and there is no judge (just the trustee and other people like you); it usually lasts approximately 15 minutes.

At this meeting the trustee will hand you payment envelopes and will confirm the date that your first payment is due. The trustee will also point out any changes that need to be made in your repayment plan.

> This meeting is not always required in Canada, although you are required to respond to requests from the trustee and to fill in certain forms provided to you.

*In many districts the meetings are more likely to be within 45-90 days of filing.

> **Note**
>
> As with Chapter 7 filings, you must give the bankruptcy trustee a copy of your tax return for the latest tax period. If this is not provided within 7 days before the initial meeting with creditors, your bankruptcy case will be dismissed. You must also provide a copy to any creditor who requests it.
>
> The new bankruptcy law also requires you to file any tax returns that are past due for the 4-year period before your bankruptcy filing. Returns must be filed before the Meeting with Creditors, although the trustee may extend this deadline. Failure to do so can result in your case being converted to Chapter 7 or even dismissed.

5. After Creditors' Meeting: Plan Amendments and Creditor Claims

It is quite common for one or more amended repayment plans to be required, usually because creditors have by now filed more precise claims showing the exact amount of money you owe them. Creditors have a set period by which they must have filed all their claims. After that set period has elapsed, and in conjunction with your attorney, you can work up an amended final repayment plan.

The amount a creditor receives will differ, and depends on a couple of factors: the priority of the debt and whether it is unsecured or secured. There is more information pertaining to this subject area and the Chapter 13 repayment plan in Chapter 16.

6. Several Months after Filing: Confirmation Hearing

You will receive at least 30 days' notice of your confirmation hearing. This is a hearing where your repayment plan is reviewed by a bankruptcy judge and, if accepted, confirmed by the court. You must attend this meeting. If your plan is not confirmed, you may file a modified plan.

> **Note**
>
> In order for your plan to be confirmed, all of your domestic support obligations that are due after your case has been filed must be up-to-date.

7. You Are Required to Attend a Personal Financial Management Course

One of the recent changes in bankruptcy law requires that you receive some instruction on how to better manage your financial affairs in the future— before your case can be discharged under either Chapter 7 or 13. This is currently a pilot project, and may not apply in the district in which you file in.

8. At the End of Your Repayment Plan: Your Case is Closed and You Obtain Your Bankruptcy Discharge

Although that is good news, there are some debts that are not discharged by Chapter 13 bankruptcy. You may have partly paid some of these debts during your repayment period (or even fully paid off some). Now you will be liable for the balance of nondischargeable debts. See Chapter 16 for more information on how to integrate paying nondischargeable debts into your repayment plan.

Starting the Process

The rest of this chapter describes, in more detail, the paperwork that you need to file and provides some further information on the process.

Take Heart

If you have read the previous chapters on property and exemptions, you should have a great deal of information on these topics already. Even so, the process of filling in the paperwork may be quite daunting and will take some time. Filing for Chapter 13 is generally not as stressful as filing for Chapter 7, because you do not run the same risk of losing most of your property. Even so, set aside an appropriate amount of time for the task—and seek support if needed.

Get Started

The Socrates Bankruptcy Kit contains all the forms you need for Chapter 7, 13 or 11 bankruptcy, and also clear instructions on how to fill them in. Visit this book's Web landing page www.socrates.com/books/bankruptcy-renewal.aspx, to find out about these and other Socrates publications that can help you.

The following forms are usually required for a Chapter 13 bankruptcy filing:

- Form 1—Voluntary Petition
  This is the form in which you ask the court to discharge your debts.

- Form 3—Application to Pay the Filing Fee in Installments
  You only need to fill this in if you are applying to pay this way. See below for more information.

- Form 6—Schedules
  The schedules are a collection of forms as follows:

- Schedule B—Personal property

- Schedule C—Property claimed as exempt

- Schedule D—Creditors holding secured claims

- Schedule E—Creditors holding unsecured priority claims

- Schedule F—Creditors holding unsecured nonpriority claims

- Schedule G—Executory contracts and unexpired leases

- Schedule H—Co-debtors

- Schedule I—Current income of individual debtors

- Schedule J—Current expenditures of individual debtors

- Summary of Schedules
  (Forms 2, 4 and 5 are not required for Chapter 13 filings.)

- Declaration Concerning Debtors Schedule
  With this form you will declare that the information contained in the schedules is true and correct. You declare this under penalty of perjury (meaning you can be prosecuted if you are shown to have been willfully misleading or have lied).

- Form 7—Statement of Financial Affairs
  This statement provides information on your financial circumstances over the past few years, and you will also be subject to the penalty of perjury if you lie or mislead.

- Mailing Matrix
  This form is essentially a list of your creditors and their addresses. It is important that you provide accurate and complete details here since the court will use it to prepare mailing labels and notices to send to your creditors.

- Income Deduction Order (if required)
  Your court may require you to submit this document with your other papers. It requires your employer to deduct your monthly Chapter 13 repayment amount directly from your wages and send it to the bankruptcy court. Before filing, ask the court if you need to do this.

- Chapter 13 Repayment Plan
  You also have to pay a fee, and there may be additional forms that apply to you. At the time of this writing the filing fee is $150. You should verify the fee with the bankruptcy court you are using.

Additional Filing Requirements During Your Case

It is also important to remember that during your case:

- you must provide copies of all tax returns that are required to be filed during this period (if they are not supplied, your case can be dismissed or converted); and

- you must also provide: an annual statement of income and expenses, detailed information regarding income sources, the names of the parties responsible for supporting dependents and any contributions to household income.

Emergency Filing

Many people filing for Chapter 13 are doing so to stop foreclosure on their home. To stop creditors quickly, file the Voluntary Petition and the Mailing Matrix. This starts the automatic stay and the filing process. Check with your local court regarding any other cover letter or form that may be required. You still need to file the rest of the papers within 15 days.

Can Someone Else Fill in the Forms?

The answer is Yes. If you hire an attorney to file and oversee your case, then filling in the forms will be their job, not yours. But many bankruptcy cases are straightforward enough that an attorney (and their fee) is not really necessary. You might consider hiring a Bankruptcy Petition Preparer (BPP) to help you; they will fill in the forms but they cannot provide you with legal advice. If you want to save money and your case is very straightforward, you may be better filing yourself.

More information and forms can be downloaded from the U.S. courts Web site (www.uscourts.gov) as well as from the individual bankruptcy court sites.

In some districts, you can call the court if you have questions and explain that you need some help with a Chapter 13 filing. In smaller districts, the trustee may be able to speak with you.

Fees—Paying by Installments

- In general, you must pay the fees, although you may apply to pay the fees in installments if you cannot provide the full amount when you file. You must pay an administrative fee in full when you file, currently $30.
- You can pay the filing fee in up to four installments over 120 days. You must fill in the form Application and Order to Pay Filing Fee in Installments before you file your petition.
- You cannot pay the fee by installments if you have hired an attorney or BPP.
- The court may waive a part of the fee if you fall below the national poverty level (this is a set level, which is very low, established by the Office of Management and Budget). You may have to appear at court to establish that you do in fact fall below the national poverty level.

Finding Your Local Bankruptcy Court

Bankruptcy is governed by federal law so it is not possible to file for bankruptcy in a state court. Instead, you must file in a federal bankruptcy court. If you are filing for bankruptcy, you will file in a federal bankruptcy court in your court district, which is usually located in the nearest major city near the place where you have lived for 180 days or more. If you run a business, you may file in the district the business is located in. All the bankruptcy courts are listed online at www.uscourts.gov. You can also look in your white pages or simply call directory assistance.

Information You Need to Get from Your Local Court

Ask the court for any information you need. Sometimes courts will not respond to letters or phone calls, so you may have to visit in person. Do not forget that the U.S. bankruptcy courts are online, and there is a lot of information at individual court sites. Often there is a Frequently Asked Questions (FAQ) page that may answer your questions.

Confirm Fees

Verify the fee with your local court, and inquire about paying by installments if needed.

Number of Copies

Check how many copies of your paperwork you need to submit. Often, you will need four copies, one of which is returned to you and stamped with the date you filed, your case number, and the date of your creditors' meeting (though this date may change).

Order of Papers and Other Details

Courts usually have very meticulous requirements concerning the particular order the completed papers are to be placed in, and whether you can staple them together or not. Usually it is not a problem if you get it wrong, but occasionally someone can decide to return your forms if you have not ordered them properly. Usually, you can visit the court to see a sample filing, which shows exactly what they want you to do. You can also try writing to the court to get this information as well (the Web landing page, www.socrates.com/books/bankruptcy-renewal.aspx has an example of a Letter to Bankruptcy Court).

Filing the Papers (and Fee)

You can do this by mail; simply enclose the papers in a large self-addressed envelope. You can also take your papers directly to the court; if you do this, you may be able to correct small errors immediately with the help of the bankruptcy court clerk. Electronic filing is rarely available for individuals.

Should You File Jointly?

If you and your spouse each meet the eligibility requirements for filing for Chapter 13, you may file jointly. Only one of you needs to meet the eligibility requirements for income; the other person can earn less or nothing at all. But you cannot double the debt limitation; your combined debts must be within the given limit.

- It is worth filing jointly if you are jointly liable for significant debts, even if only one of you has a regular income.

- If you both have a regular income you should file jointly, otherwise creditors may try to collect debts through the person who has not filed.

Common Law Marriages

In the following states, you may be considered legally married if you have lived together for a period of time as husband and wife.

Alabama	New Hampshire*	South Carolina
Colorado	Oklahoma	Texas
Iowa	Pennsylvania	Utah
Kansas	Rhode Island	District of Columbia
Montana		

*(inheritance purposes only)

If You Own a Business

If you own a small business that is formed or incorporated as a limited liability company, you will have to decide whether to file personally for bankruptcy or to take your business through bankruptcy. If you decide instead to file for Chapter 11 as a business, it is essential that you have acted and followed all the procedures for a business (e.g., taking minutes at meetings, issuing stock, conducting regular board meetings, etc). However, business bankruptcy filing is not within the scope of this book.

Effect of Filing

After filing for Chapter 13 you cannot incur new debts. You also have to stick to the payment schedule arranged in your plan. If your financial circumstances change, you can modify the plan at any time during its duration.

Continue to read on to get more information on how to create your Chapter 13 repayment plan, which you will file with your other papers. Chapter 17 of this book contains more information on what happens after you file, including details of what happens when you go to court. Chapter 17 also includes more information on how to modify your plan in the light of creditors' objections.

16 Chapter 13 Repayment Plan

This chapter provides more information on the repayment plan that you must follow after filing for Chapter 13 bankruptcy. It gives detailed information on what exactly your plan is intended to achieve and the role of the Chapter 13 trustee in implementing it.

What Is a Chapter 13 Repayment Plan?

Your repayment plan is central to your Chapter 13 case because it describes exactly how much you are going to pay creditors and the length of your plan.

Although the court-appointed bankruptcy trustee takes charge of actually distributing the money to the various creditors, your plan defines who gets what.

You must submit a plan when you file for Chapter 13. The trustee may require you to make certain modifications or amendments to it before finally approving the finished document. Although preparing a plan may seem daunting, it is actually not that difficult. If you make mistakes, the trustee can help you sort them out. And you also have the opportunity to modify your plan during its course; most people do this at least once during their repayment period due to life and financial changes.

> **Important**
>
> A realistic, approved plan is just one essential ingredient in getting your financial affairs back in order. The other necessary component is your ability to stick to the plan for up to 5 years, making the payments on a regular basis. Statistics indicate that only 35 percent of those people who file for Chapter 13 actually complete their plan. Many people drop out of filing because they cannot come up with a workable plan.

Do not be a statistic—spend time organizing a strong plan and it will help you stick to it!

How to Start

The actual format of a Chapter 13 plan is not fixed in law, but some bankruptcy courts have a specific layout that they prefer you to follow. It will make life easier for them, and probably for you, if you obtain and review their guidelines.

You can contact your local bankruptcy court for a sample plan, which usually comes with guidelines on how to fill it in. Not all courts have a prescribed format, so you can usually construct a plan from another form or make one up on your own. If you construct your own, make sure that it is typed on good quality white paper. There are examples of Chapter 13 Payment Plans on the Web landing page www.socrates.com/books/bankruptcy-renewal.aspx.

The Information Required

Your bankruptcy court will explain exactly what information they require from you. Normally you are required to provide information on how you intend to pay:

- trustee's fees
- priority tax debts
- other priority debts
- nondischargeable unsecured debts
- general unsecured debts
- post-confirmation dates (this is optional)

You also have to provide details on:

- how long your plan will last;
- how often you will make payments;
- whether you will make any direct payments to creditors outside of your plan;
- the order in which creditors will be paid (this is optional); and
- sometimes courts will ask for information on how you plan to deal with contracts and leases.a

The rest of this chapter will explain how to work out some of this information for your plan.

Fixing the Length of Your Plan

The length of your repayment plan will be between 3 and 5 years. If your gross income is greater than the median income in your state and you can pay as little as $100 each month to creditors, a 5-year repayment plan is required. However, if your gross income is less that the state's median, you have a choice: You can either file for Chapter 7 or Chapter 13, in which case your repayment plan can be 3 to 5 years in length.

Of course, your plan can be for less than 3 to 5 years if you pay in full all of the allowed unsecured claims over the shorter period. If you need more than 3 years, you can ask the court to approve up to a 5-year plan. You cannot have longer than 5 years. If you request the longer plan, you need to show why this is necessary.

Reasons for wanting a longer plan might include:

You wish to pay off a secured debt during your plan
In the case of secured debts (not mortgages—see below for more information on this subject) you may want to pay off a large amount during your plan (e.g., to let you keep your car). You may need a longer time frame to do this.

You need to meet the court-defined payment percentage
Courts differ in how much of your debts you are required to pay off. Some courts ask you to pay off at least 70 percent of your debts through the plan. If you have significant debts, this will probably take up to 5 years. At the other extreme, some courts only ask you to pay off a small amount—maybe five percent of what you owe—and are unlikely to let you extend your plan to 5 years.

Creditors request a longer plan
The trustee will pay your secured and priority creditors (more on that later) before your unsecured creditors. Unsecured creditors may object to your plan because of this, especially if you have many priority creditors. Unsecured creditors realize that they will have to wait a long time and may not get very much. In these circumstances, unsecured creditors may request that your plan be set for 5 years to increase the chance that they will receive repayment.

To repay nondischargeable debts
Remember, not all debts are discharged at the end of your Chapter 13 repayment plan. Debts that are unsecured and nondischargeable will remain. But you can make arrangements to pay them off within your plan as a way of spreading out payments. This usually means a longer plan.

A Reminder on Dischargeable and Nondischargeable Debts in Chapter 13

It is important to include all eligible debts that you want discharged at the end of the repayment period in your plan. Only these debts are affected by the final discharge of your debts at the end of your case.

Some debts are nondischargeable. These include child support arrears, student loans, drunk driving fines, criminal fines and other long-term obligations.

Most importantly, your obligation to keep paying your mortgage continues after the end of your case. Your plan simply helps you keep up payments, in addition to gradually paying off late payments and fees you have incurred.

Your Payment Schedule

Payments are typically made to the trustee once a month, but you can make regular payments according to a different schedule (weekly, every 2 weeks, quarterly, even annually or seasonally). You will need to show why this is necessary: for instance, if you are an artist, you may get royalties on a quarterly basis, and if you are a farmer, it may depend on when you sell your crops. The court will often accommodate less frequent payments but may ask you to make smaller monthly payments as well.

Remember that making less frequent payments will not reduce the amount you have to pay over the year. You will simply have to pay a larger amount each time rather than if you were paying monthly.

The Order in Which Creditors Will Be Paid

In general, creditors will be paid in the order they appear on your plan. If you want to have your creditors paid in a different order, you need to specify this in the plan.

The most usual scenario is to pay the fees involved and your debts in a particular order. As one category is paid off, the debts farther down the list start receiving payment or more payment. Unsecured creditors come last on the list after secured debts, priority debts, and support and alimony payments have been covered.

Although you may not want to pay child support and alimony before your other debts, you will need to continue to pay them. It is in your best interests to pay off secured debts as soon as possible because you are paying interest on them and also to keep the property that was put up as collateral.

What Are Priority Debts?

You are sometimes asked to identify priority creditors as part of your plan. In some cases, all priority creditors are paid in full using the information listed on your Schedule E (Creditors Holding Unsecured Priority Claims).

In general, priority debts include the following and are paid in this order:

- the trustee's fee;
- domestic support obligations, which includes alimony and child support that you owe;
- administrative fees, including filing and court fees;
- in involuntary cases, unsecured claims arising after filing but before the trustee is appointed;
- money that you owe to people who work for you (wages, salaries and commissions);
- contributions you owe to an employee benefit fund (if you employ people and pay benefit contributions as their employer);
- claims of certain people who produce grain or run fisheries (up to $4,000);

- deposits you took from individuals for goods, rental or services that you did not provide (up to $1,800);
- priority tax debts; and
- claims for death or personal injury resulting from the operation of a motor vehicle or vessel, if you were intoxicated from alcohol, drugs or other substances.

Repaying Taxes and Tax Penalties

Taxes that you owe are treated under various categories. How each of your tax debts fit into your plan depends on whether it is secured, dischargeable or priority.

Secured Tax Debts

Even though you can discharge your personal liability to pay the debt, the lien involved remains. A lien is involved if the IRS has recorded a Notice of Federal Tax Lien (usually against your house or retirement plans).

> **A Reminder...**
>
> When a debt is discharged it does not go away. The debt remains in existence, but it is your personal liability to pay the debt that is removed. This applies to all debts that are discharged by bankruptcy.

Dischargeable Tax Debts

> **Your tax debt is normally dischargeable if the taxes owed:**
> - are more than 3 years past due;
> - were filed more than 2 years ago; and/or
> - were assessed more than 240 days before filing.

In addition, the IRS must not have filed a Notice of Federal Tax Lien.

If your court only requires you to pay a small percentage of the amount of your unsecured debts, you can usually eliminate this kind of tax debt by paying a small amount during the plan and wiping out what remains when your plan ends. But if your court insists that you pay a higher percentage of your unsecured debts, you will have to pay more of the tax debt during your plan.

Priority Tax Debts

Tax debts that are not dischargeable or secured must be paid in full as a priority.

Courts generally treat interest on tax debts as dischargeable, provided the debt is. Income tax penalties are generally not considered a priority and may be dischargeable.

Paying the Mortgage

The most common reason that people file for Chapter 13 is likely because they are behind on the mortgage. Chapter 13 provides a way to catch up on late payments while continuing to make your current mortgage payments on time.

Your plan form, if you are using one, should have a section for mortgage information. Fill this in, giving full details on how much you are in arrears and exactly which payments you have missed. Also include information on your mortgage company, your normal monthly payment, and any other details you think are pertinent (fees, penalties you have accrued, etc).

You should also specify how many months you will need to pay off the mortgage arrears (including any fees, interest and associated costs). Technically, you can suggest anything from 6 to 60 months (5 years). However, mortgages are considered a priority, and most trustees will require you to catch up on the mortgage payments you owe before they start to pay off other creditors, usually within a year.

Avoiding Foreclosure

What if your mortgage company has already started foreclosure proceedings? Is it too late to pay what you owe? It may be necessary for you to cure the default (that is, pay all the outstanding mortgage payments and costs) in order to stop the foreclosure. Sometimes you have to do this up front, as soon as you file for Chapter 13. If foreclosure procedures are in progress and your mortgage company has not agreed to halt them because of your Chapter 13 filing, it is probably best to call an attorney.

Paying Other Secured Debts

Chapter 13 gives you the chance to catch up on payments for secured debts, without losing the property you pledged as collateral. (See Chapter 3 for an explanation of secured and unsecured debts.) But there are other options you might want to take, all of which can be specified in your plan.

You may choose to:

- surrender the property to the creditor instead of paying;
- pay the debt off or—if less—pay an amount equivalent to the full value of the property;
- pay up any missed payments and then continue with the current loan;
- eliminate or reduce liens on the property; or
- sell the property.

> **Note**
>
> You may have heard of people doing a Chapter 20: filing Chapter 7, and then immediately afterwards filing Chapter 13. Please note that the recent changes in the law have made this difficult to do, since you now may have to wait up to 3 years after filing for Chapter 7 before you can file for Chapter 13.

Paying Unsecured Dischargeable Debts

You are not going to be paying all your unsecured creditors in full. The most likely result is that they will all get something. You can list your unsecured creditors in order of priority, and specify what percentage of the debt you owe for each is to be met. If you do this, the court must approve your priority list. But unless you have special reasons for prioritizing, the simplest method is to propose that they all get the same percentage—this way you will not have to do the math and the court will be satisfied with your plan!

Situations Where You Might Want to Pay Back All of the Debt

Medical costs—If you or a close family member needs to keep receiving medical treatment but owe the practitioner money, the court may allow you to pay off this debt in full before paying other unsecured creditors.

Business debts—If you need to pay off a debt to a business in order to keep your own business going.

Co-debtors—If a business partner shares the debt and cannot pay it off, you may want to pay it all so that you can keep your business going.

Smaller debts—It may make sense to pay off smaller debts in full.

Paying Unsecured, Nondischargeable Debts

You have to repay these in full during your plan or pay the balance when your plan is over. The Checklist of Nondischargeable Debts in Chapter 13 can be found on the Web landing page www.socrates.com/books/bankruptcy-renewal.aspx.

Contracts and Leases

Schedule G of your Chapter 13 bankruptcy papers requires you to list any executory contracts and unexpired leases (like all other required bankruptcy forms, you can get the Schedule G form from Socrates). This includes property that you have leased (a car for instance), and also includes property that you rent, such as residential property.

You must also list these contracts and leases in your plan and explain what you intend to do about each one. Options open to you include:

1. "I will reject the contract or lease" (your obligation to the agreement ends).
2. "I will assume the contract or lease" (your obligation continues).
3. "I will assign the contract or lease" (you transfer the obligation to another person).

If you do not choose an option, it is usually assumed that you chose option 1, and the property you leased will have to be surrendered.

Making Payments Directly to Creditors

Bankruptcy courts generally do not like you to make direct payments to creditors. This is because it is a way around paying the trustee's fees (which you pay as part of your plan administration), and also because it may make it more difficult for you to meet the payments on your plan.

There are some circumstances where courts are likely to approve direct payments.

- The regular payments on your mortgage (but only if you are not behind on your mortgage).

- Payments on a car lease (but only if you are not behind on payments).

- Payments to a creditor with whom you have an ongoing relationship. This usually means payments to a medical practitioner who is treating you (or a family member) on a long-term basis.

There are a few example plans on the Web landing page www.socrates.com/books/ bankruptcy-renewal.aspx that can help you understand how the information is laid out in a repayment plan. But remember, your court will probably have a preferred format. You should contact the bankruptcy court that you intend to file with and ask for their guidelines on preparing a Chapter 13 repayment plan.

Learning the Language of Law and Finance

A short glossary is provided at the end of the book to assist in your understanding of the terms used in the book. In addition, readers are entitled to full access and use of the comprehensive Personal Law and Personal Finance Dictionaries found on the Web landing page:

www.socrates.com/books/bankruptcy-renewal.aspx

Please remember to register the first time you use this free resource. See page iv for further details.

17 After You File for Chapter 13

This chapter explains what happens after you file your Chapter 13 papers. It also provides more information on dealing with the bankruptcy trustee and about the two court appearances you are required to make. In addition, you will find an explanation of the various types of creditor objections and how they might lead to modifications of your plan.

Who Is the Trustee and What Does He or She Do?

When you file for bankruptcy you will receive a letter informing you that the Chapter 13 bankruptcy trustee will take over your case. Sometimes one person deals with all Chapter 13 cases in your district or there may be several qualified trustees. A trustee is not a judge but is an expert in bankruptcy law. In small districts, the trustee may be able to give you quite a bit of help and advice (but not legal advice).

When you file, the trustee writes to all your listed creditors so that they are aware of the automatic stay. They cannot approach you directly. You can also write to your creditors when you file to inform them immediately (the automatic stay takes effect as soon as you actually file). (An example can be found on the Web landing page www.socrates.com/books/bankruptcy-renewal.aspx.

The trustee also sends you a Notice of Commencement, which summarizes your plan and tells you three important dates:

1. the date, time and place of the Meeting of Creditors;
2. the date, time and place of the confirmation hearing; and
3. the deadline by which creditors must file any claims.

If any of this information is missing, get in touch with the clerk of your bankruptcy court.

Make Your First Payment

You start making payments before your plan has been approved and probably before the Meeting of Creditors. You must start paying 30 days after filing, so mark that date on a calendar and send a check to the trustee by then.

> **Note**
>
> If your wages are being garnished, contact the trustee before that date to get help in having the garnishment removed. Filing for bankruptcy stops wage garnishments, and you will need your full wages in order to meet the payments under your plan.

Reporting Changes—Income and Expenditure

Although you do not hand over your property to the courts in Chapter 13 bankruptcy, you do hand it over to be supervised by the trustee. So you are obliged to report any changes in income (for instance, an inheritance) and any other unusual expenditures. Generally speaking, you are free to spend your income on day-to-day expenses and general living costs, but you should not buy larger, nonessential items without first checking that this is acceptable to the court. (A trustee may not look kindly on the purchase of a top-rate stereo system.) You should also not sell property without the explicit permission of the trustee.

The Meeting of Creditors

This meeting is very short, but you must attend it, and so must your spouse if you are filing jointly. The meeting is informal and no judge is present. The trustees and creditors (if any turn up) use this meeting as a chance to ask you about your repayment plan and about any other information in your bankruptcy papers. The trustee wants to be sure that you are able to meet the repayment arrangements you propose in your plan.

If you have a legitimate reason for being unable to attend, you should contact the trustee—in advance of the meeting— for advice. You will be fined if you simply fail to turn up.

Prepare—if you are acting without a lawyer, call the trustee before the meeting (their name and number will be on the notice you received).

- Ask the trustee what you need to bring, in addition to any copies of all your bankruptcy filing paperwork (stamped copies that will have been sent back to you by the court).

- You may need to bring copies of contracts, licenses and other financial information, like tax returns, statements or checkbooks.

- Go through all your bankruptcy papers and note any mistakes you may have made. Mistakes do happen, and can be amended.

- Sit down the night before and review any questions the trustee might ask.

- Take a photo ID with you (preferably your driver's license or passport). If you have neither, contact the court to see what is an acceptable alternative. Also take your Social Security card.

- Get there on time. You will need time to park, go through security, and you will need a couple of minutes to look through the papers you have brought. However, there may be quite a few people scheduled for a meeting at the same time, so your 10:00 a.m. appointment slot may be shared with 20 other people—just wait for your name to be called. Remember, it never hurts to be early!

If you have been honest and straightforward in completing your paperwork, you have no need to feel nervous. If you are concerned that you were not honest in your paperwork, consult an attorney before the meeting.

Important

Remember that you are responsible for the accuracy of the information in your forms, even if somebody else completed them for you.

What Happens?

The meeting will usually last approximately 15 minutes. First you will be sworn in and asked your name, address and other information. You will then need to show a photo ID and your Social Security card. The trustee will then go over your papers briefly, checking that your personal details are correct and that everything appears to be complete.

What the Trustee Will Ask

The questions asked by the trustee will focus on your ability to meet the payments you propose in your plan. Also, if the trustee does not understand something, he or she will ask for clarification. For instance, if you have valued your piano at $4,000, the trustee may ask how you arrived at that figure. Remember, these queries are not accusations; they are simply requests for further information. If your paperwork is completed as honestly and as fully as possible, you have no reason to feel worried. Answer questions in a straightforward manner and as fully as you can. The trustee is actually trying to help you—his or her expert knowledge and experience makes it easier for him or her to see where a plan is perhaps not feasible.

What Creditors May Ask

After the trustee has finished speaking with you, the creditors may ask you questions. If creditors have shown up, they are most likely to be those with whom you have secured debts. They may object to the interest rate they will be getting (preferring it to be higher!) or to the length of time you will be taking to pay off money you owe them. Creditors may object to the terms of your plan, and as a result you will have to negotiate with them and submit a modified plan. This is a fairly frequent occurrence.

Creditors' Objections

Many people dismiss (cancel) their Chapter 13 case, or convert it to a Chapter 7 case (if they are eligible to do so). For this reason, creditors tend to worry that they may not get paid. In particular, the last on the list unsecured creditors will be nervous about whether they will get anything at all—and they are frequently credit card companies.

A creditor who objects will probably file a motion or an objection with the bankruptcy court. The creditor wants you to modify your plan so that you are more likely to keep paying it, and they are more likely to get some payment. A creditor can only raise an objection at your second court appearance—the confirmation hearing—if they have formally submitted a Notice of Motion or an Objection.

In reality, creditor's objections in Chapter 13 are quite limited. They can only object under the following terms:

The Chapter 13 Plan Is Not Submitted in Good Faith

The creditor doubts your intention to actually follow the plan and your ability to make payments under it. (Your previous record may be cited if you have filed for bankruptcy before and not completed your repayment plan.)

> **Note**
>
> In complex situations, it is probably best to engage a lawyer to help you. But if your plan is proposed honestly and with careful thought, and you have the ability to pay, you probably have no reason to worry. You may simply have to change the length of your plan.

The Plan Is Not Feasible

The creditor does not believe you have the means to make this plan happen. For instance, they may question the reliability of your employment or cite your previous criminal convictions as an indication that you may end up in jail during the repayment plan.

You can respond to this objection at the confirmation hearing. Bring all your paperwork and any worksheets and calculations, all in order and prepared neatly. Bear in mind that if you do have a history of nonpayment or have criminal convictions, your plan may be denied.

The Plan Fails the Best Interest of the Creditors Test

Broadly speaking, this indicates that the creditor believes they are going to receive less than if you had filed for Chapter 7, and that you could and should file for Chapter 7.

Bring all your papers and worksheets, including information on the value of the property you own.

The Plan Unfairly Discriminates

The creditor thinks they are being treated unfairly in relation to other unsecured creditors who will receive more for reasons that are not justifiable.

You can amend your plan so that all creditors receive the same percentage of the debt you owe them or you can fight to justify your reasoning.

Resolving Objections

Usually, objections can be resolved by negotiating with creditors and then making modifications to your plan.

The Confirmation Hearing

Your confirmation hearing is run by a judge. Although it is formal, there will be many others going through the same process on the same day. Do not be intimidated, and be prepared to wait.

- At this meeting the judge will ask questions about your plan and if anything seems unclear. Then the judge will ask if objections have been resolved.

- If objections have not been resolved, the judge will decide whether he or she agrees with the unresolved objection.

- If the judge does agree with the objection, you will be asked to modify your plan accordingly.

- The trustee will also say if he or she feels your plan is unfeasible and requires modification.

- The judge may order that your payments be taken directly from your wages. This income deduction order will only happen if you have regular income from employment.

- If the judge does not think you can meet the requirements of Chapter 13 and are qualified for Chapter 7, your case will probably be dismissed or converted to Chapter 7.

- If there are several issues to be discussed, it is likely that these matters will be discussed at a rescheduled hearing on a later date.

The Judge's Order Confirming Your Plan

Once your plan has been approved and confirmed by the judge, it is legally binding. Your creditors cannot object to it further and must accept the payments arranged. And you must make the payments, via the bankruptcy trustee, at the agreed rate. But you can modify your plan during its life, if your circumstances change.

Modifying Your Plan

If at your confirmation hearing it is determined that you need to modify your plan, you will usually be given a deadline by which you have to submit your modified plan. You should contact the court to make sure exactly what you must submit, how many copies and by when. After this modified plan is submitted, you will be assigned a new confirmation hearing and will need to attend court again.

After your plan is successfully confirmed, it can still be modified under various circumstances. For instance:

- if you lose your job or become ill—or other circumstances interrupt your income—you can ask for your plan payments to be lowered; and

- if allowed claims from creditors are greater than original estimations, the amount you pay may need to be increased.

Amending Your Paperwork

During the course of your bankruptcy case you may need to add information to your papers or change details if you forgot something. This is permitted by the court and there are formal procedures that you need to follow.

You will usually not have to pay to amend your papers unless the court has to send information to your creditors.

The following are some common amendments that you can make:

- Change of address amendment.

- Amend list of creditors—you will need to amend the appropriate Schedule and the Mailing Matrix.

- Add or delete property on Schedule A or B—for instance, to add inherited property, death benefits or other property that you have received within 180 days of filing.

- Schedule D—add property that is collateral against a loan.

- Form 7—you can usually change this form—the Statement of Financial Affairs—if you forgot to give details of a transaction regarding secured property.

These and other amendments must be made by filling out an Amendment Cover Sheet and by changing the relevant forms within your bankruptcy filing paperwork. Some courts allow you to amend the forms; while others ask you to fill out a new version of the form. You must check with your bankruptcy court to see what is required.

Section  Six

SOCRATES™
KNOW HOW TO DO MORE
AND SAVE

18 The Canadian Process

Although the vast majority of the information in this book is relevant to anyone filing, or thinking of filing bankruptcy, the actual process of filing in Canada is a little different from the U.S. process. The difference is largely one of terminology and, to an extent, time scale. This chapter provides an overview of the filing process in Canada and the way in which the system operates. As you will see, many of the procedures are exactly the same as in the U.S. As a helpful aid, you should refer to the chapters on property and exemptions in conjunction with this information.

As in the U.S., the number of personal—or consumer—bankruptcies has risen progressively since the late 1980s in Canada, although the number of bankruptcies per 1,000 people in Canada is lower historically. In Canada, bankruptcy offers the same opportunity to free yourself from debt and start again—provided you are eligible to file. To file you must be deemed insolvent, therefore:

- you must owe at least $1,000 (throughout this chapter only, any dollar amount will be referring to Canadian dollars); and
- you must not be able to pay your debts when payments become due.

The federal law dealing with bankruptcy in Canada is the Bankruptcy and Insolvency Act. You can consult the entire Act online by going to laws.justice. gc.ca and searching for "Bankruptcy and Insolvency." Although the law is federal, each province sets its own exemptions (see Chapter 6 for more on exemptions). A list of provincial exemptions can be found on the Web landing page www.socrates.com/books/bankruptcy-renewal.aspx.

As in the U.S., an automatic stay comes into effect when you file, stopping unsecured creditors from approaching you. Secured creditors retain liens on your property.

Bankruptcies and Proposals

Under Canadian law, you may file for personal bankruptcy (more often referred to as consumer bankruptcy, and comparable to Chapter 7) or you may file a personal proposal (often called a consumer proposal, or proposal and comparable to Chapter 13).

Mandatory Financial Counseling

Regardless of whether you file for bankruptcy or file a consumer proposal, you are required to undergo two sessions of counseling. If you do not undergo the counseling, your filing may be summarily dismissed.

The two counseling sessions must cover specific subjects.

- The first session takes place shortly after filing and is on the subject of Consumer and Credit Education. Essentially, you receive advice on improving your financial management, spending more wisely and using credit responsibly.
- The second session takes place shortly before your discharge and is called Identification of Road Blocks to Solvency and Rehabilitation. This session helps you pinpoint any major problems that might be causing you to spend money unwisely (for instance, gambling or a drug problem). There is also information on improving your budgeting skills.

Payment for the two sessions (currently $85 each) comes out of your bankruptcy estate (or is added to the amount in your repayment plan). Both credit counseling services and trustees in bankruptcy can provide or arrange the counseling sessions for you. Special training is required to provide these sessions—which are custom designed to help people who are planning to file for bankruptcy.

The Trustee in Bankruptcy

In many cases, a lawyer is not necessary to file a consumer proposal or to file for bankruptcy. But in Canada you must conduct your proposal or bankruptcy case through a Trustee in Bankruptcy. The Trustee in Bankruptcy is not a lawyer but is an individual or corporation licensed by the government who will conduct the bankruptcy process. The Trustee in Bankruptcy is paid by you or from the assets of your bankruptcy estate.

In many ways the Trustee in Bankruptcy (trustee) is extremely similar to the U.S. bankruptcy trustee referred to throughout this book. They perform the same duties and are employed as officers of the court. However, in Canada you get to choose your trustee, and he or she will assist you with your case and, in some cases, provide financial counseling.

The trustee's duties are to:

- review your situation and counsel you on any alternatives to bankruptcy that may be available;
- administer your proposal or—if you file for bankruptcy—to liquidate your nonexempt property so that the cash raised may be passed on to your creditors; and
- see your bankruptcy case or proposal through to the end, in compliance with the Bankruptcy and Insolvency Act.

How to Choose a Trustee in Bankruptcy

Many licensed trustees are members of the Canadian Association of Insolvency and Restructuring Professionals (CAIRP). You can search for a trustee in your area by using their online database at www.cip.ca. Members of CAIRP can give you a free consultation and then arrange for payment in monthly installments.

> **Note**
>
> It is important to understand that although you choose your trustee, they are an employee of the court. Once your case has commenced, only the court can dismiss the trustee.

The Consumer Proposal—How It Works

A consumer proposal is legally binding, and is administered by the courts through a bankruptcy trustee. Under Canadian law it is—technically—not bankruptcy. The idea behind a proposal is that you may be unable to meet all your debts at once but perhaps you can pay them off gradually. Normally, a consumer proposal is best suited to someone who has debts of more than $5,000 and also a steady income, (which does not have to be from employment). Your debts, or joint debts, have to be under $75,000 to be eligible (this excludes your mortgage).

Once you file a consumer proposal, you are protected from unsecured creditors and all wage garnishment must stop. You have a maximum of 5 years to pay off your debts under a repayment plan that is worked out with the trustee.

> **Advantages of a Consumer Proposal**
>
> You have time to pay off your debts.
>
> You can negotiate to only pay off a portion of your debts.
>
> An automatic stay protects you. Creditors are restricted in what they can do once this is in effect.
>
> Interest on your debts is frozen on the day you file.
>
> Wage garnishments stop (with some exemptions, notably child support and alimony).
>
> If the majority of your creditors (over 50 percent) accept your plan, it is deemed acceptable and all creditors have to abide by it.

The Process

1. You meet with a licensed trustee for an initial assessment. The trustee helps you to summarize your financial situation and how much you can afford to pay each month towards your unsecured debts. If this amount is comparable to the amount of disposable income you have, the trustee then prepares the documents for filing your proposal. The trustee also provides the court with his or her opinion on your ability to pay and sends a copy of your proposal to your creditors.

> The Socrates Bankruptcy Kit (Canadian version) has all the forms necessary to file a proposal for bankruptcy, as well as information on exactly what is required.

2. The proposal you are making is actually a proposal to your unsecured creditors. You are asking them if they will accept this arrangement as a way for you to give back at least some of the money you owe them. And you must include all of them, even family and friends who have lent you money.

The creditors have 45 days from the filing date to vote on your proposal (this differs from U.S. law). If more than half of them vote for it and there are no other objections, you can proceed to the next stage.

If more than half of your creditors vote against the proposal, it will be rejected. At this point you are no longer protected by the automatic stay and creditors can go after you as before. But normally a proposal is presented at a substantially finished stage.

3. If 25 percent or more of your creditors voted against your proposal, there must be a Meeting of Creditors. You must attend this meeting and work with your creditors and the trustee to find an agreement that suits everyone. You are also required to attend any other meetings that may be called.

- As a rule, unsecured creditors generally hope to get 50 percent of the debt back over the 5-year period (or over less time if possible). Some creditors may wish to negotiate for more, some may accept less.

- Generally, secured creditors are excluded from the terms of a proposal to creditors, unless you owe them more than the value of the collateral they are holding as security. For instance, if you owe a car loan of $4,000 but you car is only worth $3,000, the loan is undersecured and this creditor would become included in your proposal.

- Other secured creditors—for instance, your mortgage company— simply receive monthly payments from you as usual, outside the terms of the proposal. You have to keep paying them as well as your proposal payments.

Keep Up the Payments

Once you file a proposal, you start making payments. You must contact your trustee immediately if you are having problems meeting payments or other financial changes arise. You are permitted to miss two payments (they are simply added on to the end of your payment time), but if you miss three, your case will be annulled by the courts. If this happens, your creditors may immediately resume actions against you, reinstate wage garnishment and apply interest charges to the amount you owe them.

Consumer Proposals and Your Credit Rating

A consumer proposal is not technically bankruptcy but does appear on your credit report, usually as an R7. This is the code used to indicate consumer proposals, debt consolidation or credit counseling programs. It may also appear as an R9, which indicates a bad debt. At the completion of your proposal, a note remains on your credit report for up to 7 years from the date that the proposal was completed.

Bankruptcy—How It Works

Bankruptcy enables you to seek protection under the Canadian Bankruptcy and Insolvency Act. Canadian bankruptcy is in some ways similar to Chapter 7 bankruptcy. Much of the information on Chapter 7 is relevant to you if you are filing for bankruptcy in Canada. The Office of the Superintendent of Bankruptcy Canada (www.strategic.ic.gc.ca) is where you can find extensive information on Canadian bankruptcy, as well as forms and other governmental publications.

Eligibility

Anyone who lives, or did live, in Canada may file for bankruptcy as long as their debts are $1,000 (Canadian) or more.

An Overview of What Happens

- If you file for bankruptcy, many of your debts will be discharged at the end of the process—which takes 9 months (if it is your first bankruptcy).
- An automatic stay stops creditors from approaching you or taking any action while your case is in progress.
- Wage garnishment ceases while your case is in progress.

The downside of bankruptcy is that:

- you have to give your assets, or most of them, to the trustee for liquidation;
- your bankruptcy will appear on your credit report (for 6 to 7 years); and
- you have to make monthly payments, depending on your income.

Student Loans

Student loans are generally treated in the same way as other unsecured debts; during the stay, no collection action can be taken and the lender will receive a share of the distributed assets. But there is an important exception: If you file for bankruptcy within 10 years of last attending school, the loan will not normally be discharged at the end of the 9-month bankruptcy term. As a result, there is no point in filing for bankruptcy simply as a way of removing your student loan debt.

The Process in More Detail

Initial meeting—like consumer proposals, you must first engage a licensed Trustee in Bankruptcy. The trustee will review your situation, counsel you on any alternatives to bankruptcy that may be open to you, and—if you decide to file bankruptcy—administer your case from beginning to end. In bankruptcy, you have to comply with certain requirements, and must acknowledge to the trustee—in writing—that you understand these requirements.

Your Duties—when you file for bankruptcy you must:

- disclose all your liabilities and assets to the trustee;
- tell the trustee if you have sold any property in the past year and for how much;
- surrender all your credit cards to the trustee;
- attend an examination before the Official Receiver (if required—see below);
- attend a first Meeting of Creditors (if required); and
- keep the trustee informed of any changes in your circumstances.

The stay—like a proposal, a stay prevents creditors and wage garnishment once bankruptcy is declared.

Income and expenses—with your trustee, you review your income and expenses to see if you have any disposable income that can be used to contribute to payments for creditors. Your income is compared to guidelines provided annually by the Superintendent of Bankruptcy.

Property exemptions—your property, or assets, get assigned to the trustee, who may sell property to pay your creditors. But certain assets are exempt from being assigned to the trustee. Your trustee will assist you in listing your assets and exemptions, and you should be completely open and provide full information. It is very important that you discuss your exemptions with your trustee, as he or she can help you make the best use of your options. A list of provincial exemptions is provided on the Web landing page www.socrates.com/books/bankruptcy-renewal.aspx.

You may be able to make separate arrangements to keep paying secured creditors so that you do not lose your property. You should consult with your trustee on this matter.

Examination by the Official Receiver

You may be required to attend an examination by the Official Receiver after filing. You will be under oath and will be asked questions about your financial circumstances, in particular your assets. Make sure you have all your paperwork and understand how much you owe. The point of this examination is to ascertain the cause of your bankruptcy—in particular, if the court suspects fraudulent or dishonest behavior.

First Meeting of Creditors

You generally will not have a meeting of creditors unless one of your creditors requests it. If there is a meeting, at least one creditor with a proven claim must attend. You are also required to attend. The purpose of the meeting is almost identical to the Meeting of Creditors for Chapter 7 bankruptcies in the U.S.

At this meeting the trustee's appointment is also confirmed, and up to five inspectors are appointed to supervise the administration of the estate. Creditors may ask you for information and may also give directions to the trustee. If no creditors show up, it is assumed that the trustee's appointment is confirmed, and the matter proceeds forward. If there are objections, a subsequent meeting may be required.

Tax Returns

Under Canadian bankruptcy law, the trustee must prepare two income tax returns on your behalf during the year in which the bankruptcy occurs. You have to provide all the documentation needed to do this, including tax returns from previous years.

Discharge—if this is your first bankruptcy, your case is automatically discharged after 9 months unless there are objections from the trustee, the official receiver or a creditor. You will receive a copy of the discharge in the mail.

If your discharge is opposed, the trustee sends a discharge application to the court, and you may be required to attend a discharge hearing. The court listens to the trustee's report on your circumstances and chooses from the following measures:

- **Absolute discharge**—Your unsecured debts are discharged, except for those excluded under the BIA.
- **Conditional discharge**—You have to fulfill certain terms in order to get an absolute discharge. Usually this means having to pay a certain amount to creditors in installments over a period of time.
- **Suspended discharge**—There will be a delay while your case may be reviewed, but it could end in an absolute discharge.
- **Discharge refused**—This will happen if you have acted in ways that the court considers inappropriate. For instance, if you kept spending on credit during the case, continued to live beyond your means or if you sold assets without permission.

Debts Not Discharged by Bankruptcy

The debts that are not discharged include:

- court-imposed penalties or fines
- alimony and child support
- debt obtained by fraud
- student loans (if less than 10 years since you were last in school)

Your trustee can provide information on other debts that may not be discharged by bankruptcy.

Bankruptcy and Your Credit Rating

Information on your bankruptcy appears on your credit report for 6 to 7 years after your bankruptcy is discharged. A subsequent bankruptcy will be reported for 7 years.

Who Will Know?

Many people worry that everyone will find out that they are bankrupt, and that this will be embarrassing and distressing. And while bankruptcy is a matter of public record, notices of your bankruptcy are only sent to your creditors. In fact, it is unlikely that many people will know that you are bankrupt or have filed a consumer proposal, unless you choose to tell them. In general, the following are informed:

- Your employer may be notified, but only if you have wage garnishments at the time of filing; then, your employer will receive notice to stop garnishing your wages, otherwise they will not know of your bankruptcy. (It is important to remember that, by law, you cannot be fired for being bankrupt.)

- Your bankruptcy or consumer proposal will appear on your credit report for some years.

19 Understanding Your Rights

Regardless of whether you have declared bankruptcy or not, there are legal limitations on the actions that creditors and their agents can take. This chapter provides additional information on your rights with respect to creditors and your employer and what you can do to enforce them.

Remember, once you declare bankruptcy, you immediately have the protection of the automatic stay until your bankruptcy case is either dismissed or discharged. After your case has ended, creditors whose debts have been discharged may not demand further payment from you. Creditors to whom you are still liable may be able to approach you, but may not behave illegally.

If Creditors Persist During the Automatic Stay

When you filed for bankruptcy (either Chapter 7 or Chapter 13) an automatic stay went into effect. The automatic stay prohibited action from virtually all the creditors to whom you owed money.

After your bankruptcy, creditors cannot pursue you for debts that have been discharged. If a creditor harasses you by writing or telephoning you persistently, or by issuing any threats (financial or otherwise), you can take legal action. If these situations arise, it means the creditor is ignoring the notice received from the court informing them of the automatic stay and the subsequent discharge of debts. The following steps illustrate what you should do if you are being harassed by creditors:

- If you have an attorney, notify him or her of this creditor's behavior.
- Contact the bankruptcy trustee appointed to your case.
- You or your attorney should send a letter to the creditor stating that the creditor is aware of the bankruptcy proceeding and that the debt has been discharged.
- State that you will be forced to take further action if the harassment related to the continued attempts to collect the debt does not stop immediately.
- Send the letter by certified mail.

If the creditor still refuses to leave you alone, you may file a motion with the courts. The creditor may be fined for civil contempt. There is normally a fee for filing a civil action complaint in a district court, but you can apply for the fee to be waived if you are unable to pay it. See an attorney at this stage of the process. You can also find more information at the U.S. courts Web site www.uscourts.gov.

Under the terms of the Fair Debt Collection Practices Act, debt collectors are prohibited from engaging in unfair, deceptive or abusive practices. This act applies to professional debt collectors who have been hired by creditors to collect loans on their behalf. It does not technically apply to creditors who collect their own debts.

- A debt collector can only contact your employer or other people who know you in order to locate your address or to communicate with you about the debt.

- A debt collector must send written notice to the debtor after making contact. They must state the amount of the debt, the name of the creditor and the fact that the debt will be considered valid unless you dispute it within 30 days.

- Debt collectors may not harass you, be abusive, use threats or obscene language, or make annoying or anonymous phone calls. They must not publicize your debt to others.

- Debt collectors must not conceal their role from you or misrepresent the status of the debt or consequences of not paying the debt.

If a debt collector violates the terms of the Fair Debt Collection Practices Act you are within your rights to sue for damages. Your previous bankruptcy in no way affects your rights in this matter. If you are harassed by a debt collection agency or creditor, regardless of whether the debt has been discharged or not, you can ask them to Cease and Desist. If you write to them demanding this they cannot, by law, contact you further. The creditor can take action but you can no longer be harassed. If the harassment continues, you can take them to court.

The Cease and Desist Letter, found on the Web landing page www.socrates.com/books/bankruptcy-renewal.aspx, can serve as a model.

If Creditors Put Pressure on You to Reaffirm a Debt

Remember, although you asked the bankruptcy court to discharge your eligible debts, you can choose to remain legally obligated to particular debts that would have been discharged. This is called reaffirming the debt—and it is your choice.

A reaffirmation agreement has to be in writing and approved by the judge. It also has to be made before your bankruptcy is over. In addition, you have the option to cancel the reaffirmation at any time before your discharge order (the point at which your bankruptcy is completed and your debts are canceled). If a creditor puts pressure on you to reaffirm a debt, either before or after your bankruptcy has been discharged, just remember:

- a creditor cannot force you to reaffirm a debt; that option is entirely yours;

- a creditor cannot approach you after your bankruptcy and demand that you reaffirm a debt; and

- if you cancel a reaffirmation before your discharge order by following the proper procedure, the creditor is obliged to return any payments you had made during the time the debt was reaffirmed.

Once again, you can also send a Cease and Desist letter—or similar letter—pointing out the above facts, and refuse to reaffirm the debt. If the creditor is pressuring you during your case, you should inform the bankruptcy trustee and your attorney, if you have one.

Wage Garnishment

Wage garnishment, also known as wage assignment or wage attachment, is subject to certain limitations and, apart from the exceptions below, has to be court-ordered.

In order to garnish your wages a creditor must—in most cases—sue you to obtain a judgment. Your employer then deducts money from your wages and sends it directly to the creditor. Garnishment can also be taken from bank accounts.

The percentage of your wages that can be deducted as garnishment is limited in most states to whichever is less: 25 percent of your wage or the amount by which your weekly earnings exceeds 30 times the federal minimum hourly wage (currently $5.15). However, the laws and limitations relating to wage garnishment do not apply in the following specific cases:

- Student loan—the creditor does not have to sue you and up to 10 percent of your wages can be garnished.

- Child support—up to 50 percent of your wages can be taken to pay arrears (possibly more).

- Income taxes—the IRS can take most of your wages if you have ignored their attempts to collect back taxes owed.

> In Canada, the situation is very similar: a creditor must sue you and obtain a Garnishment Order from the court in order to garnish your wages. The Canada Customs and Revenue Agency—along with the Maintenance Enforcement and Student Loans—can all garnish payments directly from your wages or bank accounts.

If you have filed for bankruptcy and your case is in progress, your wages cannot be garnished. In fact, all existing wage garnishment must cease. If the debt you are paying through wage garnishing is dischargeable, the creditor cannot reinstate garnishing after your bankruptcy. If you are paying the debt through a Chapter 13 repayment plan, this replaces the wage garnishing. Any remaining amount at the end of your plan will normally be discharged and the creditor cannot claim it.

Garnishments after Bankruptcy

After bankruptcy you can object to a wage garnishment if you can show that you need the money to support your spouse and/or children. To object to any wage garnishment you should contact your local court for the relevant paperwork.

If you believe you do not owe any money to the creditor who is garnishing your wage,s you can dispute the garnishment. This does not stop the process but it does let the judge decide the matter. When a garnishment commences, you will receive a Garnishment Notice from your local court that states you may ask for a hearing to dispute the garnishment or wage deduction—it also explains the process. To dispute a garnishment in Canada, you file a Dispute Note. Contact your local court to get the paperwork for your district.

Your Rights after Bankruptcy

Denial of Credit

Under the Equal Credit Opportunity Act you cannot be refused credit for reasons based on your race, religion, color, national origin, sex, marital status or age. The same Act prevents discrimination based on the fact that you are receiving welfare, Social Security or unemployment compensation.

An application for credit cannot demand information about any of the above categories, except if you are applying to finance or refinance a home. Even in those situations, you are entitled to refuse to provide the information. In addition, a creditor may only ask information about your spouse under limited circumstances.

Prospective lenders or employers can ask how old you are but only to ensure that you have reached the legal age to borrow money (18) or to judge how much longer you are likely to work. However, they may not deny you credit because you are age 62 or older.

If you apply for credit and are refused, you have the same rights as anyone else in that situation. Your recent bankruptcy does not affect or change your rights at all. If you appear to have been refused credit for reasons that are discriminatory, you may be entitled to sue the lender for damages, as well as for any legal fees you might incur.

If you are denied credit on the basis of a credit check, the lender is obliged by law to disclose whether a denial of credit was based on information provided by a credit reporting agency. The lender is required to provide you with the name, address and telephone number of the credit reporting agency that undertook the check. You then have 60 days to contact the credit reporting agency and request a free copy of your credit report. This copy must disclose all information in the report, the source of all information, and details of who has received copies of your report in the past year (or 2 years, if for employment purposes).

For more information on your credit report and what rights you have, see Chapter 20.

Employment Rights

Your employer cannot fire or demote you because of your recent bankruptcy. Both governmental and private employers cannot fire someone simply because of their insolvency. A private employer has no right to terminate an employee's job on these grounds since this is considered discrimination under federal law. In addition, an employer cannot fire you for one wage garnishment; however, if you have more than one wage garnishment, you may not be protected.

In Summary

This chapter outlines your rights in situations you may encounter after bankruptcy. Remember that most of these rights apply to all people, whether they are bankrupt or not. Remember also that a potential lender may refuse you credit on the basis of your credit report and be quite justified in citing your problematic credit history as a concern.

Above all, do not let creditors or your employer threaten or judge you because of your bankruptcy. Bankruptcy is not a moral judgment or anything that you should feel guilty about. Assert your rights calmly and firmly, and in writing if a face-to-face confrontation would be too difficult. If you prefer, seek legal advice and ask an attorney to write to the creditors concerned. There is more information in Chapter 23 about how to get advice and support as you start out after bankruptcy.

Your Credit Report & Credit Score

This chapter provides a general explanation of what a credit report is, how it is used and interpreted by lenders, and how your borrowing and repayment affects your Credit Score. It also explains how your bankruptcy affects the information in your credit report.

You can benefit enormously from knowing just how the credit reporting system works. Once you have a clear idea of the process, you will be able to understand your credit report more easily and can monitor it for discrepancies. Anyone, bankrupt or not, can dispute inaccuracies on their credit report and ask to have erroneous information removed or corrected.

The next chapter will then take you through the nitty-gritty of a credit report, and will show you some examples. Finally, there is a chapter providing some strategies to help you actually improve or repair your credit.

Your Credit History

Whenever you apply to take out a loan, a mortgage, or a new credit card, somebody is sure to do a credit check on you. You are probably already aware of that, but you might be surprised to learn that employers, insurance companies and landlords can also ask to do a credit check, although they need your permission by law.

What exactly is the purpose of a credit check? Essentially, a credit check is the process of reviewing your credit history. Your credit history is a record of how much you have borrowed and how you have repaid your debts. This is also sometimes called your payment history. If you have ever applied for a loan, a credit card or any other form of credit, there will be information about it on file.

- If you have always paid off your debts on time and used credit wisely, you will have a good payment or credit history.

- If you have fallen behind in paying off debts, failed to pay off credit cards or defaulted on loans, your credit history will show this.

- Strangely enough, your credit history can sometimes also be deemed high risk if you have no debts and do not use a credit card—lenders are more interested in your ability to deal with credit than whether you are rich or poor.

Credit Reporting

Potential lenders are very interested in your credit history because it gives them a good idea of how much of a risk it will be to lend you money. They want to make money from your interest payments, but they do not want to lose money through your inability to pay.

Do not forget that all credit—credit cards, loans, mortgages, even insurance—is a certain kind of lending. But lenders (or, to use another term for the same thing, creditors) need to interpret a great deal of information in order to make their decision. Your credit report provides them with an overview of your financial situation, as well as general information on your employment and living circumstances.

In times gone by, a customer's financial information was much easier for lenders to confirm: people did not travel much and always worked, lived, and spent in the same community. If someone failed to pay their bills on time—or on a positive side, if they had mended their ways—the local bank knew about it or could find out pretty easily. Nowadays things are very different. It is impossible for lenders to know all their potential customers that well.

Today, lenders still decide whether or not to extend credit based on your credit history. But, since most people have quite complicated credit histories and there are other factors to be weighed, this can be a very difficult task. This is where the credit report and your credit score come into the equation.

Credit reporting has made it possible for us to move from one place to another and still obtain credit instantly wherever we may be. This wonderful convenience is naturally balanced by the fact that businesses are able to identify bad credit risks easily, enabling them to avoid customers who are unlikely to pay their bills.

What Is a Credit Report?

The credit reporting system enables businesses and lenders to make an informed decision about whether to extend credit to a customer based on their previous behavior and their current situation.

The information in your credit report includes the following information (which is covered in more detail in the next chapter):

- your name, address, and other personal information about you;

- details of accounts you are currently paying off;

- details of delinquent accounts, debts and nonpayments;

- public records information, which includes information about you that is publicly available and concerns things like child support delinquencies or lawsuits against you; and

- any inquiries showing an indication of how often, and in what circumstances, other credit reports have been requested.

Take note that credit reports are also sometimes referred to as consumer reports.

Your credit report shows both positive and negative information. So, for example, if you have always paid your mortgage on time, this will be shown on the report. Or, if you have paid off debts in full, this will be indicated. Negative information, such as debts outstanding or bills that were paid late, will also be noted.

The Credit Reporting Agencies (CRAs)

The information in your credit report is usually collected by one of the three major credit reporting agencies (also known as credit bureaus or consumer reporting agencies). The main agencies are:

Equifax

Equifax Credit Information Services, Inc.
P.O. Box 740241
Atlanta, GA 30374
To order report: 800.685.1111
Web site: www.equifax.com

Equifax Canada Inc.
Consumer Relations Department
Box 190 Jean Talon Station
Montreal, Quebec
H1S 272
To order report: 800.465.7166
Web site: www.equifax.ca

TransUnion LLC

Consumer Disclosure Center
P.O. Box 1000
Chester, PA 19022
To order report: 800.888.4213
Web site: www.transunion.com

Canadian Residents Outside Quebec

TransUnion Canada
Consumer Relations Centre
P.O. Box 338, LCD 1
Hamilton, ON
L8L 7W2
To order report: 866.525.0262

Canadian Residents in Quebec

TransUnion (Echo Group)
1600 Henri Bourassa Boul Ouest
Suite 210
Montreal, PQ
H3M 3E2
To order report: 877.713.3393
Web site: www.tuc.ca

Experian (U.S. only)

National Consumer Assistance
P.O. Box 2002
Allen, TX 75013
To order report: 888.397.3742
Web site: www.experian.com

What Happens in a Credit Check?

The following sequence of events happens whenever a business, landlord or lender does a credit check on you:

- businesses or, as they are referred to by the credit reporting agencies, merchant subscribers, pay the CRA for your credit report on an as needed basis;
- the CRAs collect and provide the information; they use it to work out a credit score for you and provide this and the credit report to the merchant subscribers. The score is not part of the credit report but is usually provided with it;
- once they have the credit report, lenders or merchants use the information to make their decision on whether to extend or deny credit to you; and
- in turn, they furnish the credit reporting agency, or CRA, with information about your financial record with them, which is added to your file.

It is important to remember that the CRA plays no part in the decision of whether to offer you credit or not. Each lender makes an individual decision, using the information as a tool. This is why one lender may refuse you credit and the next day another may be quite happy to give you a loan. Even so, the credit score provided plays a significant part in their decision making process, so your aim should be to improve your credit score as soon as you can.

Tip

Some lenders are very happy to offer credit to someone with a very poor credit report but they are typically the lenders who will charge exorbitant interest rates and make money from your vulnerability—so beware!

How Your Credit Score Is Calculated

Your credit score is a numerical value that is calculated by weighting the information in your credit report in various ways and using it to calculate a three digit number.

Despite recent moves to make access to your credit score easier, the method for calculating the score is still rather mysterious. The three leading credit reporting agencies each generate the credit score slightly differently, so you may have a slightly different credit score from each. In all cases, the following criteria are considered, with the following approximate weighting for each:

- 35 percent—Your payment history
- 30 percent—The amount you owe
- 15 percent—The length of your credit history
- 10 percent—New credit
- 10 percent—The types of credit you use

As expected, your payment history is most important. The information taken into consideration includes not only your outstanding debts but also more specific details on how late your payments have been in the past. Remember that your credit score takes both positive and negative information into account, and any debts you have paid off in full will be recognized.

The major credit reporting agencies use the FICO credit score system. Credit scores are commonly called the FICO or FairIsaac score because the software used to calculate them was made by Fair, Isaac and Company. Though the range is from 300-850, most FICO scores usually fall between 340 and 820.

- The higher up the scale you are, the less of a risk you pose to lenders.
- Lenders are often willing to offer credit to those with lower scores but are likely to ask for higher interest rates or to put other restrictions in place.
- Some lenders decide what interest rate to charge you on the basis of your FICO score alone—or whether to lend to you at all.

How Do Lenders Interpret Your Credit Report?

Most potential lenders keep several broad criteria in mind when they decide whether to extend credit to you. They consider these criteria along with your credit score in assessing what kind of risk you pose. The following are just a few of the criteria looked at:

Ability to pay—Looking at your income and current debts, a lender evaluates whether you have the ability to make payments on the credit you are requesting. They will consider your job, the amount of credit you already have and your payment history.

Assets—Lenders look to see if you have assets that they can take possession of if you fail to meet the payments on a loan.

Stability—Lenders like to feel that your situation is unlikely to change abruptly, and can only improve. It is therefore viewed positively if you have been at the same address for some time or if you own the property. They also take other factors into account, such as the length of time in your current job and if you have had a bank account for a long time.

How Does Bankruptcy Affect Your Credit Report and Credit Score?

Once you have declared bankruptcy, it will appear on your personal credit report for a specific period of time defined by federal law. Information about bankruptcy is generally a matter of public record, so there is nothing you can do to stop it from being noted in your credit report.

- If you filed Chapter 7, the information remains on your credit report for 10 years.

- If you filed Chapter 13, the information remains on your credit report for 7 years.

Your credit report will indicate when a debt has been written off, or discharged, due to bankruptcy. There is more information on how that is indicated in the report in the next chapter.

Normally, negative information can remain on your credit report for 7 years after you have paid off the debt or had it written off. However, bankruptcy is the exception. Information relating to your bankruptcy can remain on your credit report for up to 10 years.

The most immediate impact of bankruptcy is the negative effect your payment history will have on your credit score. When you become bankrupt, and for some time after, you will almost certainly find it difficult to get a loan, a mortgage or other credit.

If Your Bankruptcy Should Have Been Removed by Now

The bankruptcy court itself has no authority over the credit bureaus. The credit bureaus and CRAs are controlled by the terms of the Fair Credit Reporting Act (FCRA). In addition, the largest credit reporting agencies belong to an organization, the Associated Credit Bureaus. If your bankruptcy should have been removed from your credit report—for instance, if the period above has now expired—you can contact the Federal Trade Commission (FTC) to question why it has not been removed. The FTC can also give you general information on credit problems.

Federal Trade Commission

Bureau of Consumer Protection
Education Division
Washington, D.C. 20580
202.326.2222

You should examine your credit report regularly to ensure that that information is removed at the due date.

How to Get a Copy of Your Credit Report

You are entitled to ask for a copy of your own credit report from any or all of the major CRAs that apply to you—either directly or via one of the many online bureaus. In fact, you should do so on a regular basis, and certainly when you are considering applying for a loan or mortgage and know somebody else will want to do a credit check on you.

To get a copy of your report, visit the Web page of any of the major CRAs listed above or phone them for further information.

How Much Will It Cost?

In the U.S., a recent amendment to the federal Fair Credit Reporting Act required that all three of the major CRAs provide anyone who asks with one free copy of their own credit report every 12 months. In many states you can already obtain a free annual credit report, and by September 1, 2005, all Americans will be able to do this.

In Addition

• in most cases, you are already entitled to one free report a year if you are unemployed and looking for a job within 60 days of being unemployed; on welfare; or your report is inaccurate because of fraud;

• you are also already entitled to an additional free report if you have been refused credit on the basis of a credit report. Anyone who refuses you credit for this reason must, by law, provide you with a letter explaining this and how to get a copy of your report; and

• you can obtain additional copies of your credit report for a fee, currently around $9.

Note

In Canada, you can obtain a free copy of your credit report by mail from both Equifax and TransUnion. You simply mail in a request on a form provided or write a letter with the same information (Request for Credit Report is included on the CD). You can also pay a small fee (currently around $15 CDN) to have immediate online access to both your credit report and a credit score.

If you have filed for bankruptcy or are thinking of doing so, you have particularly good reasons for analyzing your credit report. But you do not need a specific reason to obtain a copy. The CRA must provide full details of everything in your report, including the sources of the information. The CRA must also provide details of any requests for your credit report in the past 2 years that have been made by potential employers.

Your Rights When Disputing Your Credit Report

Remember, the FCRA provides you with rights regarding your credit report. Here is a summary of your legal rights:

- You may challenge the accuracy of your credit report at any time.
- The credit bureau must reinvestigate anything you challenge within 30 days of notice of a dispute.
- If the credit bureau cannot confirm that the adverse information in dispute is correct it must delete it from its files.
- If the credit bureau finds errors in the information you have disputed it must delete it from its files.
- If the bureau does not confirm that the information you challenged is correct within a reasonable time it must also delete it from its files.
- If the creditor verifies that the information is correct and the bureau confirms this to you, the information remains in your file. However, you may also give your side of the story—you have the right to send a 100-word consumer statement disputing the information. You can ask the credit bureau to help you write it. They must attach it to every copy of your credit report that is requested from them. See the letter, Addition of Consumer Statement, found on the Web landing page www.socrates.com/books/bankruptcy-renewal.aspx.

In summary, there is no doubt that a bad credit score can make it difficult for you to obtain good credit or other services where proof of your financial responsibility is important. But this need not be a permanent situation; as you will see in the next chapters, there is a lot you can do to repair your credit and to show lenders that you have a firm grip on your financial circumstances.

Free Forms and Checklists

Registered readers can visit www.socrates.com/books/bankruptcy-renewal.aspx for free forms, letters and checklists. See page iv for details on how to register. Among the many items available are:

Request for Free Credit Report

Request for Removal of Outdated Information

Demand for Corrected Credit Report

Debt Consolidation Schedule

Analysis of Cash Available for Debt Repayment

Monthly Expenses (Worksheet)

Examples of Credit Reports (TransUnion & Experian)

Loan Worksheet

And more . . .

21 Cleaning Up Your Credit Report

Monitor Your Credit Report

This chapter explains how to interpret some of the more important aspects of your credit report and what to do if you find an error. It also describes a few strategies for cleaning up your report.

As someone whose bankruptcy has recently been discharged, it is particularly important to do whatever you can to improve your credit rating. As a starting point, you will need to ensure that all the information in the report is accurate. If you find an error in your credit report or out of date information, dispute it. Your goal after filing bankruptcy should be to reestablish your creditworthiness and to straighten your financial affairs. Understanding what is in your credit report can help you in this endeavor.

Keeping Your Cool

Finding an error in your credit report can be very aggravating, and it may make you understandably angry. Whatever you do, do not lose your cool and send a rude or angry letter to the CRA that provided the report. This may give you some brief satisfaction but will not get the result you need. Remember that credit bureaus are simply businesses and they must comply with laws governing their operation. They have no other special authority but focus simply on providing a good service to their customers—them being the businesses or merchant subscribers who ask for information. As a result, the individual consumer is pretty low on their list of priorities. Generally, if the information the CRAs collect indicates a possible problem with your payment history, they will err on the side of caution and mark this problem on your credit report.

How To Proceed

The rest of this Chapter provides some guidance on how to proceed. You can also get more detailed information and useful forms and sample letters from the Socrates Kit Starting Over After Bankruptcy. As you proceed make sure to:

- obtain a copy of your credit report (see previous chapter);

- make several photocopies as you do not want to mark the originals;

- review and note any errors on your credit report (using one of your copies);

- list any questionable items;

- dispute incorrect personal information; and

- request corrections.

You can also:

- add a Consumer Statement; and

- ask for positive information to be added.

Review Your Credit Report

An example of a credit report can be found on the Web landing page www.socrates.com/books/bankruptcy-renewal.aspx. Each of the three main CRAs has a slightly different way of formatting a credit report—but they contain the same information.

Personal Information and Employment Details

Check that the following are all present and correct:

- name and any aliases (if there are other names you go by)
- address
- Social Security number
- date of birth
- state ID number
- spouse information (if applicable)
- employer(s) information

This information is used to help verify the other items appearing on your credit report, so it is very important that it is up-to-date. If this information is out of date (in particular, addresses) you may find items that do not actually belong to you turning up on your report. In this case, make a note of the information that is wrong. Do this for each credit report you are reviewing.

Other Information

Information that is public record (including any bankruptcies less than 10 years old) will be listed. Check to make sure that none of the following appear in error:

- Bankruptcies that are older than 10 years.

- Bankruptcies that are less than 10 years but do not have the specific chapter identified (for instance, you do not want people assuming you filed for Chapter 7 if you actually filed Chapter 13).

- Lawsuits or judgments that are over 7 years old or have expired due to the statute of limitations.

- Criminal records older than 7 years.

- Paid tax liens.

- Delinquent (unpaid) accounts that are older than 7 years or which do not state when the account became delinquent.

- Credit inquiries that were made without your knowledge when you were simply comparison shopping (for instance, visiting different mortgage companies in person or online or test-driving a car). See below for more information on what an inquiry is and how it affects your report.

- Commingled accounts—information that indicates that your report has information that belongs to another person (probably someone with a similar name to yours).

- Duplicate accounts—something listed twice, perhaps under different categories in your report.

- Accounts listed as open when in fact they are closed. Also, if you closed an account yourself, you want the report to state "closed by consumer." Otherwise, it may look as if the account was closed by your creditors because you did not pay them.

- Voluntary surrender of vehicle listed as repossession.

- Erroneous charge-off codes.

Charge-offs

If you find this code, it indicates that the creditor charged the account off to profit and loss. This means that the creditor thinks your debt is uncollectible. You will see this code against many debts that were discharged when you became bankrupt. You cannot dispute these since the code is correct in this case.

But you may have agreed to pay off some longstanding debts as part of your bankruptcy. If you have paid off a debt, the charge-off code should no longer be there, and you should ask for it to be removed. Most often the creditor has not provided the updated information to the credit bureau when you paid off the delinquent account.

It is beyond the scope of this book to go into detail about every code or listing that can appear on a credit report. These are the more common errors and omissions you should look for, although there can certainly be others. If there is any information that you think is wrong or should not be there, make a note of it.

Inquiries

Why should you worry about inquiries regarding your credit report? Whenever someone asks a credit bureau for your credit report, this generates what is known as an inquiry. Inquiries are noted on your credit report. If too many inquiries appear in quick succession, it looks as if you may have been applying for a great deal of credit. This flurry of activity can be interpreted negatively and may result in your being refused credit. Although this seems, and perhaps is, somewhat unfair, there is little you can do about it unless the inquiry was made without your knowledge or permission.

Take Note

Creditors are not allowed legally to request your credit report until you indicate a desire to enter into a sale or lease. Some creditors—especially car sales companies—tend to interpret this rule rather broadly.

Some people worry that requesting copies of their credit report will generate an inquiry. They feel that they will damage their own credit simply by requesting to look at their report. This is not true. When you request a copy of your credit report you generate what is sometimes known as a Soft Inquiry, which does not affect your credit rating.

Dispute Only Erroneous Information

You have the legal right to dispute information that is incomplete or inaccurate. But remember, there is no point in disputing negative information that is correct and for which the statute of limitations has not yet expired.

Under the terms of the Fair Credit Reporting Act, you may have the right to send a letter to the CRA (also known as the credit bureau). In this letter you can dispute erroneous information and ask for it to be reinvestigated. In fact, the credit bureau is legally obliged to reinvestigate in response to your dispute and to get in touch with you within 30 days. Reinvestigation is quite an easy process; even so, credit bureaus find ways not to do it. In order to get the results you want, you need to be careful when writing your letter.

What Is a Frivolous Request?

Credit bureaus can refuse to investigate a dispute if they deem your request to be frivolous.

- Most often, credit bureaus will immediately say your request is frivolous if you write that you are trying to repair your credit or start over after bankruptcy rather than specifying exactly what information you are disputing.

- Credit bureaus also do this if you send a series of letters, each disputing one error that you have found. Instead, scrutinize your credit report carefully and note every single discrepancy or error. Then make a list that ranks these errors in order of importance and write one letter that covers them all.

Your Dispute Letter

The Request for Removal of Outdated Information letter can be used as a model for this situation. Use the Complaint Letter to request removal of erroneous information.

- Your letter should be written in your own words and handwritten neatly or typed. Use the examples provided as models only.
- Explain that you would like erroneous information removed, and specify exactly what it is and why it is erroneous.
- Do not go into any other details.
- Say that you are exercising your rights under the Fair Credit Reporting Act 15 U.S. Code Section 1681.
- Enclose a copy of your credit report and any other relevant paperwork.
- Provide full personal details—name, address, Social Security number and spouse's name.
- Be courteous, straightforward and firm, and provide as much detailed information as you can.
- Get a trusted close friend or spouse to read your letter and check it for mistakes or errors.
- Always make a copy of your letter and file it where you can find it.
- Send your letter by certified mail with return receipt requested so that you have a record of its delivery.
- Wait 30 days for a response, and if no response is provided, send a reminder with all the information again. Point out that you are sending a reminder and that the credit bureau is legally obliged to reinvestigate the information you are disputing.

Ironically, an official looking letter on headed notepaper is less likely to get a good response than a straightforward, simply written letter. Credit bureaus will assume the more formal letter has come from a credit repair agency and are likely to deem it a frivolous or irrelevant request.

Things You Can Do to Improve Your Credit Report

In addition to correcting erroneous information, there are actually a few things you can do to improve your report. You want to explain mitigating circumstances for negative information and, where possible, also add information to show that your finances are now under control and you are dealing with credit wisely.

Add a Consumer Statement

You have the right to add a consumer statement that explains items on your report (you are the consumer here). This short statement (up to 100 words) is a chance for you to explain any mitigating circumstances or a particular reason why something negative appears on your report. It goes without saying that the reasons should be true, accurate and verifiable.

- Do not use consumer statements as a way of venting your anger about a situation (for example, saying "That lady ripped me off and I decided not to pay" will not help you). Just give the facts and a brief explanation.

- Use the statement to explain how a temporary blip in your life, now over, was the cause of a financial problem (e.g., "I was called up to active duty in March 2003 and was not able to deal with paying off and closing this account. By the time I had the chance, the account had been closed by the creditor.")

If someone requests a copy of your credit file, the CRA is only obliged to provide a summary of your statement. So make sure to keep it short!

Examples of Consumer Statements

"I am disputing the debt I owe to Kandy Computer Store. I ordered a computer from them but it arrived with a broken monitor. Because they would not let me return it at the store, I am negotiating a solution with the manufacturer instead."

"The late payments against my account with Metrobank Co. should not be on my file. I sent them notification of my change of address on January 3, 2002. They failed to note this change and sent bills to my old address for a year, so I did not receive them. The problem has now been sorted out."

Add Positive Information

Sometimes accounts that you are actually paying on time and regularly over a long period do not show up on your credit report. These missing credit histories tell stories that you want people to know. In particular, some major lenders just do not bother passing on information on mortgages and car loans to the CRAs. In these situations, make copies of your recent statements and any canceled checks, and ask the CRA to add this information to your file.

Note

The CRAs are not obliged to do this and may charge you a fee to do it; and;

You need to send a letter of request. (See the Request for Addition of Credit Information on the Web landing page www.socrates.com/books/bankruptcy-renewal.aspx.

Other Positive Information You Can Add

Making sure that all your personal details are listed can inspire confidence in lenders who are reading your report. If you have not been at your current address for very long, ask to have your previous address listed too (if it is not already). Make the same request with your employment history. If you have a bank or savings account—or both—you can add the account number(s). Similarly, if you own your own home, you can make sure your mortgage company is listed.

Important

Do not list your bank or savings account number, or your mortgage company, if you think you may be sued by a creditor. It will give them additional information that you may not want known.

Section Seven

22 Other Strategies to Repair Your Credit after Bankruptcy

As you come out of bankruptcy, you are going to find that having a record of it on your credit report will make it difficult for you to get credit. It does not matter how wise or frugal you are being now; lenders will still feel nervous about giving you money based on your previous record. In order to be able to obtain credit again, you will need to show creditors that you have learned from the experience and are now managing your finances wisely.

To improve your credit score as quickly as possible you need to start adding positive information to your credit report. Gradually, as your payment history gets better, your credit report will continue to build up with positive information and your credit score will improve.

You may reasonably think that the best way to recover from bankruptcy is to stop using credit and to deal only in cash and check payments. This is not the best choice though, because if you have no credit activity at all, no new information will be added to your credit report. The best way to improve your credit score—commonly known as Repairing Your Credit—is to show that you are capable of making full and prompt payments to lenders. Although it may seem strange, one of the best ways to improve your poor credit rating is to get credit and use it!

This chapter suggests some ways in which you can do this and provides some strategies for building a new credit record.

Remember that repairing your credit will take time. It might take a couple of years, but with a bit of work you may be able to get loans on good terms before then.

Get a Loan

As soon as you can you should try to get a small loan.

- Borrow only a small amount and do not expect great rates initially.
- Remember that the purpose of the loan is not to buy expensive or inessential goods, but rather to improve your credit.
- Avoid loans with hidden fees and ridiculously high interest rates. Read Chapter 23 for more information on the kinds of financial predators to avoid.

Once you have a loan—for instance, to buy a TV or a piece of furniture—be scrupulous about paying it off on time. Even if the terms of the loan allow missed payments, do not miss a single one. Keep paying regularly every month—on time and in full. Each time you send that check, think of it as another positive mark on your credit report.

When you have paid off the loan, take out another loan for a similar amount. This time see if there are better loans available to you; you may be pleasantly surprised.

Remember—do not shop around too much for loans. Each time a lender runs a credit check on you, this will generate a credit inquiry on your report. At this stage you want to avoid too many inquiries appearing on your report.

Open a Savings Account

Opening a savings account and putting aside a small amount of money each week or month can do a lot to improve your credit since this information appears on your credit report. Additionally, you can use the savings account as collateral against the small loan you will take out and pay off in regular installments.

One of the benefits of bankruptcy is that your release from previous debts may mean that you have some money in hand. The whole point of bankruptcy is to be able to start out again, without becoming completely destitute. Although you still have to pay off your secured creditors, you will have been released from many long standing unsecured debts. So, if you find you have a little more money than before, breathe a sigh of relief but do not spend your extra cash on luxuries.

Even if you are still paying many secured creditors and your finances are very tight, you should budget to save each month. Do not consider saving as simply an optional extra that you will do if you have the money—instead, make it a priority to save and cut back if necessary to make saving possible.

- Aim to save five percent of your pay. If that is not presently possible, decide on a set amount and stick to it each month. Remember, it is the regularity of the payments that will have an impact and will gradually afford you extra credit on your credit report.
- If possible, arrange for the money to be automatically taken out of your pay and transferred to your savings account. That way you will not be tempted to divert it to other items that seem more important.

- If you get a raise at work, transfer the extra money to your savings rather than increasing your expenditure allowance. You can manage without that extra money for a while.

- Accept the fact that you are going to have to live a very simple life for quite a while, and that saving money is going to make life far easier in the long term—even if times are lean right now.

Remember that the wonderful thing about having a savings account is that, not only is it improving your credit rating, but it is also providing you a buffer if things get tougher down the road. If your bankruptcy was brought about by sudden financial disasters that were beyond your control—like loss of employment or sickness—then you know just how useful savings could have been.

Use Your Credit Card to Improve Your Credit Rating

As you start over after bankruptcy, you may never want to own a credit card again. Even if you think you can do without one, there are many advantages to having a credit card and using it wisely. The main advantage is that your responsible use of the card will appear positively on your credit report. If you are using your card sensibly and paying off your balance every month, you will be offered more credit and will be approached by other credit card companies. But do not take extra credit unless you need it and can afford it.

Keeping Your Old Credit Card or Getting a New One

If overspending on your credit cards contributed to your bankruptcy, those cards will have been taken from you and the accounts closed. Of course, there may be some cards that you did not overspend on. Although these credit card companies will be aware of your bad credit rating, they may allow you to continue holding the card. It is possible that they will impose terms that are unfavorable, but you may have to live with this for a while. You should certainly check to see if better deals exist.

Types of Credit Cards

There are two main types of credit cards: Secured and Unsecured.

A secured credit card is essentially a charge card. It is a safer gamble for the credit card company or bank. A secured card requires that you open and maintain a savings account with the bank or card company. The amount you put in this account acts as a deposit. The spending limit on your card will be a percentage of your deposit, typically between 50 percent and 100 percent. You usually have to pay an annual fee and you may have to pay interest rates that are higher than those associated with an unsecured card.

You can see that a secured card does not offer many advantages. However, if it is the only kind of card you can get, use it wisely and only occasionally. Your good behavior will register on your credit report. After 6 months or so, you can try to reapply for an unsecured card.

An **unsecured credit card** is preferable but may be more difficult to obtain if you have bad credit. On the other hand, some credit card companies will give you a card if they see that your previous debts are now discharged as a result of your bankruptcy—which means that other creditors are not waiting in line for payment. However, the companies know that you are desperate, and will probably demand a high rate of interest.

Note of Caution

Watch out—there are many unscrupulous and fraudulent lenders out there. See Chapter 23 for some important tips on avoiding credit card scams.

Getting a New Card

Shop around for credit cards but do not submit too many applications. If you apply for several credit cards, this sudden activity will not look good on your credit report.

Instead, spend time looking at all the cards out there. Apply selectively for one card that offers a good deal and that, realistically, you stand a good chance of being given. Once you have the card, remember that you are using it as a credit repair tool and a way to spend wisely.

You can also look on the Internet to see credit card comparisons. Good Web sites include:

www.bankrate.com
www.cardweb.com
www.consumer-action.org

If you are a member of a credit union, see if they will offer you a credit card. The rates are often favorable. Similarly, if you are a member of a professional organization or university (or used to be), see if they offer credit cards to alumni at favorable rates. However, you need to accept that you are not in a strong position at present and may have to pay higher rates or fees to get a credit card.

Here are a few pointers on how to use your credit card wisely:

- Do not treat your credit limit or allocation as the amount you are going to spend. Remember, this is the upper limit defined by the credit card company, which would like you to incur ongoing debt so that they can receive interest payments from you.

- Only use your credit card for essential or planned purchases. As you start out you can even limit the use to one particular regular expense, such as your weekly trip to the supermarket.

- NEVER buy on impulse. If you are worried about your self-discipline, do not take your credit card shopping with you.

- Keep receipts for all purchases made by credit card—and do not forget any automatic payments (for instance, for cable TV) or any Internet or telephone purchases.

- Pay off your credit card bill in full each month. It is essential not to build up an increasing amount of credit card debt if you want to repair your credit.

Above all, remember that credit is not extra money on top of the money you earn or receive from other sources. A credit card simply lets you access some of that money in advance. It seems obvious, but it is easy to forget this when shopping!

Checking Your Credit Card Statement

If you are using your card wisely, you will be able to pay off your monthly credit card bill. Just think how great it will be not to have that sinking feeling when that familiar envelope arrives each month! But it is still important to check your credit card statement carefully. Mistakes do happen, and you want to catch them quickly. You also want to be on the lookout for any fraudulent use of your card number—it can happen to anyone!

Ask for Clean Credit Letters

If you have been making payments regularly and on time for at least a 12-month period, you can ask for clean credit reference letters from companies you pay regularly, such as:

- an auto insurance provider
- a home telephone provider
- a mobile/cell phone provider
- the utility companies (water, gas and/or electric)

Most companies are used to providing such letters, and will respond favorably to your request. If you receive no response to your letter, telephone the customer service number for the company concerned and politely ask again. You may have to pay a small fee for the service. Make sure to ask that they date the letter, provide your full name and address, and details of your prompt and full payment of account balances.

23 Getting Good Support & Avoiding the Sharks

Although this chapter is in the after bankruptcy section of this book, good support and financial counseling is important both before and after bankruptcy. In fact, you are required to receive credit counseling from approved counselors as part of a Chapter 7 and Chapter 13 bankruptcy filing and, in Canada, a consumer proposal filing.

While credit counseling prior to bankruptcy is important, you may also have a need for it after bankruptcy as you start out again. This chapter explains what kind of counseling is available and how to choose a reputable company. Because credit counseling has quite a few financial predators trawling for vulnerable customers, there is also advice on how to avoid the sharks.

Whether you are considering filing for bankruptcy or have emerged from it, make sure to read this chapter for some more information on how to get valuable support.

What Is Credit Counseling?

If you file for bankruptcy or file a consumer proposal under Canadian bankruptcy law, you must obtain credit counseling from an approved counseling service. As already mentioned, you must do this within 180 days before filing for Chapter 7 or Chapter 13, and you must receive a certificate from an approved nonprofit counseling agency.

Prior to bankruptcy, the counseling agency will help you to perform a budget analysis. This essentially involves analyzing how much you spend and how much you have coming in. Together you and your counselor work out a way to plan for your day-to-day expenditures and to put aside money for bills and other known expenses.

After bankruptcy you may have very different financial circumstances. You may actually have more money in hand than before, yet still have to cover debts that you remain liable for, as well as plan for normal expenses and savings. A credit counselor can help you set up a new budget and plan for the future.

What Is a Nonprofit Counseling Service?

This is actually a rather confusing term. Many people, quite understandably, think that nonprofit services must have no interest in making money from them—it sounds as if they are charitable operations. In fact, these services do not function as charities but are run as businesses—sometimes they simply ask for a donation rather than a fee.

Debt Consolidation or Debt Management Plans

On the whole, debt consolidation is not usually a good idea. What happens is that you go to the debt consolidation company and they will help you obtain a loan to pay off all your debts. You are then left with one big loan instead, which you start paying off in installments. Though in one sense this kind of plan can help get the pressure off your shoulders, it is usually not a good idea—the new loan is likely to be secured against your home or other important property and the interest rates will be high or liable to change. It is usually better to approach your individual creditors to see if they will let you renegotiate your payments.

Choosing a Reputable Company

There are various ways to check if a company has a good reputation and is approved as a pre-bankruptcy counseling service.

To find reputable counseling services, you can contact the following:

1. Visit www.consumer.gov for information provided by the federal government on credit and other general consumer issues.

2. The Council of Better Business Bureaus
   4200 Wilson Boulevard, Suite 800
   Arlington, VA 22203
   www.bbb.org

3. National Foundation for Credit Counseling
   801 Roeder Road, Suite 900
   Silver Spring, MD 20910
   Phone: 301.589.5600
   Fax: 301.495.5623
   www.nfcc.org

When you have found a counseling service you would like to use, check with your local Better Business Bureau to see if there are any complaints listed for that company. You can also check with the clerk of your district court for a list of approved credit counselors. Each district is required to maintain a list of approved credit counseling agencies and instructional courses on personal financial management. Also, make sure to:

• choose a service based in your state where you can sit down face to face with the representative;

• get everything in writing. Never rely on verbal promises;

- go to a good, reputable service that provides a free assessment of your needs and gives you information on what they can offer you—without requiring any kind of fee or upfront payment; and

- read all paperwork, especially contracts, very carefully. Do not sign anything until you agree with the terms. Be very suspicious of aggressive sales techniques and any pressure to sign quickly to get a special offer or deal.

Avoiding the Sharks after Bankruptcy

As soon as your bankruptcy is discharged, you may be surprised to find that people will start offering you credit. Beware—most, if not all, of those enticing cards or phone calls will be from people who are anxious to make money from your vulnerable situation. They know that you are going to have difficulty obtaining good credit for a while and how eager you will be to repair your credit.

Here are some companies to avoid:

Credit Repair Clinics—These services offer to repair your credit quickly so that once again your credit report will be whiter than white, and you will have no problem getting instant credit. Can they really do that? Simply put, no they cannot. At most, they will write to the main CRAs for you, which may only make the situation worse.

Guaranteed loans—These companies will offer you a loan as long as you pay them a fee up front—ignore them. While some legitimate lenders require a fee, they will never guarantee that they will offer a loan—a legitimate lender needs to check your credit first.

Instant credit card, anyone?—If a company offers a credit card without even asking your name, you would be wise to hang up the phone politely or put the flyer in the trash. The card will probably be at a very high rate or require a huge upfront fee. A credit card company that raves about its low APR will suddenly increase it to inflated rates without warning—credit card companies can legally do this.

Most importantly, you need to be realistic. While you will find it harder to get a new credit card for a while, these are not the companies to turn to. Instead, see if you can get a secured credit card—perhaps at a not so favorable interest rate—from an established and reputable company or from your bank. If you belong to a credit union, see if they can help you.

Face the fact that you will probably need to pay a higher interest rate for a while, but after 2 years, or perhaps even sooner, your responsible use of the card will pay off. Your credit card company is likely to agree to a higher spending limit or even to lower your interest rate—just ask them.

Additional Resources

If you are looking for more advice on how to manage your finances after bankruptcy and the situations you may face, there is more detailed information in the Socrates kit Starting Over after Bankruptcy, as well as useful forms, worksheets and sample letters to help you keep track of your finances.

24 Onward & Upward

The information in this book can help you determine the type of bankruptcy that you are eligible to file, and whether doing so is in your best economic interest. In most straightforward cases, personal bankruptcy does not necessarily require the expense of hiring a lawyer. This book provides tools to help you prepare for filing and also explores a variety of strategies to help you get maximum protection and so you can benefit from bankruptcy.

Resources

There are many online resources dealing with the subject of bankruptcy, some good and some not so good. Recent changes in bankruptcy law mean that you need to be particularly careful in what sites you go to, because you need to visit reputable sites with updated information.

You can stay up-to-date by visiting the special Web page that has been set up to accompany this book. You will find additional information on bankruptcy matters and updated versions of the forms and other materials at the Web landing page www.socrates.com/books/bankruptcy-renewal.aspx.

Some Other Useful Web Pages

The U.S. Courts
www.uscourts.gov

Bankruptcy Act
www.law.cornell.edu/uscode/html/uscode11/usc_sup_01_11.html

Fair Credit Reporting Act
www.ftc.gov/os/statutes/fcra.htm

Fair Debt Collection Practices Act
www.ftc.gov/os/statutes/fdcpa/fdcpact.htm

Equal Credit Opportunity Act
www.ftc.gov/bcp/conline/pubs/credit/ecoa.htm

Social Security Online
www.ssa.gov

Bureau of Labor Statistics
www.bls.gov

Cost of Living Index
www.coli.org

Information on Credit and Credit Counseling Concerns
www.credit.about.com

Canadian Bankruptcy Law (search for bankruptcy)
http://laws.justice.gc.ca

Canadian Information on Tax and Filing
http://strategis.ic.gc.ca

Forms and Other Information on the Web Landing Page

Consult the Appendices for lists of property exemptions and other information. There are also several checklists and forms that can help you collect the information you need. For official filing forms, you should consult the Socrates Bankruptcy Kit, which provides all forms, as well as instructions for completing each form.

Section Eight

Appendices

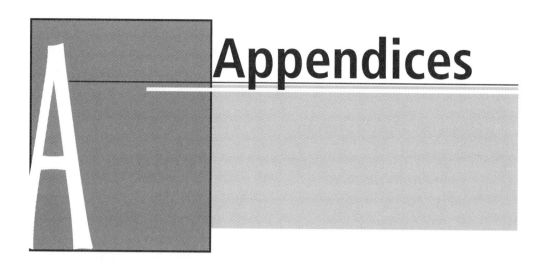

Appendices

Would You Lend Money to Yourself?

Score Yourself

Test yourself with this sample scoring system to get an idea of how lenders evaluate an applicant's risk. Add up your points for each question, and then compare your total to the scoring list below.

Factor Points

1. Years at present job:

a. Less than 1 year	0
b. 1 to 2 years	1
c. 2 to 4 years	2
d. 4 to 10 years	3
e. Over 10 years	4

Lenders have found that people who move frequently, do not have telephones or cannot keep steady jobs are poor credit risks.

Factor Points

2. Monthly income level:

a. Less than $1,000	0
b. $1,000 to $1,500	1
c. $1,500 to $2,000	2
d. Over $2,000	3

3. Present obligations past due:

a. Yes   0

b. No   1

4. Total monthly debt payments compared to income (after taxes):

a. 50 percent   0

b. 40 percent to 49 percent   1

c. 30 percent to 39 percent   2

d. under 30 percent   3

5. Prior loans with lender:

a. No   0

b. Yes, but not closed   0

c. Yes: closed, or with two or fewer 11-day notices per year   1

6. Checking account:

a. None   0

b. Yes, but with more than five rejected items over past year   1

c. Yes, with no rejected items over past year   2

7. Length at present or previous address:

a. Less than 3 years   0

b. 3 years or more   1

8. Age of newest automobile:

a. Over 1 year old   0

b. Less than 1 year old   1

9. Savings account with lender:

a. No   0

b. Yes   1

10. Own real estate:

a. No   0

b. Yes   3

11. Telephone in own name:

a. No   0

b. Yes   1

12. Good credit references:

a. No   0

b. Yes   1

In this example, you could score a possible 22 points. The guidelines provided to the loan officer might read like this:

- 0-11 points (0-50 percent of possible points): Reject outright.

- 11-13 points (50-60 percent of possible points): Review very carefully. Do not approve unless there are other strong indications that credit should be granted.

- 13-15 points (60-70 percent of possible points): Review with a bias toward approval. (This is the profile of the typical consumer, indicating a reasonable risk.)

- 15-20 points (70-90 percent of possible points): Grant the loan unless there is good reason to deny.

- 20-22 points (90-100 percent of possible points): Automatically grant credit within reasonable limits.

Obtaining Credit

Although it is possible to get a credit card without a good credit history or a high income, few people know how to do it. Most go through the ordinary channels and get turned down, so they incorrectly conclude that a Visa® or MasterCard® is unavailable to them. Sometimes even people with good credit histories and high incomes get turned down—even though they know people who are less creditworthy that have numerous credit cards. The credit card world can be simple when you understand the rules it works by, but to the uninformed it is challenging, even mysterious.

The Credit Card System

You certainly do not need dozens of credit cards to be successful. Though there are advantages to having many credit cards, it is the proper use of credit cards, rather than the total potential dollar amount of credit available, that is important. At the same time, to get the more valuable credit cards, you must know how the credit card system operates.

By studying how the banks interrelate, you will understand how to deal with credit card companies. Banks work together; many share a computer connection that trades vital cardholder information. Most banks want to know how many credit cards you have before considering you for one of their own cards.

It is how you use your credit card(s) that gives you wealth, not the number of cards you possess.

When banks decide you have too many cards (each bank has its own policy on how many is too many), they automatically reject your application(s).

Many banks offer the same card and will not allow a single cardholder to have more than one card from the same issuer. You may, therefore, receive only one card from an interconnected network of cooperating banks.

The Bank Card System

When you apply for a credit card at your local bank, much more is going on than you realize. Although the name of your local bank may be proudly displayed on your card, chances are your card was issued by another bank behind the scenes. Banks trade favors and reciprocate functions. Most often, however, banks hire each other to perform different services as a way to save money.

The bank card system is complicated. First there is the process of accepting the new applications, asking for credit reports and setting up approved accounts. Then there is card printing and embossing, not to mention the ongoing paperwork involved in year after year of statements, sales brochures, late payment notices and the countless other details that make a credit card program successful.

All of this is costly. That is why smaller banks act as credit card agents for larger banks. In other words, smaller banks contract with larger banks for card related services. Huge card processing centers do all the accounting, credit checks, mailings, statements, collections and administrative details for a large number of small banks. The smaller bank pays a fee and that is a percentage of the annual credit volume.

The main advantage of this system is that it allows smaller banks to stay in the game. Because there is fierce interbank competition—and because offering customers the convenience of credit cards is such an important part of bank promotion—many banks make their credit card packages a major advertising tool to attract new customers from the competition.

The larger banks also benefit from this system, because their overhead is partially subsidized by collecting annual service fees from the smaller institutions using their card processing services. In fact, card processing centers often realize handsome profits.

Some bank networks link different parts of the credit card process in a kind of chain. One bank may offer the card while another does the credit checks and a third or fourth does the card embossing and monthly statements. Some of these chains may be short and some may be surprisingly long.

Applying for More than One Credit Card

What happens if you simultaneously apply for different credit cards from a dozen banks in your area? Inevitably, many of the banks will be connected to the same major bank. This raises two possibilities:

1. The major bank will approve your credit. But because duplicate accounts are seldom allowed, of the 12 applications processed by the major bank, the first one accepted becomes your account and the other 11 are automatically canceled out. The credit card will reflect the name of the local bank that was on the accepted application. Unfortunately, you have needlessly generated 11 useless and potentially harmful inquiries on your credit report.

2. The smaller agent banks approve your credit. The major bank may issue several cards to the same individual if the agent banks assume responsibility for your credit; that means the agent banks would also have to assume responsibility for any defaults in payment.

Many major banks offer cards directly. If you have not already received a solicitation from one, you can look them up on the Internet or call them. That way you know you will not be generating unnecessary inquiries that appear on your credit report.

Shopping for Credit Cards

You have many choices when it comes to selecting a bank credit card, so examine all your options carefully before selecting the cards to apply for. There are great credit card bargains all over the nation—as well as deals you should avoid. Use the Credit Card Comparison form to compare the following three features that are part of all bank card terms:

Credit Card Comparison Chart

	Transaction Fees	Annual Membership Fee	Introductory APR	Final APR (When Changes)	Cash Advance Policy	Originating Bank	Restrictions on Use of the Card
Card 1 (name)							
Card 2 (name)							
Card 3 (name)							
Card 4 (name)							

1. **Transaction Fees.** Banks have discovered that 50 percent of all cardholders pay their total balance at the end of each month. This naturally limits the service fees each customer will be required to pay. To increase their revenues, some banks have designed transaction fees. For example, one major bank charged 12 cents for each use of the card. The cardholders felt they were getting a deal because the annual fee for this card was only $10 per year. However, for people who use their cards regularly, transaction fees can add up fast. Many cards charge no transaction fees, making them far less costly.

   It is a myth that all credit cards are alike, or that you must live in the same area to get a certain bank's credit card. Also, do not be misled into believing that you must have an account with the bank to which you are applying.

   It is important to check for transaction fees before applying for a bank card.

2. **Annual Membership Fees.** Annual fees are designed to boost sagging credit card income for the banking industry. However, some banks waive annual fees if you keep a minimum balance in your checking account. To evaluate the

worth of this offer, check what the interest rate would be on your balance. If it is too low, you would be losing more in the income you could make from a deposit in another bank at a higher interest rate than what you save by not paying an annual membership fee.

3. **Finance Charges/Annual Percentage Rate (APR).** These rates vary widely. Although there are legal limits—caps above which rates cannot go—these limits have a very high ceiling; they may also vary by state. Many credit card companies now offer adjustable percentage rates as a way to entice the new cardholder to transfer existing account balances. This introductory rate is often limited to as little as 6 months—after which the rate zooms back up to the card's regular rate. Do not be taken in by offers of low balance transfer rates, because within a year you could wind up paying more interest than you did before the transfer.

Many banks do not put an annual percentage rate on their application forms because their rates often change, and these changes are usually based on other interest rate indicators and the interest charged by competition. You often do not find out the actual interest rate you are asked to pay until the credit card arrives in the mail and you sign on the dotted line. Before you sign, check the interest rate and if it is not acceptable, return the card.

The new cardholder seldom has the willpower to return a new card, even one that arrives with a surprisingly high interest rate.

Debit Cards

The plastic card your bank issues for use in automated teller machines (ATMs) is not a credit card; it is a debit card. Each card has a magnetic strip that is activated when you punch in your personal identification number (PIN). Never keep your PIN number anywhere near your ATM card. Instead, try to pick a PIN number you do not have to write down: But do not use any part of your Social Security number or your address. These are the first numbers a thief will try if they get your ATM card and other identification.

Although these cards may carry the Visa or MasterCard logo, when you use them, you are not borrowing money, as you do with a credit card, you are using your own money. But they can still get you into credit trouble, because it is all too easy to forget to note card withdrawals in your checkbook; whether for cash at an ATM, to pay bills or order from catalogs, or for a product or service

If you report a stolen ATM card within 2 days of the theft, you may face a maximum liability of $50. However, if the theft goes unreported, you may be held responsible for up to $500 of any resultant loss. In fact, if unauthorized withdrawals are not reported within 60 days of their initial appearance on the bank statement or your liability is unlimited, you could even lose your entire deposit.

Although they are highly convenient, ATM cards do not offer the same degree of consumer protection enjoyed by regular credit cards.

Bankers prefer debit cards over checks because check processing is generally unprofitable. Merchants like the debit card system because they get their money immediately, electronically transferred into their company account. This system exists electronically, supported by a minimum of paperwork. With debit cards, the merchant does not have to worry about a check being misplaced or lost, nor do they have to worry about losing any checks from a store robbery.

How to Get Your Credit Cards

Here are 13 essential tips to help you obtain the credit cards you want:

1. Make a list of banks from which you will request application forms. Sometimes it is easier to get credit cards in the area in which you live, but the very large national banks are generally aggressive in seeking new accounts. Do not overlook savings and loans and credit unions.

2. Ask for an application form for Visa and MasterCard accounts, either by telephone or in writing. Be sure to request information about finance charges and fees, because these points often are not included in the application.

3. Obtain your credit report from the credit bureaus. If your credit report reveals negative marks against you, follow the procedures outlined later in this guide to remove them. If the report lacks details of your positive credit history, ask the bureau to add that information to the credit bureau. The credit bureau can charge a fee for entering these reports, but it may be worth the expense if it allows you to improve your position in the credit world.

4. If negative marks cannot be removed, apply for a secured credit card. You may discover, however, that not all credit bureaus have negative reports on you. If you find a credit bureau that does not have a negative report on you, apply for credit with an institution that uses this credit bureau. Most of the large credit card issuers subscribe to the major credit reporting agencies, but you may be able to find a smaller institution that subscribes to the credit bureau that makes your credit history look more favorable.

5. If your total income from all sources is less than $1,000 a month, apply for an unsecured credit card—unless you score very high on all the other credit criteria and show that you can pay your debts from other assets. To obtain secured credit cards, you will generally need to show some income, but it does not need to be from a job. For example, pension or other retirement benefits, income from investments or alimony may be sufficient.

6. Get the number of inquiries on your credit report down to three or four in the past 6 months. If you have a number of active inquiries—inquiries that have been added to your report within the past 6 months—either wait until they automatically come off your report or attempt to remove them following the procedures outlined later.

   If you want to enter the credit world on your terms, work at building your income. If you have no income, it is sometimes possible to get a credit card by obtaining a co-signer—someone who has good credit and agrees to assume responsibility for your debts.

   Applying for credit with negative marks on your report invites refusal. Do everything possible to remove the negative marks before you submit your application for credit.

7. Apply for credit cards from retailers in your area. Department store cards, gas company cards and other retail credit cards are usually easier to obtain. Check to see whether your payments are reported to a credit bureau. Sometimes they are not, but if they are, then using this card and repaying on time will boost your credit record.

   Even if payments on these accounts are not reported to a credit bureau, many applications for credit ask about your other credit card accounts. A good payment record on more easily obtained accounts can give you some recommendations on which to build more credit. Often, having a secured Visa or MasterCard is sufficient to get credit from these other companies.

8. Have your loan officer help you get a Visa or MasterCard. Ask what your chances are of qualifying; also ask what your chances are elsewhere. Different institutions have different policies and your loan officer is likely to know about them.

   Sometimes a lending institution will offer cards at a lower than average annual percentage rate but tighten its requirements to reduce the chance of loss through bad loans. If your bank does this, the loan officer may recommend that you go to another institution that charges higher rates but has more lenient credit requirements.

   The amount of credit you can qualify for is usually directly dependent on the amount of your income.

9. Review the terms of the card issuers and decide which terms are important to you. For example, if you plan to use your credit cards to finance consumer purchases or investment opportunities, a low annual percentage rate is desirable. If, on the other hand, you are going to use a card for the convenience of day-to-day purchasing and intend to pay the full amount at the first billing to avoid finance charges, a no annual fee card with a long grace period is what to look for.

   It is ideal, of course, to get cards with no annual fee, low APR with a long grace period, and no other surcharges. Unfortunately, banks are in business to make money, so no credit card provides all these advantages.

10. Complete the application forms for those credit cards that meet your requirements. Answer all questions truthfully—remembering that you are not required to give any more information than is requested. Type or print clearly. Use a street address, not a post office box number, and in care of, or general delivery.

11. Do not send more than two or three applications at the same time to card issuers that use the same credit bureau. Otherwise, you may be turned down for too many inquiries. Most credit card issuers will automatically request your credit report from the credit bureau when they receive your application. These will appear on future credit reports as inquiries. More than a few inquiries showing up in a short period may result in your being refused credit.

12. Send out applications for unsecured credit cards to the issuers you have targeted. Record your responses and keep track of approvals, declines and requests for further information, as well as your response, if one is called for.

13. If you are denied credit, federal law requires that you be told the reason in writing, as well as the name of the credit bureau that was used. You have the right to request a free report on your file from that credit bureau, but it must be done within 30 days (order it only if you need one from that credit bureau, because your own requests generate inquiries, too, although these are usually not held against you).

    You have a right to know why you were turned down. Once you find out, you will know exactly what you need to do to get approval, or at least to get to the next step of approval. If you do not understand why you were denied credit, contact the lending institution and ask for a specific reason so you can act on it using the strategies contained in this product.

Credit Card Alternatives

If you did not pass the tests for unsecured credit, do not give up hope. Even if there are some negative marks on your credit report that you cannot remove, it is still possible to get credit. It is also possible to get a loan with a low income level if you do not have a negative credit history. However, the loan usually must be secured with collateral.

Remember, lenders want to lend money because they make money on the money they lend. But also remember that they make money only if the loan is repaid. Therefore, bank policy is strict and loan officers shy away from approving questionable loans. If your income is low or your credit history is either insufficient for evaluation or decidedly poor, you will not be approved for an unsecured credit card.

If you have a good credit record with a particular credit bureau, it is wise to attach a copy of that credit report to your application form.

You may still qualify for a secured card. You may be a borderline case that does not qualify for unsecured credit but will qualify if some form of security or collateral is left with the lender to ensure payment (usually in the form of a savings account at the bank issuing the card).

If you cannot get a secured credit card on the strength of your collateral, try to get someone to co-sign for you. The co-signer should have strong enough credit to act as security for the credit line on the card and some extra, just in case you turn out to be a poor risk.

Becoming a co-signer is a big responsibility. Do not ask a person to co-sign for you if you cannot live up to the obligations for which he or she will be responsible.

Your positive credit history from using a secured credit card or a debit card may not be reported to the credit bureau. Your possession and responsible use of these cards does, however, create references that you can use in the future.

There may be other forms of collateral acceptable to a bank: a pledge of stocks or bonds, a lien on an automobile or boat or you may have other equally valuable collateral to use.

Credit Card Brokers

You may have noticed ads in national magazines guaranteeing Visa, MasterCard, or other credit cards even if you have a poor credit history. These companies are merely taking advantage of the consumer's lack of knowledge. They simply furnish applications for secured credit cards, sometimes collecting a nonrefundable processing fee for doing so. Others send a booklet or an instructional sheet explaining secured credit cards. Save the $25 to $50 these firms will charge you. Use the information in this section to obtain credit cards on your own.

Credit Card No-Nos

Credit card debts can and most often do spiral out of control without diligent management. Here are some suggestions to prevent you from getting caught in the credit card trap:

- Do not use credit cards to live a dream lifestyle.
- Should you find yourself with financial problems, never use a credit card to make ends meet—except in the direst of circumstances.
- Do not get into a minimum payment syndrome. In many cases the lender offers a minimum payment to fit your budget and keep you in good standing. However, when you calculate the total pay down on the lender's minimum payment basis, you will eventually pay about 700 percent more for your purchase and thousands of additional dollars in interest.
- Do not use teaser interest rates. These interest offers are usually incredibly low rates, sometimes even zero interest rates, which are offered on an introductory and time limited basis, generally allowing you enough time to incur substantial debt. After the introductory period expires, the interest rate soars up to at least the regular rate listed on the offering.

- Do not get caught in suicide rollovers, using one or more credit cards to pay off another debt. This puts you in even greater financial jeopardy.

- Never put off making your credit card payments on time.

- Stay away from special offers for goods and services promoted by credit card merchants.

- Be wary of increases in credit card spending limits.

- Do not wait to report a lost or stolen credit card. It is easier for the merchant to freeze that account and issue you a new one than to wind up in a dispute over lost or stolen card charges.

Always dispute, in writing, any discrepancies on your monthly statements.

Get Your Debt in Perspective

If you owe more than you can comfortably pay, you are in debt. For most people, bank loans and credit cards are the most common forms of debt, but there are many other ways to take on more debt than you can comfortably handle.

Debt is not credit. When you are in debt, you have exhausted your credit. Mortgages, rents, car payments, food, clothing, and some educational loans are not considered to be debts; because they must be paid on a regular monthly schedule over a long period of time—they are considered expenses.

The following shows how to help get your debt in perspective:

Learn Exactly What You Owe

- Collect all your unpaid bills and any other evidence of outstanding debts.

- List them all together with name of creditor, account number, date due and amount due.

- Total the number of creditors and the amount due.

Unpaid Bill List

Creditor	Account Number	Total Amount Due	Monthly Payment	Amount Overdue	**Date Due**

Even if the total seems scary, at least you know where you stand. This accounting is something that has to be done if you are going to move forward out of debt.

Mentally Consolidate Your Bills

It is the totals that matter: the total amount due, and the total amount you need to pay out each month. Important: The total amount you are supposed to pay out may not be the same as the total amount you can pay out, given your income. In the next section we will talk about how to budget and decide how much is actually available to pay your bills, and how to allocate the money. For now just keep in mind a couple of things:

- No matter how well you think you are doing as you go along, allocate the same amount to monthly payments every month.

- Pay off the smallest bills first, leaving more to allocate to the larger ones as you go along. Example: You have two bills due immediately, one for $250 and one for $750, for a total of $1,000. You can afford to pay $500 a month. Pay off the smaller one, and put the remaining $250 on the larger one, which you can pay off in the following month. (This is of course an oversimplification, but there is a positive psychological effect to knocking off each bill.)

- Give yourself reasonable deadlines. Many people sabotage their own financial well being by adopting unreasonable goals, ones they cannot possibly hope to accomplish given their financial circumstances. Monitor what is happening and do not be afraid to alter your goals as necessary to align with reality.

Alter Your Spending Habits

If you keep doing what you have been doing, you will just dig a deeper hole. If you want to get out of debt, you will have to change your spending habits—and perhaps seriously alter your lifestyle.

Set reasonable short and long term financial goals and put deadlines on them. You cannot wish yourself out of debt; you can only work yourself out of it. The more you practice meeting even limited financial goals, the more confident and in control of your life you will feel. This will make it possible for you to meet longer term goals successfully.

- Recognize that short term means 24 hours: During the next 24 hours you are not going to incur any new debt. And then do the same for another 24 hours. Preventing your debt from expanding is the first step in getting it down to nothing.

- Recognize that long term may mean years, if you are in really deep debt. But as you master debt reduction techniques, you are committing to permanent change in your financial condition.

Once you are in control of your financial well being, you are no longer a debtor, you are a debt buster!

In order to eliminate your debts, you must satisfy only your needs—not your wants. There will be time to buy what you want after you are in control of your finances.

Cancel Your Credit Cards

If you cannot resist temptation, you have to remove the temptation. Trying to conquer debt with your credit cards handy is like trying to pilot a rowboat through a hurricane.

- If you feel you need a credit card as identification for when you pay by check, keep the card with the least available credit on it.
- Return, revoke, cancel, destroy, or otherwise make unavailable all the remaining sources of credit: credit cards, revolving lines of credit and credit extensions.
- Stop carrying your checkbook.
- Give yourself an allowance. Write yourself one check every week and live on it.
- When credit card offers come in the mail, tear them up and throw them away.

This will not be easy. Credit card offers will keep rolling in, and some of them, the most dangerous, will be preapproved. Do not bite.

Use Cash Only

Yes, it can be done, though it is not easy.

- If you do not have enough cash to pay for an item, you cannot afford it. Do not buy it.
- If you use a check or an ATM card to get cash, enter it into your checkbook immediately.
- Do not ask your bank for overdraft protection. This is a line of credit with a very high interest rate and is a great temptation to abuse.
- If you do not know how to balance your checkbook, do not write another check until you find out how. You must avoid bouncing checks (writing checks that you do not have enough money to cover). The bank charge for a rubber check can be $30 or more each time, and the merchant you give the bad check to will also charge you. This is a great way to run your credit into the ground—where it will stay for a very long time.

Living on cash means you have to prioritize your spending. You have to keep asking yourself—Is this something I absolutely must have? What am I willing to give up to get this object?

Make a Budget

This subject has, as it deserves, its own separate section. For now, just keep in mind that your budget is your lifeline. It can guide you to the safest and shortest route to your ultimate goal—total control of your finances.

Trim Expenses

First, look at variable expenses. Could you be spending less on food? Hamburger instead of steaks? The whole family may have to change its lifestyle in order to get back in a position where you can afford steaks more often.

When your budget is complete, look at every item and see where it can be cut.

- Maybe you need to get videos and DVDs by mail instead of locally; the mail services usually do not charge late fees.
- Are you driving a car that you can afford? Is it a gas guzzler?
- Have you talked with your insurance agent about ways you can cut costs on your insurance?
- Do you file all insurance claims promptly?

You have the right to appeal the payment of an insurance claim. If you feel your reimbursement is inadequate, do not hesitate to contact the next higher level of authority in that insurance company.

- Does anyone owe you money? If they do, collect it and do not lend any more.
- Are your expense reimbursements at work current?
- Analyze your payroll deductions. It may be time to put less in a 401(k) if you are paying heavily in interest on late bills.
- If you are renting, maybe it is time to downsize: find a place where the rent includes the utilities, get a roommate or just get a smaller place in a less desirable neighborhood.

Ultimately, you need to reduce your total expenditures to about 80 percent of your take home pay so you can use the other 20 percent to get your debt load down.

A budget is seldom permanent because the budget must necessarily change to reflect the realities of change in your own life.

See If There Are Ways to Increase Your Income

Getting a better job is the obvious way to get more income, but it is not the only way. Someone in the family may have to get a second part-time job. Older children can work part-time on weekends to help out. See if you are eligible for:

- any government assistance programs; and/or

- church, civic or charitable programs.

This is no time to let your pride stand in your way. It is important to get back on your feet, and if you need a helping hand, take it.

See If There Are Some Debts You Are Not Obligated to Pay

You are not legally obligated to pay:

1. Illegal finance charges. Your credit card issuers must make sure the bill is sent to you at least 14 days before the interest is due. If the bill is late, contact the issuer immediately.

2. Charges for:

   - merchandise you did not receive;

   - merchandise that does not meet reasonable standards of quality or performance;

   - merchandise that is below advertised standards; and

   - merchandise sold to you on the basis of false or misleading claims.

3. More than $50 in charges after you notify the card issuer within 30 days that your card was stolen.

You also have some rights. You have the right to:

1. a refund or credit for any overpayment you made;

2. cancel any of the following contracts within 3 business days of signing it:

   - a contract to join a health club;

   - a contract to join a mail order discount book or CD buying club;

   - a door to door sales contract for more than $25;

   - a loan where you pledge your home as security; and

   - a contract signed anywhere other than the seller's normal place of business.

(If you were not told you had a right to cancel within 3 days, you may have even longer. In any case, if you do cancel, your money must be refunded within 40 days.)

3. cancel any contract where the seller took advantage of you (an unconscionable contract). This can happen where the terms of the contract are so one-sided favoring the seller that the average person and the courts would be shocked, or where the circumstances prevented you from having any meaningful choice.

Never sign anything you do not completely understand. And be skeptical if something sounds too good to be true—it probably is.

The more deeply indebted you are, the more frantic you are likely to be, and the more easily victimized by fear. Be aware of the temptations of frustration and desperation. Force yourself to be patient.

Create a Working Budget

If you are to reduce your debt and survive, you must have a highly specific budget and you must adhere to it tightly. Since most expenses and debts are paid on monthly basis, a monthly budget usually works best.

Use this secret financial tip from the pros, the simplest way known to prepare for unexpected financial difficulties: Establish an emergency fund and make saving for that part of your monthly financial exercise. Many financial consultants recommend you set aside a minimum of 3 months' salary in an emergency reserve. Obviously, if you are already deep in debt, that will be impossible immediately, but budget for even a small contribution every month.

Begin the Budgeting Process

Begin by listing all of the income you receive. If you are paid weekly, multiply your gross by 52 and then divide by 12; if you are paid biweekly, multiply by 26, then divide by 12. Do not over estimate incentive earnings, such as gratuities, overtime, bonuses or commissions. This monthly amount is the total you will have available to both exist on and to pay down your debts.

An emergency fund is only for emergencies, so plan for it in your budget, but do not use it unless there is a genuine emergency.

Next, precisely detail all your expenses, debts and any other expenditures. Leave nothing out. Start with the necessities of life such as mortgage, auto payment, sensible and necessary food, minimal clothing allowance and utilities. Then dig deep in your mind to detail every other necessary expenditure you must incur. Do not leave out anything.

Let's say you add up your available monthly income and you get $2,500. The total of your bare necessity living expenses is $2,000. That means you have $500 available to pay down debts. Now, as outlined in the next section, your must set up an order of repayment—and live by it. You may need to get the cooperation of your creditors, but the success of your debt survival depends on it.

When you set up your budget, also set up your goals so that you can start planning to achieve them.

Once a debt is paid off, many people begin to think they are free to spend what they had been paying on that debt. WRONG! The secret of debt survival is to continue paying down monthly on any remaining obligations, upping their payments until they are all paid in full. Only then will you be debt free and able to enjoy the fruits of your struggle.

The Order of Repayment

A good way to decide which debt to repay first is to give priority to creditors who would be quickest to take an action that would hurt you.

If you own a home, you must keep your real estate taxes current. Some municipalities start collection proceedings as early as 3 months into delinquency—should your home be confiscated for nonpayment of taxes, it will be sold at auction.

Light, water, and sewerage are the key utility payments. While many consider telephone service a necessity, it is still more expendable than these other utilities. If necessary, you can always ask your telephone service provider to give you an emergency only service that allows you to place emergency (911) calls out and receive incoming calls.

The law requires that you always make child support payments. This type of debt can only be relieved by court order or by the children reaching the age of emancipation.

The IRS has many collection rights not afforded to other creditors, but the agency is usually quite receptive to setting up a time payment arrangement as long as you are cooperative. The interest can be high but it may be necessary to roll out payments, and it sure beats having your wages garnished.

Never move a debt up in the priority list simply because the creditor is pressuring you harder. Even if repossession of a car is threatened, it is never more important than rent or mortgage, food and other basic necessities.

Secured debts incurred for household goods are usually a low priority on the debt repayment schedule.

Unsecured debts without any collateral attachments have the very lowest priority. Such debts include most credit cards, debts to lawyers, hospitals and other professionals, and open end or revolving charge accounts with merchants. While all of the above will file a bad credit report, most will not file suit for collection.

Creditors will seldom attempt to seize household goods through collateral repossession, as these items generally have little or no resale or market value.

If you co-signed for someone else's debt, put it on your list as if it were your own debt. When someone defaults on a co-signed debt, the co-signer immediately becomes liable for the entire debt.

Where to Find the Money?

Friends and Family. Whether to try to borrow money to repay your debts is always a question. You can approach friends or relatives first, since their interest rates will be competitive. They are likely to have the most lenient credit terms. If you go this route, always be honest. Tell them which creditors you plan to pay with the loan and how you will implement your budget in order to pay them back. Be sure to offer them a reasonable interest rate—but be aware there are hidden costs of borrowing from relatives.

- Is your loan going to be a burden to others?

- Can you deal with the emotions attached to such a loan? Will your spending habits be monitored? Is it difficult to live with constant reminders of your financial difficulty?

- Are you willing to expose your weaknesses? Will you feel humiliated or belittled by having to ask for a loan?

- Will you have to start paying the loan back immediately?

- Are you positive the borrowed money will get you out of debt once and for all—or are you just delaying an inevitable bankruptcy?

Consumer Finance Companies. Many consumer finance companies lend to financially burdened consumers on both a secured and unsecured basis. However, the interest rate is high. So be leery of unscrupulous lenders who look to exploit those in financial difficulty.

If in the back of your mind you are thinking of filing bankruptcy, do not borrow to pay bills that might get discharged in bankruptcy anyway.

Common Reasons for Credit Denial

When prospective lenders inquire about your credit standing, they examine your record with certain expectations. The six most common reasons for credit denial based on a credit report are:

1. **Delinquent credit obligations.** Late payments, bad debts, or legal judgments against you make you look like a risky customer.

2. **Incomplete credit application.** Any large discrepancy between your application and your credit file can count against you. If you left out some important information or made an error on the application, the lender will wonder if you are hiding something.

3. **Too many inquiries.** Inquiries are made whenever you apply for credit. As few as four inquiries within 6 months' time may be considered a sign of excessive credit activity. The creditor may then presume you are trying desperately to get credit and are being rejected elsewhere.

4. **Errors in your file.** These can arise simply from typing mistakes or from confusing your name with someone else's. Since the credit bureaus handle millions of files, the possibility for error is substantial. Errors can be corrected only if you carefully and regularly review your file for accuracy and then taking the necessary steps to correct any errors that you do find.

5. **Insufficient credit file.** Your credit history is too scanty for the type or amount of credit you requested. You need to build your credit history more fully, as we discussed earlier, before qualifying for the level of credit you are now requesting.

6. **Legal action.** Tax liens, bankruptcy, foreclosure, or repossession of collateral will kill your credit fast because they are so serious. But do not despair, they too can be overcome.

Always examine your credit record before applying for credit. A credit bureau may confuse you with another individual, carry erroneous information in your file, or perhaps include false, incomplete, or one-sided information provided by a creditor. Most of these problems can be resolved using the procedures discussed below.

If you have moved, this can also create problems in your credit history.

The 10-Step Plan for Cleaning Up Credit Reports

Step 1. Identify Your Credit Problems

The information on credit reports is usually coded like your bank statement, but consumer reporting legislation requires credit bureaus to explain anything on the report that you cannot reasonably understand. Each report contains a key to the coding symbols. Familiarize yourself with the symbols, then look for the negative remarks, the dings, in your credit file and circle them in these four sections of your report:

1. The Historical Status is a record of your monthly payments. Ideally, this should be free of past due symbols, which may be 30, 60 or 90 day periods. Almost 90 percent of the bad marks are likely to be from past due symbols. These could have been entered accidentally, or because the mail was late, or because of delays in processing your payments. (Of course, you may actually have made late payments.)

2. The Comments section may contain remarks like Charged to P&L (profit and loss). That means a company has charged an account off as a bad debt loss, and that it does not expect to collect. This, of course, implies that you are a bad credit risk.

3. Inquiries made by any bank, store or other company to which you applied for credit will be listed in the report. If there are too many of these, a potential creditor may begin to think you are in financial difficulty and may be seeking credit as a solution and refuse to give credit. How many is too many is a subjective judgment made by each creditor. As few as four or five in 6 months may be too many for some.

4. Public Records may appear in your credit report as tax liens, bankruptcies, or court judgments that affected you. These entries should also be examined for accuracy.

Step 2. Determine Your Credit Score

Somewhere on your credit report you will find a column with a title like Account Profile. This column contains a summary rating for each of your accounts. A summary may read positive, negative or nonrated. Positive means you are okay; your payments are all on time.

You must have your payments credited to your accounts before the due date, not just mailed by that time, if you are to avoid past due symbols.

Negative means you have a serious credit problem; perhaps you have defaulted on a debt. Nonrated may mean you have a few late payments here and there. Nonrated entries still put you in a weak position, even though there is nothing strongly negative against you. Each negative or nonrated entry has a code reflecting the nature of the problem.

Step 3. Analyze Possible Protests to the Credit Bureau Disputing Each Ding

To exercise your legal rights, you must aggressively challenge any bad marks. The credit bureau will only verify the facts if you assert that they are in error, so do not be shy. Draft a strong but polite protest for each item you want to challenge, and tell the credit bureau you are exercising your rights under consumer reporting legislation.

For example, suppose you find the code Charge Off. This means that the creditor charged your account off because it thinks your debt is uncollectible. You could protest that this comment should be removed because, in fact, the debt was satisfied and therefore should not be reported as a Charge Off.

Another problem might be a series of Past Due notations. You could protest that those payments were delayed due to a mix up with the post office when you changed your address. Most often the credit bureau and creditor will state that the payment was in fact late, and therefore it is correctly reported. However, if a post office mix up occurred, you could submit a consumer statement to the effect that the account is in dispute because bills were not delivered by the creditor even though a change of address was furnished.

Step 4. Send Your Letter of Dispute

Using the sample letters included in this section as a guide, write or type a letter of dispute to the credit bureau. Your letter should not look like a form letter. List each incident that you want to challenge and enclose photocopies of any documents that support your claims. These might include correspondence with your creditors, canceled checks indicating payment or receipts. The law gives you the right to dispute any citation on your report if the information contained in that citation is inaccurate or incomplete.

Your goal is to protest—and eventually remove— all negative or nonrated profiles.

Make a copy of your completed letter for your records and send the original by certified mail with return receipt requested to be sure the bureau receives it. It is also a good idea to include a copy of your credit report to make sure the bureau checks the right file.

The only limitation to a dispute of items on your credit report is that your claim should not be frivolous or irrelevant.

Use the Complaint Letter to Delete Inaccurate Information to dispute errors on your credit report. Use the Request for Removal of Outdated Information to request that old information be taken off your credit report. If there are too many inquiries, you may also use the Request to Merge Inquiries with Account; this helps eliminate excessive inquiries, which can be red flags on your credit history. Write a consumer statement if you have good reason to challenge a given problem.

Step 5. Record Your Actions

As soon as you mail the letter, log the date for each protest you have made on any incident or negative entry. Keep related disputes together in a file with copies of the letter, the credit report, and any other documents you sent copies of to the credit bureau.

Step 6. Wait for a Response

By law, credit bureaus must respond within 30 days.

Step 7. Send Follow-Up Letters

If the credit bureau does not respond within a reasonable time, write follow-up letters. Using the Reminder to Respond and point out that the law requires the credit bureau to respond to a consumer dispute within a reasonable period of time or the agency is in default. Should the credit bureau fail to respond within 30 days of the reminder, use the Demand for a Corrected Credit Report.

If the credit bureau fails to respond in the time allotted, you are entitled to have deleted any negative mark on your report that you challenged.

If the credit bureau fails to provide an immediate updated credit report, free of the disputed entry, you have several methods of recourse. The:

- Federal Trade Commission can bring legal action against the bureau;
- bureau may be liable to you for damages resulting if it continues to issue the old report; and
- bureau may also be liable for any attorney fees you incur.

It is often possible to eliminate negative marks simply by disputing entries. Since many creditors will not take the time or make the effort to defend the negative entry, you can eventually repair your credit through the default of your creditors.

Step 8. Ask for an Updated Credit Report

At the end of each letter you send there is a request for an updated copy of your credit report. Consumer reporting legislation requires the bureau to send a free notification of any updates to anyone who has received a copy of the report within 6 months previous to any corrections or statements that are added to the report. When you request it, remind the bureau to send an update to anyone else who has recently inquired about your credit.

The bureaus are not required to send a copy of the entire report, but they will often do so because that is more convenient for them.

Step 9. Compare the New Report with the Prior Report

Most bureaus will send you an updated report. Carefully compare the updated report with the original one. Mark with a star any negative entry that has moved up to nonrated, or any nonrated or negative entry that has moved up to positive.

Notice that the bureau may delete some items if a creditor failed to respond to its investigation promptly. This is common; the creditor's failure to deal with a bothersome piece of paperwork has now been turned to your advantage and is helping to clear your record.

Step 10. Repeat the Process

There are probably still some bad marks left. Also, it sometimes happens that a dispute results in an update to an account that is even more negative than before. For example, reinvestigation could uncover the fact that you actually had more late payments than were previously reported.

The Extravagant Spouse Problem

It may happen that one spouse is more extravagant than the other—more prone to run up bills. To keep peace in the family, and to keep the credit record clean for at least one member of the family, you can ask the credit bureau to separate the files, using the form letter supplied.

So what do you do? Now it is time to go back to the beginning of the process and start over again. You should put your credit record through this process at least twice before going on to the next phase. Remember that during this process you must be very careful not to allow any new problems to appear on your record. Keep all your accounts current or pay ahead of schedule.

Turning around Your Credit

Many negative remarks cannot be deleted without creditor cooperation because the incidents are accurate and the creditor persistently cooperates with the bureau's request for verification. There are two methods to achieve this kind of cooperation. One is to explain what caused the problem—if there is a reasonable explanation. The other is to work with the creditors to negotiate repayment plans so that they realize you are sincere in your intention to pay them back.

Cleaning Up the Credit Report

For the first method your goal must be to persuade your creditors to soften their stance by either toning down or entirely deleting their remarks on your credit report. Here are eight steps to follow:

Step 1: Set Up a Worksheet for Creditors

Accurate record-keeping is essential in dealing with creditors who still give you bad marks. Use a creditor worksheet containing names, account numbers, credit remarks, and any other documents, correspondence or notes you have on your dealings with them.

Creditor Worksheet

Creditor Name	Account Number	Amount Due	Last Payment	Last Contact (Date & Name)	Notes

Step 2: Write to Each Creditor

After studying all the facts about each account and the nature of the credit complaints, write each creditor explaining your version of how the problem arose. Use the Explanation for Delinquent Payment as a guide, but do not be afraid to expand upon it. Be specific: give all the details, including a full documentation. Perhaps, for instance, your company went bankrupt suddenly, or you lost your job.

Remind the creditor that you eventually paid and mention that you appreciated their services and products in spite of the payment problems that arose. Appeal to the creditor's compassion; ask that the bad marks be removed now that the account is settled, or ask that the creditor put a statement into your credit report stating that the account is paid up.

As you write the letter, consider it in light of other accounts that may have been affected by the same circumstances. Each letter you send should be consistent with the others so that if your creditors' new comments appear on your credit file, they will appear reasonable and consistent. Do not send in weak excuses for late bill paying. Send the letter by certified mail, return receipt requested. Keep a copy of each letter and the receipt in the file with your worksheet.

Step 3: Order an Updated Credit Report after 30 Days

Your letters may convince your creditors to cooperate. Allow about 30 days for them to respond, and then order a new credit report to see if the creditor has made any changes in your report.

Step 4: Contact Creditors by Telephone

If letters prove to be futile, use the telephone. This will allow you to interact with the creditor in a more personal way. Before you call, study the information you have gathered from your credit report, your creditors' responses and the worksheet you have compiled. Then write a simple outline of all the points that you want to make during your call.

Step 5: Be Persistent

Sometimes the first call to a creditor will have no effect. Do not be bashful or discouraged, simply try again. Be persistent, maybe talk to a different person. Large companies will have many people working in their customer relations departments.

In both letters and calls, be factual, but appeal to the creditor's sense of goodwill. Offer to send the creditor a letter with the agreement to update your status in writing, along with a self-addressed, stamped envelope. (Be certain to obtain the creditor's name and office address.) The creditor should sign the letter and return it to you for your own records. This letter is important if the creditor forgets to change your status or later decides not to help you. You can send this letter to the credit agency yourself to repair your credit.

Step 6: Send Your Statement to the Credit Bureau

If the creditor has not improved the marks on your report, write directly to the bureau and ask it to add your consumer statement to the account in accordance with consumer reporting legislation. Your comments as to why the bill was not paid on time will then be submitted with your credit report in response to any credit request. Your comments may greatly mitigate the damage of a particular entry.

You may not want to comment on any particular entry but you may want your credit record to reflect reasons for a generally poor record caused by:

• a layoff from work	• divorce
• personal or family matters	• tax problems

Once a creditor agrees that a change in your report is justified, call to ask that the change be made in your credit status.

Step 7: Wait for a Reply

Now the ball is again in the bureau's court. You must wait the estimated time that you established when you initially persuaded the bureau to remove the dings. In a few weeks the bureau should reply and may also send you an updated copy of your report. If your statement appears positive, you may be ready to start using your credit again.

Step 8: Try Again

Remember persistence. If these efforts do not work, wait a few months and repeat the process. Over time the situation may have changed. See what happens when you try the creditor again. You may find a new person in the office who will be more cooperative and willing to help you regain a good credit rating.

Point out your prior track record. Be convincing that these problems are behind you and are not likely to recur.

Negotiating a Repayment Plan with All Creditors Together

Installment plans are effective because when your alternative is probably bankruptcy, that threat forces creditors to the negotiating table. Creditors understand that under a bankruptcy proceeding they realize (will get) little or nothing. For any plan to work for you, however, a majority of your creditors must agree to it. The key to an installment plan is your willingness to repay the entire debt over time.

There are several ways to work out a repayment plan:

1. **Self run program.** You directly contact your creditors, present your plan, and convince them to accept your long term payment proposal. Couple the threat of bankruptcy with your own sincere belief in the plan. Send a certified, return receipt requested letter containing your budget and repayment plan to each creditor. Explain your financial circumstances and request a reduction of payments until your financial condition improves, a settlement for a lesser amount than the total you owe, an installment payment plan if you owe a lump sum, or an opportunity to discuss an out of court settlement.

2. **Credit counselor administered plan.** You turn over your paycheck to the organization and they give you back an allowance to live on. They use the rest of the money to pay creditors. Make sure all creditors agree to the plan, in writing. This binds all parties to the contract. Do not waive any of your legal rights as a condition of the agreement.

3. **Conditional discharge from bankruptcy.** Ask the court to allow you to pay your creditors money over a period of time. Keep in mind that you have to convince the court of your ability and intention to make the payments. Once these payments are finished you will receive an absolute discharge from the bankruptcy.

4. **Consolidation order.** A consolidation order sets out the amount and the times when payments are due to the court.

5. **Compromise agreements.** These also work because of the threat of bankruptcy, but differ from installment plans because you offer to repay only a percentage of your outstanding debt, perhaps 20 percent to 30 percent. For this settlement to work, you need to convince your creditors of two things:

   1. You have little income; and
   2. You have few assets.

   In other words, if you filed for bankruptcy, your creditors would get very little and if they sued you, they would probably not even recover lawyer's fees.

Your creditors will examine your budget very carefully. You must show ample evidence of a dramatically reduced standard of living and significant sacrifices. Otherwise, they will doubt your sincerity and honesty.

Paint the darkest financial picture you can. Detail all of the hardships you have endured—job layoffs, deaths in the family, serious mental health, car repossessions and home foreclosures. Your creditors must believe you are judgment proof.

Negotiating Repayment Plans One by One

Working with creditors to negotiate repayment plans will help you demonstrate your ability to make regular payments on time, pay off the debts you owe and revive their interest in you as a customer. In return you are going to ask your creditors to restore your positive credit rating.

Even if your account has already gone to a collection agency, deal first with the original creditor. The creditor will not be as persistent as a collection agency; it may have already given up any expectation of full payment. Dealing with the creditor provides more flexibility to negotiate the time or the amount to pay.

Often, because of an agreement with the collection agency, the creditor may not deal with you. Collection agencies are not consumer oriented and will be more difficult to negotiate with, so whenever possible get to the creditor before the debt is turned over for collection.

A collection agency receives a percentage of what it collects from you, so it will try to get as much cash as possible from you.

Whether you are dealing with the collection agency or the creditor, use these five pointers:

1. **Make a win-win offer.** Your goal is to trade money for a positive credit rating. For example, you could agree to pay 100 percent of what you owe in 12 monthly installments in exchange for the creditor agreeing to recognize your new bill paying commitment with better credit ratings. To be specific: Perhaps you can agree that after 3 months of punctual payments, a negative rating could be raised to a nonrating.

2. **Obtain open account status.** It looks bad when your account is closed to further purchases, even if you are making regular payments. When you are negotiating an offer, ask that they reopen your account as long as you uphold your end of the agreement. If the creditor will give you a clean bill of credit health, your extra effort to pay him or her is certainly worth it. Caution: Make sure the terms you finally agree on are within your budget so you can faithfully keep your promise.

3. **Put it in writing.** Once you have reached an agreement, it is vital to put it in writing. Type up the agreement as a letter, sign it, and send it with a second copy and a stamped, self-addressed envelope. (Before you send the letter, you may want your lawyer to check the wording if the amount in question is significant.) Once the creditor signs the agreement and returns it to you, it can become part of your credit record (see Creditor Settlement Agreement).

Before putting your agreement in writing, carefully verify all the points of agreement with the creditor over the phone.

You can be very persuasive if you offer to pay 100 percent of the debt, even if it is over a fairly long period, perhaps with some interest or a service charge added.

4. **Honor the agreement.** Be punctual. Make every payment on or ahead of time. If your ability to meet the agreed payment schedule should be threatened by unemployment or illness, inform your creditor right away, before you miss any payments, and explore ways to solve your temporary setback that will meet everyone's needs.

5. **Verify your credit upgrade.** Allow a reasonable time period from the date the creditor agreed to make changes, and then request your updated credit report. If the changes have not been made, call whoever made the agreement

to remind them. If the agreed changes are not made, you can dispute the information on your credit report using a copy of the creditor signed agreement as supporting evidence for the change.

Tax Liens and Your Credit Rating

A tax lien on your credit report will definitely hurt your chances for a loan to buy a home, business, car, boat, or any other major purchase as well as affecting your ability to obtain credit cards.

Unfortunately, the fact that you had tax liens may not be erased from your credit report until 7 years after the taxes have been paid. However, a past lien is not nearly as damaging as a current tax lien. That is why you must be certain every credit bureau updates your credit history to show that your outstanding tax liens have been fully paid. To check:

- ask the IRS, the state tax department, and the municipality for copies of every lien they have filed against you if you have not kept their notices; and

- search the public records in your jurisdiction.

For each recorded lien that is not noted as discharged, insist that the reporting agency contact the appropriate revenue agency or check the public records to confirm that the lien has been released. Follow up to make sure your credit report reflects the discharge of all tax liens against you.

You can even help your credit picture even if you are only now resolving your tax problems. For example, if you are paying the revenue agency in installments, your credit report can reflect the anticipated discharge of your lien because an agreement has been reached with the agency. You can submit a Consumer Statement to the credit bureau explaining that.

It is possible to erase existing (and unpaid) tax liens by following the same strategies used for erasing other negatives. If you challenge a tax lien, the government does not always substantiate the lien within the required 30 days; often, the government will not respond for 45 to 60 days. But since the documentation was not provided within the required 30 days, the credit bureau must delete the tax lien notice and cannot later reinstate it.

You will be most successful if you attempt to erase the tax lien after your tax file has been transferred to governmental archives. This transfer usually takes about a year. Having your tax file in the archives often increases the turnaround time beyond the required 30 days.

Bankruptcy, Repossession and Foreclosure

Serious problems in your financial past, such as bankruptcies, court claims, repossessions or foreclosures may stick to your credit report even after you try every method we have discussed. For these major problems we can only recommend the virtues of patience and persistence. You will be surprised at how much you can accomplish merely by sticking it out. As these events drift further into your past, they will become less significant in your credit history.

Fortunately, any adverse information that is more than 7 years old (other than bankruptcy, which stays on for 10 years) must be deleted from your file, whether it is challenged or not. You cannot be penalized forever for past mistakes. Another exception is that if you request credit or life insurance worth $50,000 or more, or apply for a job paying $20,000 or more, the credit bureau may release an unexpurgated version of your credit history. This otherwise deleted information is kept in a separate file that can only be released in these circumstances.

Terms That Can Lead to Common Pitfalls

The fears of debt and/or bankruptcy often lead to hasty decisions. You must remain calm and painstakingly aware of:

1. Suicide rollovers—this devastating strategy is actually recommended by some financial advisors: Take a cash advance on one credit card and use it to repay other credit cards. The more credit cards you have, the more credit cards you can manipulate. In the business of debt, these are called suicide rollovers because you choose to commit financial suicide instead of facing your debt.

2. Prepayment penalties—if you should pay the loan before it is due, the lender forces you to pay a penalty. This costly provision, usually found in the fine print of a loan agreement, is designed to keep you forever in debt. Negotiate it out of your contract! To pay a five percent penalty on the remaining $50,000 of your mortgage would cost you an extra $2,500.

3. Uncapped variable interest rates—a capped variable interest rate is an interest rate that fluctuates with the federal interest rate, but never rises above a certain point. In contrast, an uncapped interest rate has no fixed ceiling. An uncapped interest rate leaves you without any protection whatsoever.

Dealing with Debt Collectors

At this stage in your financial condition, there is not much more damage a debt collection service can do to your credit rating, so do not let collectors put more pressure on you. Keep in mind that they are subject to fairly stringent laws.

Dealing with Threats and Lawsuits

Creditors and collectors often use heavy tactics and threats in their attempt to collect a debt from you. You must never make special efforts or move a debt up on your priority list unless a lawsuit from the creditor is likely and could seriously hurt you.

Will the Creditor Actually Sue Me?

Because the lawsuit process is usually slow and more costly, the creditor will try every other available remedy; especially if you are considered judgment proof (have no assets).

- If your debt is less than $1,000, it is unlikely the creditor will pursue a lawsuit.
- If you have a presentable defense, the creditor will likely withdraw.
- Unless the creditor has a history of local collection suits, it is unlikely the creditor will follow up. Check with the court clerk to see if the creditor has brought other suits in your area.
- When the creditor is out of state and the debt is relatively small, it is highly unlikely that a lawsuit will be filed against you because the cost to the creditor is usually prohibitive.

Almost without exception, the suit must be filed where the defendant lives or where the contract was signed. If it was signed some distance away, perhaps at a place where you used to live, check the local laws there, as requirements may vary. They may require the claim be filed where the defendant lives or has a business, where the contract was signed, where the contract was broken or where the merchandise was purchased.

What to Do If a Suit Is Filed against You

If it seems possible that a creditor may file suit against you, there are some basic courses of action you can take. Always collect your certified or registered mail, and accept any notices about court action; you cannot escape consequences or subsequent actions by being uninformed, so the earlier you know what is going on, the better. In fact, you do yourself injustice by allowing actions to occur without your complete knowledge.

Seek professional advice or counseling when a suit is threatened or instituted. If your financial situation is desperate, call the local bar association and ask if they have pro bono (for the good of the citizenry) services.

Always respond to any summons or action in a timely manner.

Read the court summons carefully. Some require a telephone response, while many require a written response within a certain number of days or a personal appearance on a specific date and time. Some may have preprinted forms that you can fill out and return.

Should you fail to meet the stipulated deadline, the court may award full claim to the creditor—plus legal fees and court costs. You would also forfeit any rights to raise a defense or explain why you should not have to pay the full amount due.

Even if you should reach an out of court agreement with the creditor beforehand, make all required appearances and meet all deadlines until the court order is adjudicated, perhaps by acceptance of your agreement. Make sure all agreements and stipulations are in writing.

Always submit a defense or counterclaim. A defense is the reason you claim you should not have to pay all or part of the debt to the creditor. A counterclaim is an attempt to prove the creditor owes you money. Should you not file any defense, the court will have no alternative but to find for the creditor—which could again include court costs and legal fees.

Some common defenses include the:

- creditor is attempting to collect more than the agreed amount;
- merchandise was defective;
- merchandise was never delivered;
- creditor used misrepresentation or pressure to create the debt;
- debt was paid but not credited;

- account (yours) is current or the debt is not owed;
- signature (yours) was forged;
- debt was discharged in bankruptcy;
- suit is too late; the statute of limitations has lapsed; and
- creditor violated laws in making or attempting to collect.

An oral agreement or settlement, if challenged by the creditor, carries no merit with the court.

Saving Your Property from Foreclosure and Repossession

The worst thing you can do if you cannot pay your home mortgage is play ostrich and ignore the problem. If you are to avoid foreclosure you must not only communicate with your lender but you must also propose sensible solutions. Some possible solutions include the following:

1. **Sell your house.** If you simply cannot afford to own your house, then sell it as quickly as possible to pay the loan. A sale preserves your equity and avoids a bad credit report and costly lawyer's fees.

2. **Make the lender your partner.** Explain the situation to your lender. If you cannot afford the mortgage, the lender may accept some equity in the property, and in return cancel part of the loan. This works best if the property is quickly appreciating in value.

3. **Equity share with a third party.** If the lender will not partner with you, it may be an attractive investment to some other investor who can help handle the mortgage.

4. **Offer additional collateral.** If the loan value is close to the value of the property, and the lender believes it might take a loss on foreclosure, offer additional collateral as an alternative.

5. **Refinance.** If you have a short term or high interest loan, refinancing may substantially reducre your monthly mortgage payment.

6. **Secure a second mortgage.** If you have some equity in your property, a second mortgage may provide you the money necessary to bring the first

mortgage current. But this makes sense only if you know you can handle both mortgages.

7. **Borrow against other assets.** If you cannot refinance or obtain a second mortgage, than perhaps you own your car free and clear and can get a loan against it. But watch the interest rates on these loans, they can be expensive.

8. **Offer to pay interest only for a short time.** Some lenders will accept interest only if you can prove that your problem is temporary. This can reduce your mortgage payment considerably.

9. **Renegotiate the interest rate.** If your interest rate is below the current rate, the lender will, of course, not be interested in negotiating with you on any terms because it is not making money on your loan. Renegotiating higher interest, while costly, may be more feasible than refinancing.

10. **Offer a bonus.** If you cannot convince the lender to accept interest only for a short time, offer a few points as a bonus. This can be attractive if the interest on your loan is below prevailing rates.

11. **Negotiate a complete payments moratorium.** A lender who believes you have adequate equity in your property may be willing to negotiate a short term hold on your payments (interest and principal).

12. **Reduce the term.** Offer to shorten the term of the loan and the lender may cooperate with a moratorium on principal and interest. For example, a 20-year loan may be shortened to 5 years, but the payments may be based on a 20-year loan.

13. **Seek a co-signer.** A lender who is concerned about the safety of the loan may be more lenient if you offer a co-signer for the loan.

14. **Check the loan documents.** If the lender insists on foreclosure, have a lawyer check your loan documents to see if clauses in them may violate lending statutes. Even if this does not stop foreclosure, it can at least improve your negotiating position.

Refinance Your Way out of Trouble

Refinancing works well if you have the equity in your property for additional borrowing power. You can use the proceeds from a new mortgage to pay the arrears on the first mortgage, or you can refinance with a larger first mortgage at a lower interest rate.

Interim second mortgage financing is a good solution when your negative cash flow is temporary, but the second mortgage holder may bargain for a bonus: Some equity? Higher interest? Negotiate!

Sell Your Property for No Cash Down

When you face foreclosure you can no longer afford to offer your property for sale on conventional terms (a high price and big down payment). The goal is to sell your property before you lose it, so you must sacrifice price, down payment, or both. If you have a reliable buyer and can secure yourself with a mortgage on the property, you will sell fastest with a small or no down payment. This is more important to most buyers than a lower price.

> **In Sum**
>
> Set new priorities. A speedy sale is more important than a higher price or larger down payment. Greedy sellers often end up with nothing but foreclosure.

If you will inevitably lose your property, this is the time to tap any equity in the property that you can salvage either by refinancing or selling. You may not be able to squeeze much from the property, but whatever you can salvage is money to bring down your other debts. A second mortgage lender is your best money source.

Attract Cash Bearing Partners to Bail Out Your Loan.

Do you have real estate in financial trouble and heading for foreclosure? Your headache may be just the right medicine for wealthy investors looking for a tax break and long term appreciation.

Many investors fit this bill: Individuals who want real estate tax shelters but do not have the time or expertise to manage their own investment properties. You will need the right approach to lure these investors.

- Advertise for investors. Your best bet is to look for professionals, like physicians, lawyers, executives and successful business owners.
- Form a limited partnership where the investing partners have their liability limited to the loss of their investment. Limited partners participate in profits and in tax write off losses.
- Give your investors 100 percent of the tax write offs so they can deduct all the taxes, interest, depreciation and negative cash flow.
- In exchange for these tax benefits your investors will advance all the funds necessary to cover the negative cash flow and keep the property out of foreclosure.
- Set up your deal so that when it comes time to sell, the profits are split 50/50. This is permissible even if you own only one percent of the partnership.
- Serve as general partner and manage the property—for a fee. This deal attracts many passive investors to real estate, even those that operate precariously with a negative cash flow. Your accountant can show you the benefits investors may reap and how you must sell the idea.

Three Pointers to Win Back Your Property after Foreclosure

All is not necessarily lost even after foreclosure. You may convince the lender to sell you back your home, automobile, boat or other foreclosed asset. Why would a lender sell you back your property after all the trouble of foreclosing? Here are three reasons:

1. The lender may have hoped to sell the property for a higher price but did not succeed. The only reasonable alternative may be to sell the property back to you.
2. The lender may now see you as being in a stronger financial condition, particularly if the foreclosure eliminated other liens and attachments against the property or you filed bankruptcy to cancel other debts.
3. The lender may want to quickly dispose of the property to avoid storage or maintenance costs.

To get your property back, convince the lender that you will not default again. If the collateral was your home, ask the lender to rent the house back to you for the amount of the mortgage payments. Make timely payments for 6 or 9 months, and the lender may develop enough confidence in you to mortgage the property to you again.

How to Avoid a Deficiency Judgment

If your property is foreclosed upon or repossessed, you may lose far more than the property. You may also be liable for a deficiency, the difference between what you owe your lender (including lawyers' fees and court costs) and what the lender sells the collateral for.

Your lender must usually go to court to obtain the deficiency judgment. The lender can then enforce it like any other judgment. To avoid a deficiency judgment, follow the points below:

- Offer the lender the collateral before foreclosure, waiving rights of redemption. Be a cooperative borrower and help your lender avoid hassles and legal costs. The lender will be more inclined to accept the property and forget about deficiencies, particularly if you can convince the lender you are judgment proof.

- Find a buyer for the collateral. You will get a much higher price and incur less of a deficiency if you can sell the property and avoid a distress or auction sale.

Do Not Be Victimized by a Sham Foreclosure Sale

Always attend any auction of your property so you can be certain the auction is conducted in a commercially reasonable manner to bring the highest possible price. This is vital when you are responsible for any deficiency and want the sales price to cover the mortgage. Lenders do conduct bad auctions. They may intentionally suppress the price so they can end up with your property at a bargain price while you end up with a jumbo deficiency. Look for:

- rush bidding, with insufficient time for counter bids;

- discouraging bidders with negative remarks about the property;

- unrealistic terms of sale, such as a high deposit or fast closing; and

- insufficient notice of the sale at auction.

How a Foreclosure Can Work Miracles

Foreclosure of your real estate, personal property, or even business assets can be the ideal way to safely transfer your property with the fewest questions raised by other creditors.

If your objective is to save the property with the least possible trouble from other creditors, have your lender conduct a friendly foreclosure. The lender can resell the property to a new corporation or some other entity you organize. The lender may cooperate if you offer incentives such as higher interest, but may happily participate if only to keep the property, and the mortgage, out of bankruptcy court. This tactic works especially well with a secured lender who holds security interest (mortgage) on a car, boat, airplane or even a business.

Why Lenders Hate Repossessions

If you default on the payments even one time, the lender can take the personal property that you pledged as collateral for the loan. Read your security agreement carefully. Comply with all it's terms. If you make your payments on time but violate other loan terms, you may still be in default and can lose your property.

Banks and finance companies have very little patience with defaulted secured debts because their mortgage on the property makes collection easier and they know that the longer they wait, the harder it will be to collect and the less they may collect.

So what can you do if you are falling behind on your loans? Refinancing is often an option with auto loans. If you appear to have the ability to pay the new lower monthly payment, finance companies will keep refinancing.

If you are past due on a bank loan and have a checking or savings account with that bank, they can collect the amount due from your account. They usually do this after 2 months of nonpayment. Still, banks and finance companies do not want to go to court or seize assets. If you communicate with them and show a sincere willingness to make good on the loan, you can usually work matters out.

The strategies used to avoid a real estate foreclosure can usually prevent repossession of an automobile, boat, or other personal property because all these lenders are in a similar position.

However, it is important to understand your rights in the event of a threatened repossession. Repossessions are controlled by law.

Your creditor can personally take possession of collateral on default only if it can be done without breach of the peace. If property to be repossessed is inside your home, you must first give your consent to the creditor to enter your home and remove the property. You do not have to surrender the property unless a law enforcement officer delivers a court order instructing you to do so. If the creditor damages the property while it is being unlawfully repossessed, this will probably be considered a breach of peace. Also, if you or someone in your family asks the repossessor to leave your property and he or she refuses, this would also breach the peace.

However, if property, such as your car, is located outside your home, the creditor can repossess it as long as you are not guarding it or are not inside it. It is also legal for them to use a master key or hotwire the vehicle and simply drive it away. If the car is in a garage or carport, the repossessor cannot take the vehicle.

Some other points about repossession:

- If you have paid 60 percent of the cash price of the goods, the creditor must dispose of the collateral and return you any recovered amount in excess of the debt (and reasonable expenses incurred by the creditor). For example, if you buy a boat with a secured boat loan and have paid off 60 percent or more, the creditor may sell the boat but must return to you any profit made from the sale. The creditor has up to 90 days to sell the property.
- The creditor must notify you before disposing of the collateral.

After seizing your property, the lender can sell it, lease it, or dispose of it in a commercially reasonable manner. This means that the property must be sold following the prevailing trade and business practices for that type property. The creditor can sell it as is or make reasonable repairs to obtain more money.

The creditor must give you reasonable notice of the sale. The property can be sold by one of two methods. (1) In a public sale open to anyone—you must be notified of the date, time and place of the sale. (2) In a private sale—the creditor invites people most likely to be interested in buying the property. In this case you may be notified only of the date.

The creditor can buy your property if he or she is the high bidder and the terms, including price, are commercially reasonable. You can fight what you feel is an unreasonable sale of repossessed property, but only by going to court and proving that that the creditor's method of resale was unconscionable.

You have the right, up to the time the creditor sells the property, to redeem the collateral by paying the remaining debt plus any expenses.

Bargain for Lender Concessions

What points may you and your lender negotiate when you cannot make payments on your loan? Here are the five most common concessions:

---

1. **Extend the loan.** This is most acceptable to the lender because your loan remains earmarked for full payment.
2. **Defer payments of principal.** This concession provides little relief on newer loans that are heavy on interest for the earliest payments.
3. **Defer interest payments.** Lenders more actively resist this request as it produces a nonperforming loan.
4. **Concession of interest payment.** In more severe cases a lender may concede 1 year's interest. Beyond that, the loan should be completely restructured.
5. **Freeze all loan payments.** This is the most difficult proposition to sell to a lender, but when borrowers have acute cash shortages, lenders often have no choice but to temporarily suspend all payments.

Lender concessions during a loan workout frequently change. Both you and your lender must show flexibility and constant reassessment of the situation to ensure your workout plan is fair to both.

Lenders more willingly suspend payments when they are adequately secured, the collateral will retain its value and the freeze is only short term.

How to Recover Repossessed Property

If your car or other property has been repossessed, there is often a short period of time where you can get the vehicle back by reinstating your contract. This means you can get the property back and resume the payments under the same terms of your original contract by paying all late payments and fees, including the costs of repossession (storage, etc.).

However, you cannot reinstate the contract if:

- the contract has been previously reinstated;
- you tried to avoid repossession by hiding the property;
- you abused the property and its value decreased excessively; and
- you were violent toward the creditor.

In most states the creditor must notify you of your right to reinstate the contract after repossessing the property. If you are not notified, you can possibly get the property back without payment on arrears. Of course, you must resume future payments on the loan. If you have not been notified and you want to reinstate your contract, simply contact the creditor and work out the arrangements. You have between 60 and 90 days to reinstate the contract. If you decide not to, the lender will notify you of the sale. You will then have time before the sale to redeem your property or pay off the entire loan balance to get your property back.

Recovering Property Left in a Repossessed Vehicle

If your car is repossessed with personal property inside it, you have the right to get that property back, but read your loan papers immediately. Some loans say that you must request your personal property within 24 hours of repossession.

Lender Liability—How to Wave the Big Club

Lender liability lawsuits have become a major weapon for beleaguered borrowers. The courts have increasingly sanctioned lenders for a wide number of violations. Lenders are now extremely sensitive to a possible liability claim. Depending upon the nature of the violation, the court can award you considerable damages and even discharge your loan obligation to an over bearing lender. The most common violations to look out for are:

1. fraudulent lender conduct or misrepresentation in either making or handling the loan;

2. changes in loan terms without your consent;

3. unreasonable control exercised by your lender, as when a lender asserts management authority over a business;

4. failing to make future advances as promised;

5. making derogatory comments about you;

6. calling a loan into default without good reason; and

7. negligence in the administration of your loan, particularly in disposal of collateral.

These are only a few of the infractions that can put your lender on the defensive. Carefully record all dealings with your lender, highlighting actions you consider questionable. A lawyer knowledgeable in lender liability can review the merits of your claim.

How to Capitalize on Lender Mistakes

Never assume your lender holds a valid mortgage against your property. You and your lender may think the mortgage is airtight, yet there can be legal defects in it that make the mortgage (but not necessarily the obligation) worthless. At the least, they may delay foreclosure for months until the defect can be corrected. Whether a mortgage is valid or defective requires professional review by a lawyer who will check for these five common defects:

1. Incorrect name of the mortgagor.

2. Missing mortgagor's signature.

3. Incorrect property description.

4. Incorrect filing in the public records.

5. Failure to file in the public records.

Faulty security interests in personal property are more prevalent than errors in real estate mortgages. The most common errors with security interests include:

- The security interest lapsed because the financing statements were not refiled after 5 years.

- The debtor's name is incorrect.

- The collateral is incorrectly described, or fails to include major assets (i.e., inventory or accounts receivable).

- The financing statements are incorrectly filed in the public records or not filed at all.

These defects may render the mortgage or security interest void against third parties but not necessarily the debtor.

Uncovering a serious defect in your mortgage gives you enormous bargaining power with your lender. Your cooperation is usually needed to correct the problem.

Sidestep Dangerous Balloon Mortgages

Many mortgage defaults involve balloon mortgages where the borrower must pay the entire principal of a mortgage on a fixed date. Sellers, for example, often accept balloon mortgages from buyers who can only afford interest payments in the early years. This arrangement assumes that the buyer will refinance several years after the sale.

Balloon mortgages make sense when you anticipate an increase in property value and can refinance to pay the balloon mortgage. Unfortunately, property values do not always increase and buyers cannot always refinance their property. If that happens, there are two options:

1. Offer the mortgage holder a higher interest rate for an extension. This proposal is reasonable when there is sufficient cash flow to handle a slightly higher payment.

2. Seek an equity investor who will put in the cash to pay the mortgage. In exchange, give the investor part equity plus a mortgage on the property. Plan ahead—allow yourself time to find an investor and negotiate a sensible deal.

Bulletproof Yourself before You Battle Your Lender

Never battle your lender with other assets in case the lender attaches those assets without warning. Ideally, you sheltered your assets before you accepted the loan. If you are not judgment proof, make a last minute effort to place your other assets out of the lender's reach. Most vulnerable is money on deposit with your lender. A bank can, without notice, apply all funds in your checking or savings accounts against your loan. The lender also can set off deposits of any guarantors to the loan. Transfer these accounts to other institutions at the earliest opportunity.

Once your loan becomes shaky, your lender is likely to demand additional collateral for the loan. Should you agree? Usually not. When a lender questions whether the present collateral is sufficient to cover the loan, the chances are it is not, so why jeopardize more of your assets? This only improves the lender's position and weakens yours.

Lenders do make valuable concessions for additional collateral. They may offer moratoriums on payments, lower interest, or even additional cash advances, but these concessions are seldom in your best long term interest.

How do you gracefully refuse your lender's demand for more collateral? Best approach: Have your other property titled with your spouse. While you may be willing to grant the lender's request, perhaps your spouse and you are having marital problems and your spouse (and his or her lawyer) refuses to encumber more property. This face saving story politely refuses a lender—and it works! Do not assume a secured lender will not go after your other assets. It can be a costly mistake. Refusing to pledge more collateral will not prompt the lender to foreclose faster.

Eviction

Once your rent payments are in arrears, you will be faced with the possibility of eviction, confiscation, loss of your personal property, and relocating your family and possessions to more affordable housing. Use extreme caution when dealing with anyone who claims to be able to postpone eviction indefinitely. Many of these services never even file papers on your behalf. Then, when the eviction process continues, they simply tell you they were not successful. Others file incorrect papers or unsatisfactory defenses, worsening your current financial position and placing you in greater debt. The best way to avoid eviction is to pay the rent on time, but there are times when that is not possible. No matter what the circumstances, if you are sued for eviction, you have the right to a fair trial.

Negotiate with the Landlord

A Notice to Quit or Notice to Vacate does not mean you have to leave at once; it is a warning. It is generated whenever you have failed to pay your rent or broken any agreement you may have made with your landlord about payments. The notice will sometimes give you a number of days in which to cure or erase the arrearage. If you do not meet that time frame, the landlord may petition the court to start eviction proceedings. The landlord may also specify any other breach of the rental agreement—such as a pet violation—that might have been previously overlooked but now demands enforcement.

Once you receive a Notice to Quit, you must move at once to negotiate a mutual solution to the problem—possibly with weekly or biweekly payments. In some cases, a landlord may even consider lowering the rent for a specified time (like in times of extreme hardship). But always be aware that landlords are not required to make concessions or help you work out your financial problems.

One possibility is to ask for a lower rent for a specified time while you seek more reasonable housing. This would save both you and the landlord the cost of the eviction process, and let you leave on your own terms.

Temporary/Permanent Rent Assistance

In some areas, community service agencies and welfare assistance may be available to you and your family. Some programs offer assistance in paying back rent; others offer assistance in paying moving expenses and security deposits.

Although the waiting lists are quite long, tenants who do not already receive a government housing subsidy may apply for government housing assistance programs—including special rental assistance, nonprofit housing programs, and even traditional housing—when they have problems with:

• homelessness	• being a member of a minority group
• debilitating illness	• small children in the household

The length of waiting time and other priorities will vary from program to program, but do not hesitate to apply for assistance if you fall on sudden hardship. That is the purpose of the programs. For additional information about these and other programs, contact your local housing authority and community social services offices.

Respond to the Courts

If you have not paid the back rent or negotiated another agreement with your landlord in the time allotted, the landlord may proceed to file the eviction action in court. (Eviction actions are also known as forcible entry, detainer, or ejectment actions.)

Generally, hearings on evictions are heard quickly. The law requires that you receive a copy of the landlord's complaint along with a summons to appear before the court—usually delivered by a process server. As few as 5 days may separate the date of court appearance from the date you are served.

If you disagree with the landlord's complaint or feel you have a sufficient defense to protect yourself against the impending eviction action, you must immediately contact the court and file a counterclaim.

More often than not, eviction hearings are less formal than other cases, meaning you do not have to become familiar with all the legal jargon. This makes it easier to communicate with the court and file the proper documents.

Attend the Eviction Hearing

If you are served with a notice of eviction, it is imperative that you attend the hearing, even if you have already moved out. You need to protect your interests. For example, the landlord could misstate the amount of back rent you owe, or claim damage to the property that is not there or that was not caused by you. Make sure you are completely prepared for the hearing. Have your defense strategy planned out on paper, and bring everything you need with you, such as:

• the lease	• any photos that validate the state of repair
• any witnesses	• rent receipts, money order stubs or canceled checks

Even when no defense is available, your presence at the hearing indicates your concern, and you may find the judge willing to listen to extenuating circumstances or to consider possible solutions other than eviction.

Any defense not raised at the hearing will be lost. In most courts, the landlords must comply strictly with the laws regarding content and timing of notices. Should you prove the landlord wrong or find any misstatements, the eviction may be dismissed or the landlord may be forced to start the entire procedure from the beginning.

Another defense may be peaceable possession. This defense could be used when the landlord has failed to file an eviction action before the time prescribed in the Notice to Vacate has expired. Since the landlord has inadvertently consented to your continued occupancy despite the late payment, peaceable possession may result in the eviction being dismissed. Rest assured that a landlord who loses on this point will immediately reinstitute the procedure.

Another defense would be that the landlord has previously or continuously allowed your payments to be paid late and now suddenly commences an eviction proceeding. The eviction procedure would now be considered improper because the previously accepted timeline was altered without proper notice to you.

It may be necessary to seek legal advice to completely understand specific procedural requirements regarding your landlord's actions and your responses to those actions. Contact your local social services offices, legal aid or local bar association. Many communities have clinics and pamphlets concerning tenant's rights.

Substandard Housing Defense

Most courts will recognize defenses and counterclaims where the tenant claims the property is not habitable (in suitable living condition). You can prove this defense by producing copies of letters to the landlord requesting that repairs, etc., be made, or by photographs, video and witnesses. One of the best witnesses is a building or housing inspector who has responded to your complaint and will certify the premises has the faults you claim.

Where no building code violation exists but other problems are present (such as air conditioner or heating deficiencies), the courts may decide that you are only responsible for a portion of the back rent. Although you may still wind up being evicted, the amount you would have to pay back could be reduced or even eliminated. Many jurisdictions require that prior notice of such deficiencies have been presented to the landlord in writing before a housing deficiency defense will be accepted. You must send such notices of deficiency by certified mail, keeping a copy of the notice and attaching the receipt of certified mail to it. Always consult with a lawyer on such matters.

Sometimes evictions are brought in retaliation against a tenant who attempts to organize other tenants in an action against the landlord. Or a landlord may commence an eviction proceeding against a tenant who has contacted the building inspector or housing authority. This can be a good defense, but again you should consult with and possibly retain a lawyer.

Appeals

Should you lose the eviction case, if possible, immediately file an appeal to a higher court—but only if you feel you have a substantial case. Frivolous appeals, like frivolous lawsuits, could result in a fine or other sanction assessed against you.

The threat of an appeal can provide you bargaining ground in settling a back rent or rent lowering problem. The time lapse until your appeal is scheduled also allows you to relocate in a more orderly manner.

In some courts, filing an appeal requires payment of filing fees, but if your rental arrearage is due to financial hardship these fees may be waived.

The Eviction

Should you receive a court order for eviction, you must immediately begin making arrangements to relocate. Never disregard the court order or you may be forcibly removed at any time, and your possessions confiscated for sale or auction as part payment against the back rent due, or they may be left out on the street.

Many jurisdictions will advise you of an actual eviction date. Contact the sheriff or local court clerk to find out how long you have to vacate. More often than not, once you receive the notice you have very little time to prepare before you are evicted.

Should you not move out by the ordered date, you may be forcibly put out. The landlord may put a lien on all your possessions to cover the costs of the moving and storage. You have to reimburse the landlord for those costs or post a bond to retrieve your possessions.

Unauthorized Lockouts and Seizures

Some jurisdictions do give the landlord the right to seize your belongings when you are behind in the rent—without obtaining a court order. You would then have to go to court to obtain the right to get back your property or pay money or post a bond to have your property released to you.

Should your property be confiscated in this manner, you must immediately seek legal counsel. Even where seizure is allowed, certain property remains exempt from seizure. In some cases you may challenge, on constitutional grounds, the very seizure itself.

Self help evictions (lockouts, utility shutoffs, and eviction related harassment) are almost always illegal. In any of these cases, you must immediately seek a lawyer. You will be entitled to re-enter the property and have the harassment terminated. In some cases, you may be entitled to compensation or damages.

Often in the self help eviction the landlord will claim the tenant had moved out. You must immediately contact the landlord in writing, advising that you have, in fact, not vacated. Should the landlord refuse to allow you back in, your written notice will serve as proof to the court that you have not vacated.

It is a much better situation for all parties if you have voluntarily vacated the premises by the scheduled eviction date.

Suit for Back Rent

A landlord's suit for back rent may or may not be included in the eviction case. Should you be sued for back rent, you must treat this as you would any suit for money by a creditor.

Some defenses that you presented in the eviction hearing may also be defenses against a suit for back rent. Common defenses include:

• substandard housing conditions	• illegal lockouts
• improper calculation of amount due	• illegal seizures

The landlord's management company, lawyer, or collection agency may also be in violation of debt collection harassment laws.

Rental Unit Problems

Rental properties must comply with local housing ordinances, fire ordinances and health regulations. Additionally, heat and hot water must be available to the tenants. Appliances provided in the rental unit must be safe and in proper working condition. Rental units are usually required to be free of vermin and infestation. Should these conditions not exist in your unit, you should:

- Make a written request to the landlord.

- Contact the housing inspector. After giving the landlord a reasonable time to make repairs, your second action is to contact the housing inspector or code compliance officer in your community. Make your complaint in writing, attaching a copy of the notice you send the landlord.

- Beware of retaliatory eviction procedures. Some landlords respond aggressively to tenants taking complaints to the authorities. While the law usually protects tenants from retaliatory evictions or lockouts, some landlords may attempt them anyway. Should this occur, seek advice from a local legal services office or a lawyer who specializes in rental laws.

- Seek a court order. Persistent requests and even building inspectors do not intimidate some landlords. Your next step is to seek a court order; the courts can force the landlord to make repairs and sometimes award you compensation in the form of rent reductions or abatements.

Some jurisdictions allow tenants to withhold rent in an attempt to force the landlord to make necessary repairs or replacements. These laws generally set out specific steps you must follow or your tenant's rights may be jeopardized.

Breaking a Lease

Comfortable rent payments can quickly become stressful when you lose your job or another financial disaster strikes. One solution is voluntarily relocating.

If your landlord is not sympathetic to your plight, you may wind up with another financial problem. You may not only owe rent for the months you were unable to pay, but if you move you could also be liable for rent payments on the remainder of the lease.

Read the lease. If your rental agreement specifies that either party may terminate the lease with notice, all you have to do is give your landlord that written notice. Unless something is drastically wrong with the premises, like rendering it unsafe to inhabit, most laws allow for a 30-day written notice. Some leases start out on a 1 year term and then automatically convert to a month to month lease if another lease is not signed after the year has expired. Some landlords will waive back rent payments or reduce any lease breaking penalty in exchange for a written agreement to move as soon as possible.

Negotiate what you owe. When your lease calls for all rent to be paid until its expiration, try to get a break from the landlord. Sometimes it is less costly for the landlord to negotiate the balance than to hire a lawyer, skip tracer, or collection agency to come after you once you have moved.

Sublet. There are two methods for subletting your apartment. One is to find someone to take over your apartment who will pay the rent to you so you can then pay the rent to the landlord. This method leaves you completely liable and at risk if your subtenant reneges on the rent.

The second method is to find someone to completely take over your lease. Once the paperwork is complete, the new tenant becomes completely liable and you are totally released—whether the new tenant pays the rent or not.

Landlords are much more receptive to a sublease assumption of an apartment where there is no loss of revenue than having you rent to a third party.

Break the lease. If you have exhausted all options and your landlord refuses to negotiate an early termination or sublease assumption, you must carefully evaluate the cost—and risk—of breaking the lease. There are financial consequences to breaking a lease, but the penalties of eviction or paying rent you cannot afford may be considerably worse.

If you break a lease, the landlord is obligated to try to rent the apartment immediately. Should the landlord not do this immediately, this could be a defense for you in any future suit.

Other advisable methods to help you break your lease are to:

- give your landlord as much advance notice as possible—at least 60 days notice allows the landlord to secure another tenant;

- consider doing your own advertising for a replacement tenant;

- make sure the premises are spotless and in a perfect state of repair when you vacate;

- check newspaper ads daily to make sure the landlord is advertising the apartment; and

- periodically stop by the apartment to see if the landlord has rented it. This protects you against a claim that the landlord was unable to rent the unit in a timely fashion.

More than likely, you will lose your security deposit if you break the lease, but if you have time to plan carefully and you can accomplish the transfer without it costing the landlord any rents or unplanned expenses, you could possibly recover all or at least part of your deposit.

25 Credit Traps

People who are most anxious for credit are those who are most likely to fall into credit traps. Many credit traps are scams and are illegal. Others stack the deck so heavily against the borrower that, while legal, they are simply unconscionable.

Some of the largest corporations in America are nothing more than sophisticated pool hall loan sharks who routinely fleece their clients. Because credit is big business, all the pressure that Madison Avenue and modern technology can bring to bear is used to convince you to sign on the dotted line and enter into a credit deal that is rarely in your best interests.

Your defenses are patience, knowledge and suspicion. Learn to be patient—even when desperate. And understand thoroughly anything that requires your signature. Aggressively question and be an educated skeptic!

Seven key points to remember:

1. If monthly payments are low, the interest rate is usually high.

2. Always figure the total cost of your loan at the end of the loan period.

3. Have all charges explained to you and put in writing.

4. Be sure any merchandise you buy on credit is competitively priced.

5. Be wary of deals that seem to good to be true.

6. Do not be afraid to negotiate.

7. Seek credit from those who report to the credit bureaus.

We are each motivated by the fear that we will be denied something we need, want or deserve. We also are motivated by greed. These two powerful motivators often blind even the most honest and sensible person. Each month thousands of credit complaints to Better Business Bureaus prove that point. What about you? Have you fallen into one of the following 25 traps?

1. Catalog Credit Cards

Issued by mail order catalog companies, these cards allow you to buy from the company catalog. Often called gold or platinum cards, they sound like bank credit cards but are not. You will be offered a high credit line without any credit check—and if this offer sounds too good to be true, it is, because:

- The merchandise in their fancy catalogues is overpriced by 50 percent or more, so you vastly overpay.

- You must often make a large down payment (40 percent to 85 percent of the price) to cover the seller's product cost. The company thus loses nothing by offering extensive credit—even with no credit checks—because later payments are pure profit.

- Other credit offers inevitably accompany the cards: expensive application, memberships or order processing fees. While these companies claim there are no interest charges, the interest is hidden within the inflated price.

Catalog companies seldom report to credit bureaus, so despite their claims, you cannot rebuild credit by dealing with them.

Credit rackets flourish because they cater to the two basic elements to every credit scam—fear and greed.

2. Telephone Credit Scams

900 or 976 numbers are leased from the phone companies by other companies that want to sell you a product or service by phone. When you call these numbers you pay an additional charge above the normal call costs. This charge can top $20 per minute!

How does this relate to your credit? Well, credit is the item most commonly advertised by companies who use these 900 or 976 phone numbers; they may invite you to call their 900 or 976 number to obtain a secured bank card or catalog credit card. All you get for your money is a credit application—plus a very large phone bill.

3. Advance Fee Loans

Though it is illegal in many states, hundreds of thousands of people are still victimized by this scam each year. In its simplest form, someone (a loan broker) promises to find you a loan in exchange for an advance fee. After you pay this fee, the broker disappears with your money.

Legitimate loan brokers usually collect their fee after they obtain your loan, with the fee paid from the loan. An advance fee loan broker, in contrast, collects before the loan is found.

Many sophisticated techniques are used to get you sucked into this scam. You might answer an ad from a professional sounding firm urging you to call a 976 number for more information or to receive an application. The price of the call could be the fee, or you may be asked to pay the fee by credit card, check or money order. These advance brokers often advertise via cable television, radio, newspaper, fliers, and handouts. Before you hand your money over to these people, contact the Better Business Bureau, your state Consumer Protection Agency, and/or the Federal Trade Commission.

It is virtually impossible to recover your money if the broker fails to deliver. Be suspicious of anyone who asks you to pay for services before delivery.

4. Bogus Credit Repair Companies

These companies promise to fix your credit, often for an exorbitant fee that can run into thousands of dollars. Remember, a credit repair company cannot do anything more than you can do yourself with patience, persistence and knowledge.

Credit repair companies often disguise themselves as a legitimate financial aid company, debt counseling service, loan consolidation company, or a credit fix it company, but you can look for certain warning signs: impossible claims and false promises in the company's advertising, such as "No Credit Beyond Repair," "Eliminate All Negative Reporting Including Bankruptcies," or "We Can Get You Unlimited Credit Now, No Matter How Poor Your Credit History." Also, be wary if the company claims it can get you a major bank card even if you have poor or no credit.

Bogus credit repair companies use many techniques to draw clients, from lists of court reported bankruptcies and telemarketing to direct mail advertising. Once they contact you, they often prey upon your fears with these lies and deceptions:

- They may claim the company is affiliated with the federal government. In truth, the federal government is in no way connected with any aspect of credit repair.
- They may tell you that file segregation is a legal credit repair technique. But file segregation is an illegal technique used by companies to create a separate identity for a client. This is a federal crime that may also involve mail or wire fraud. You may also be sued for civil fraud.

They may also trade on your fear that bankruptcy destroys your ability to obtain credit for 10 years. This is not true. Most creditors consider bankruptcy situations case by case and take into account the reason for the bankruptcy and whether it was due to circumstances beyond your control, such as illness or job loss.

Some states have laws that regulate credit repair companies. These states usually require that the companies be bonded or have insurance to cover upfront deposits in case they are sued by clients; to abide by the FCRA; to inform clients of their legal rights; to give clients a written contract; and allow clients three to five days to change their mind after they sign a contract. The 15 states that regulate credit repair companies are:

Arkansas	Louisiana	Oklahoma
California	Maryland	Texas
Connecticut	Massachusetts	Utah
Florida	Nevada	Virginia
Georgia	New York	Washington

Disguised as a debt consolidation company, the credit repair company also may offer you—a very high interest loan with large upfront fees, possibly secured with your home as collateral. A bankruptcy attorney may also be disguised as a debt counseling service as a front to attract clients. Another firm may offer you a national bank card that is only a secured bank card easily obtained by yourself without having to pay fees to the credit repair firm.

What should you do if you do decide to work with a credit repair firm? First, contact the Federal Trade Commission, Better Business Bureau, the state attorney general, or the Department of Consumer Affairs to see if complaints have been filed or legal action taken against the company. Second, meet personally with a representative of the company to find out what it can and cannot do for you; get this information in writing. Finally, do not under any circumstances give the company money in advance.

5. Credit Card Cash Advances and Cash Advance Checks

Madison Avenue has given cash advance checks fancy names, but they are still just different ways of using your credit card.

These are used by some banks to trap you into a high interest loan. Here is how the process works: You try to cash a check at a branch of the bank where you have your account. The teller refuses because it is against bank policy to cash checks from its other branches, so he or she suggests that the bank instead give you a cash advance on your bank card. But of course, you may pay a huge advance fee to the bank for issuing the card, and also pay high interest the minute you receive the money—because banks often eliminate the interest free period with cash advances. If the bank eliminates the interest free period because of the cash advance, it can do so for the entire balance of your bill. You could therefore pay as much as 285 percent interest, even though you fully paid the entire cash advance within 30 days. Some banks will charge you additional interest on any unpaid balance in your credit card account. This ploy is known as pyramiding.

Cash advance checks work exactly the same as credit card advances. The charges still appear on your monthly credit card bills and are subject to the same high interest rates.

6. Overdraft Protection

This so called protection, which can easily destroy you financially, is a variation of the cash advance trap. Here is how it works: If you write a check that exceeds your account balance, the bank honors the check and charges the difference to your credit card account. The bank will point out that since you avoided bouncing a check, you avoided a bounced check fee.

But here is what you will pay: Because protection is usually rounded to the nearest $100, if you exceed the balance in your checking account by even five cents, the bank advances you the full $100. You are now also liable for all the other costs associated with credit card cash advances. The bank will apply the extra $99.95 it forced you to borrow and reduce your credit card account, while it also collects interest on your loan.

7. We Waived Your Minimum Monthly Payment

This is one of the most destructive traps laid by credit card companies. It is particularly attractive at times of increased spending, such as Christmas.

Even though no minimum payment is required for a certain month, you continue to accrue interest. If your debt is already high, and you accept this offer several times a year (sometimes you will receive this offer for 6 consecutive months), you will seriously increase your debt and make the bankcard company considerably wealthier. A minimum payment plan (an average of 18 percent interest with a 2.5 percent minimum payment) will have you pay $4,230.83 on a $2,000 debt over the 12 years and 9 months it will take you to pay it down. Imagine how much longer it will take, and how much more it will cost, if every one of those 12 years includes months in which you omit the minimum payment.

A popular variation is when you walk into a store in August to buy a big ticket item and the salesperson explains that if you buy the item today, you need not make payments until January. What the salesperson does not mention is that January's bill will include finance charges from August.

8. Insurance from Your Credit Card Issuer

Insurance offered by a credit card issuer is usually unnecessary, and always overpriced. The terms are the worst to be found anywhere, whether the insurance be life, disability, unemployment, hospital or any other type of coverage.

Be particularly skeptical about credit insurance. Banks love to sell this overpriced insurance because they are the beneficiaries; the payment is used to pay your outstanding balance if you die, while they collect hefty premiums in the interim.

If you want insurance, see an insurance broker who is independent of any bank card.

9. Credit Card Registration Services

These companies offer you protection from loss of your credit cards with just one phone call. If you pay $15 a year for this protection, it will ultimately cost you hundreds of dollars to have avoided a few toll free phone calls. And each time you add or subtract a credit card from your list, you must still notify the registration service by mail. It is far easier and cheaper to keep your own list and notify the credit card companies yourself.

10. Mail Order Loans

Some banks will eventually send you a non-negotiable check. You just have to fill out the short application and the bank will send you a real check for the stated amount.

Beware

This is yet another cash advance mail order scheme. The bank will tempt you with very low minimum monthly payments but the annual interest is likely to be the highest possible legal rate.

For instance, a $3,000 loan at 1.8 percent interest per month paid in monthly installments of two percent will take 77 years and 3 months to fully pay. And you will have paid $24,734.58 in finance charges.

11. Advance Tax Refunds

This loan against an anticipated tax refund only begins to make sense if you have a large tax refund coming. Why? Because the fee charged is computed on an annualized rate, as though you borrowed the money for an entire year, even if you are borrowing it for a maximum of four weeks. If you expect a $1,100 refund and pay a flat fee of $84, your effective annual interest rate is 92 percent. However, if you expect a $3,000 refund, the annualized rate drops to only 12 percent.

12. Second Mortgage Scams

These are most common in the home improvement industry where con men offer to make home improvements in poor neighborhoods to people who have considerable equity in their homes. The contractor arranges financing for his or her victims with lenders who offer second mortgages with very high interest rates and loan origination fees. Sometimes a contractor can convince the home owner to sign a trust deed to secure the work on the home. Even if the owner is dissatisfied with the work, the contractor can force the sale of the home to collect his or her money.

Avoid contractors who offer package deals with second mortgage companies; they usually involve kickbacks.

13. Bait and Switch Conversion Loans

Here unscrupulous loan brokers offer you a below market rate mortgage—if you first accept a mortgage loan with very high interest. You are promised that it will be converted to a lower interest mortgage, but until that happens you must continue to pay the interest.

Beware
Conversion to the low interest loan seldom happens.

14. Waiving Your Rights

Always read finance agreements carefully. Some agreements contain clauses stating that in the event of legal action, the consumer waives all legal defenses. Never waive your legal rights.

15. Illegal Finance Charges

Any credit card issuer that gives an interest free grace period must mail your bill at least 14 days before interest is due. This gives you the chance to pay the bill without incurring a finance charge. If you receive the bill too late, essentially you are forced to accept a finance charge—and this is illegal.

16. Invasion of Privacy

This is a serious credit problem, one that continues to grow. It usually involves a technique called prescreening or prequalification for credit. Here is how it works:

Suppose the issuer of a new bank card wants to find people with perfect credit who also earn at least $50,000 per year. The credit bureau, from its own files, can generate a list of potential customers meeting those qualifications. The company can also send its own list to the credit bureau and the credit bureau can delete nonqualifying names. You may be on such a list with neither your knowledge nor consent. Companies can thus uncover your financial characteristics without seeing your actual credit report.

The only way you can discover this is by inspecting your own credit report. If the word promotional or letters PRM appear in the inquiries section, it means your file was prescreened. You can ask that the credit bureau not include your file in any prescreening program, but presently the bureau is not obligated to honor your request.

> **Other examples of irresponsible data collection include the following:**
>
> • A company maintains a computerized list of persons who file malpractice suits against doctors and hospitals. This list enables medical personnel to screen out potential troublemakers.
>
> • A company keeps an index of patients who do not pay their bills and hotel guests who damage or steal property and do not pay their lodging bills.
>
> • A company offers landlords inside information on tenants.

These bureaus and services do not notify you when your name is used by a third party. You are thereby denied your right to question the agency and have it reinvestigated. This is illegal.

17. Suicide Rollovers

This trap plays on the pressure of mounting debt and pretends to be a simple debt reliever: Take a cash advance from one credit card and use it to repay other credit cards. The more credit cards you have, the more credit cards you can manipulate. No cash is required. If you have a large portfolio of credit cards, you can continue to make minimum payments for a long time.

In the credit business these are called suicide rollovers because instead of facing your debt, you choose to commit financial suicide. Some financial advisors suggest that in good times you obtain as many credit cards as possible so you will be prepared for the tough times. This is one of the most dangerous traps on the road to sound credit management.

18. Shotgunning Credit Applications

This is just not a smart technique to follow. By mailing in as many credit applications as possible, you end up with a massive inquiry list on your credit report. That will only further hurt your chances for credit.

19. Debt Consolidation

You apply for more credit to combine your debts into one payment. However, this immediately signals to a lender that you cannot meet your monthly payments. Also, interest rates are usually high or you must put up collateral to guard against default. This is a good strategy if you can repay the loan but a bad strategy if you cannot.

20. Mortgage Reduction Information Kits

These expensive kits, which cost hundreds of dollars and are peddled door to door, contain no information that you cannot find elsewhere for free or for a few dollars. They all tell you the same thing—cut your mortgage payments into biweekly installments to save interest. The problem is that only a few banks will accept biweekly payments.

21. Prepayment Penalties

This costly provision, usually found in the fine print of a loan agreement, is designed to keep you forever in debt. If you should fully pay the loan before it is due, the lender then forces you to pay a penalty. To pay a five percent penalty of the remaining $50,000 on your mortgage will cost you an extra $2,500. Negotiate this out of the contract! Also find out if your state restricts this type of clause.

22. Prepaid Interest

The fine print may also include an add on interest clause. The interest is added to the total amount of your loan before the lender calculates your monthly payments. The total amount of the loan is then divided by the number of required payments. There is no advantage to discharging the loan early, because the fine print says interest will not be refunded, so you do not save if you pay early. For example, if you borrow $5,000 and the interest for the term of the loan is $500, your total loan is $5,500—whether you pay in 20 months or 2 months.

23. Uncapped Variable Interest Rates

A capped variable interest rate is one that fluctuates with the prime interest rate but never rises above a certain point. In contrast, an uncapped variable rate may start at nine percent but with no ceiling it can rise to 20 percent or more, as happened in the early 1980s. Variable rates are always dangerous, because this type of rate leaves you without any protection whatsoever.

24. Noninterest Bearing Deposits

These deposits do draw interest—but not for you! Insist that if the terms of the contract are not satisfied by a certain date, any monies you deposit will begin to earn interest at prevailing money market rates.

25. Food Freezer Plans

This plan has many interesting variations. Some sell you food with low monthly payments. Others force you to buy enormous quantities, while others discount only your opening order. Still others are not transferable outside your geographic area. These plans eagerly extend credit because they all have one goal—to get you to buy the freezer at three to five times what you can buy a comparable freezer for at a local store. These plans are even more grateful if you lease the freezer, because at the end of the contract you must return it.

Be very careful with food plans. Read the fine print carefully and do the math. Joining these plans is rarely a good deal from a credit viewpoint.

Avoid quick fix solutions. If it sounds too good to be true, it probably is.

Things to Keep in Mind

There are, of course, many other credit scams. And new ones are conceived daily. But how do you avoid them? You need to:

- be patient
- be suspicious
- read the fine print
- not sign anything that you do not understand
- check references
- practice good credit management

Online Resources

American Bankruptcy Institute, The

> www.abiworld.org

American Consumer Credit Counseling

> www.consumercredit.com

Center for Debt Management

> www.center4debtmanagement.com

Commercial Law League of America

> www.clla.org

Debtors Anonymous

> www.debtorsanonymous.org

Employee Benefits Security Administration

> www.dol.gov/ebsa

Federal Trade Commission-Consumer Protection

> www.ftc.gov/bcp/menu-credit.htm

Findlaw's Bankruptcy

> www.findlaw.com/

InterNet Bankruptcy Library (IBL)

> http://bankrupt.com

Myvesta

www.dca.org

National Association of Personal Financial Advisors

www.napfa.org

National Foundation for Consumer Credit (NFCC)

www.nfcc.org

Legal Search Engines

Catalaw

www.catalaw.com

FindLaw

www.findlaw.com

Hieros Gamos

www.hg.org/index.html

LawAid

www.lawaid.com

LawCrawler

www.lawcrawler.com

Internet Legal Resource Group

www.ilrg.com/

LEXIS/NEXIS

www.lexis-nexis.com/default.asp

Meta-Index for U.S. Legal Research

http://gsulaw.gsu.edu/metaindex

USALaw

www.usalaw.com/linksrch.cfm

WestLaw

http://creditcard.westlaw.com

(Registered users only. Fee paid service.)

Glossary of Bankruptcy Terms

Please note: The terms described below are just part of a much larger Bankruptcy Dictionary available to readers of this book at www.socrates.com/books/bankruptcy-renewal.aspx. To gain access to this information, you must register at Socrates.com using the eight digit registration code printed on the enclosed CD-ROM.

AAA See American Arbitration Association.

abandonment In relation to a child: The failure by a parent to provide any financial support or to communicate with her or his child over a period of time. In these circumstances, a court may terminate that parent's parental rights. If a child is physically abandoned by both parents, the child may be made available for adoption. In relation to a spouse. See desertion.

accommodation party A person who gives the strength of his or her credit to another person by signing a negotiable instrument as a co-signer or endorser.

accord In contracts, an agreement to settle a claim.

acknowledgment A statement made by an individual in the presence of a notary public or other official authorized to administer oaths confirming that a document with the individual's signature was actually signed by her or him.

actual cash value The theoretical value of a property, which insurance companies calculate by deducting depreciation from the current replacement value.

admissible evidence Evidence that a trial judge or jury may consider because it is deemed reliable under the rules of evidence.

ADR See alternative dispute resolution.

adult Generally, any person 18 years of age or older.

affiant The signer of an affidavit.

affidavit A signed written statement of facts, confirmed by the oath or affirmation of the signer before someone authorized to administer such an oath (e.g., a notary public).

age of majority Legal adulthood, when one becomes a major rather than a minor: usually the age of 18 years. Upon reaching this age, a person can vote, buy alcohol, join the military, make a will and sign binding contracts—and the person's parents are no longer required to make child support payments. The age may vary, depending on the activity: in some states the voting age is 18 years, but the age for buying alcohol is 21 years.

agent A person who, by mutual consent, is authorized to act for the benefit of and under the direction of another person when dealing with third parties. The person who appoints the agent is the principal. The agent is in a fiduciary relationship with the principal, can enter into binding agreements on behalf of the principal and could potentially create liability for her or him. See attorney-in-fact.

aggravate To worsen or make more serious.

agreement An understanding between two or more parties about a particular issue, covering their obligations, duties and rights. The term can also mean contract (i.e., a legally binding agreement) but has a broader application and extends to understandings that are not legally binding.

alimony Payments made by one ex-spouse to the other for support under the terms of a divorce. "Permanent alimony" is indefinite in duration and usually follows from a marriage of 10 years or longer or in the case of an ailing spouse. "Rehabilitative alimony" usually lasts for a defined period, by which time the recipient spouse is expected to have prepared for financial independence and become self-supporting. Also known as spousal support or maintenance.

alternative dispute resolution (ADR) The various methods of resolving disputes through means other than the judicial (i.e., court) process. These include negotiation, conciliation, mediation and arbitration. ADR methods are faster, less formal, less expensive and often less adversarial than a court trial. Recently, the term has come to be used to mean Appropriate Dispute Resolution, emphasizing that ADR methods are positive ways to settle disputes and are more than just alternatives to litigation.

American Arbitration Association (AAA) A private nonprofit organization established to provide education, training and administrative assistance to parties using alternative dispute resolution (i.e., nonjudicial methods) for resolving disputes.

amortization Method of paying off a debt with a series of regular, periodic partial payments of interest and principal. See mortgage.

annulment A court decree canceling a marriage because of some defect that existed when the marriage took place, in effect treating it as if it never happened. Annulments are rare since the no-fault divorce has become the norm, but are obtainable for misrepresentation, concealment (e.g., of a criminal record), misunderstanding and the refusal or inability to consummate the marriage.

appraisal An estimate of the fair market value of something, such as real estate, valuables or stock. A professional appraiser (a neutral expert) makes an estimate by studying the property and comparing the initial purchase price with recent sales of similar property. Appraisals are often ordered by courts in probate, bankruptcy and other proceedings in which market values need to be established for a property. Banks and mortgage companies use appraisals before making loans, and insurance companies use damage appraisals before settling claims.

appraiser A professional expert who is hired to determine the current market value or full cash value of real estate or other property.

appreciation An increase in value, particularly of property that has risen in value since it was acquired.

arbitration A method for resolving disputes using a neutral third party or parties (the arbitrator or arbitration panel) rather than a court. Arbitration uses procedures that are less formal than those of trial courts, and can be a faster and cheaper way to resolve conflicts. There are a number of types of arbitration: In binding arbitration, the arbitrator has the power to impose a decision, sometimes within previously agreed limits (e.g, a maximum or minimum award). In nonbinding arbitration, the arbitrator can recommend a decision but not impose it. Many contracts, including those used by large manufacturers and finance companies, require mandatory arbitration in the event of a dispute.

arbitrator See arbitration.

arrearages Overdue payments for alimony or child support. State laws now make it very difficult to get rid of arrearages: bankruptcy will not discharge them. A temporary modification of the payments should be sought by those unable to make full payments.

as is A phrase indicating goods or property that are sold without warranty as to quality or condition.

assignee A person or company to whom rights in a property are transferred. An assignee may take over a lease from a tenant who wants to move before the expiration of a lease. The assignee assumes the legal rights and responsibilities of the tenant, including paying the rent, but the original tenant can be held legally responsible if the assignee fails to keep her or his side of the bargain.

assignment The act of transferring to another (the assignee) all or part of one's property, interest or rights.

attachment The act of legally seizing property to bring it under the custody of a court.

attestation The act of watching the signing of a legal document, such as a **will** or **power of attorney**, and then signing one's own name as a **witness**. When an individual witnesses a document in this way, she or he is attesting (i.e., stating and confirming) that the person whom the individual watched sign the document did in fact do so. Attestation does not mean that one is asserting the accuracy or truthfulness of a document, only that one saw it being signed by the person whose name appears on the signature line.

attestation clause The clause of a will in which the witnesses certify that the will was properly executed.

attorney fees Payments to a lawyer for legal services. Fees may be charged in a number of ways: by the hour; per the job or service (e.g., a stipulated fee to draw up a will); on **contingency** (in which case the lawyer receives a proportion of any sums awarded to the client—or receives nothing if there is no award);or on retainer (i.e., an advance or down payment on an hourly or per job fee). Attorney fees are normally paid by the client who has done the hiring, but sometimes a law or contract requires the losing **party** of a lawsuit to pay the winner's **court costs** and attorney fees. In family law cases (**divorce, custody** and **child support**) a judge often can order the more affluent spouse to pay the other spouse's attorney fees, even where there is no clear victor.

attorney-client privilege The right of a client to keep communications with his or her lawyer confidential and free from disclosure, either as **evidence** in a trial, or by being presented to the opposing party during discovery.

attorney-in-fact The individual named in a **power of attorney** document to act on behalf of the person (the **principal**) who signs the document; the attorney-in-fact is an agent of the principal. The responsibilities given to the attorney-in-fact depend on what is specified in the power of attorney document.

avails Amounts available to the owner of an insurance policy other than the actual proceeds of that policy. These include **dividend payments, interest,** cash, **surrender value** (i.e., proceeds from selling the policy back to the insurance company) and loan value (i.e., the amount of money that can be borrowed against the policy).

bad faith The deliberate failure to fulfill some duty or contractual obligation owed to another, such as a seller refusing to honor a guaranty.

balloon payment A lump sum due at the end of a period of time during which payments on a loan have consisted of interest payments only, with little or no principal paid off—often a mortgage or car loan. Many states prohibit balloon payments for certain sorts of goods, and may insist that the lender let someone refinance the balloon payment before forcing collection.

bankruptcy Proceedings under federal law whereby a debtor can discharge (i.e., wipe out) his or her debts or have protection from creditors while trying to repay them. Liquidation bankruptcy (Chapter 7) involves discharging debts by the surrender of assets. Reorganization bankruptcy (Chapter 13) involves providing the court with a plan for repaying the debts. Reorganization bankruptcy for businesses and for consumers with very large debts is called Chapter 11.

basis The value of a property for income and capital gains tax purposes: the value that determines profit or loss when property is sold. The basis may be what was paid for the property. For example, a house bought for $300,000 has a tax basis of $300,000. If it is later sold for $400,000, the taxable profit is $100,000. The original tax basis may be "adjusted" to reflect improvements or damage to the property during the period of ownership. Inherited property has as a basis the market value of the property when the will-maker died. Property by gift, however, has the same basis as the giver's. See **stepped-up basis**.

beneficiary A person or organization entitled to receive benefits through a legal device, such as a **will,** gift, trust or life insurance policy. Also a third party who receives the benefit of a contract between two other persons.

bequeath A term sometimes used in wills to mean "leave," as in, "I bequeath $10,000 to the West Side Cats' Home."

breach The breaking or violation of a law, contract, duty or guaranty by commission or omission.

breach of contract Failure without legal excuse to perform a promise made under a valid agreement.

brief A written statement of position prepared by each side in a lawsuit, typically setting out the facts of the case, points of law and authoritative case support for each **party's** respective position. Briefs may be submitted to a trial court (a trial brief), but they are more commonly used in the **appeal** process (an appellate brief).

case A controversy or dispute brought before a court for decision. The broad categories are: case at law, in which monetary damages are sought and in which a jury may be used in reaching a decision; and case in equity, in which some action (e.g., an injunction, a divorce) or the cessation of an action is sought, rather than monetary damages, and which is decided by a judge alone. The term also describes the evidence a party submits in support of a position.

cash surrender value The amount of money available on the voluntary termination of an insurance policy before the policy's benefits become payable (i.e., what one gets from selling a policy back to the insurance company). See avails.

certified check A check drawn by a depositor but stamped and signed by a bank official to indicate that sufficient funds are on deposit and set aside to pay the check when it is presented.

certified copy A guaranteed exact copy of an original document issued by a court or government agency. Many organizations require certified copies of legal documents before particular transactions can take place. For example, a certified birth certificate may be needed as part of a passport application, and a bank may require a certified death certificate before releasing funds to a beneficiary.

Chapter 7 bankruptcy Liquidation or straight bankruptcy, the most familiar sort, in which many or all debts are discharged (i.e., wiped out) completely in exchange for an individual's or business' nonexempt property. Proceeds are distributed to creditors. Chapter 7 refers to the relevant section of the federal Bankruptcy Code.

Chapter 13 bankruptcy Reorganization bankruptcy for individual consumers that may allow the full repayment of debts. Individuals keep their property and use their income to pay their debts (partly or fully) over 3 to 5 years, according to a plan presented to the court. The minimum amount to be paid is approximately equal to the value of the individual's non exempt property. In addition, the individual's disposable net income (minus reasonable expenses) must be used to pay debts during the period. At the end of 3 to 5 years, the outstanding balance of the debt owed is erased. Chapter 13 refers to the relevant section of the federal Bankruptcy Code.

child support The requirement that all children be supported by their parents until the children reach the age of majority (usually 18 years) or become emancipated (by marrying, joining the military or living independently). Full-time students beyond the age of majority have child support entitlements in several states. Parents living separately must each support their children. The typical arrangement is that the parent with custody fulfills his or her support obligation by having responsibility for the child on a daily basis, and the other parent makes payments to the custodial parent on behalf of the child. In a divorce, the noncustodial parent is almost always ordered to make payments to the custodial parent of child support amounts fixed by state law. If the parents are sharing physical custody, courts sometimes order the parent with the higher income to make payments to the one with the lower income.

civil case A noncriminal court action, usually a lawsuit between two parties to enforce a right or obtain redress from some wrong, often concerning property rights. Examples include actions involving breach of contract, probate, divorce and negligence. Also known as civil action or civil dispute.

cohabitation Living together as husband and wife without first getting married.

collateral Money or other property that serves as security for the guaranteed payment of a debt. The creditor has legal right to the property, if not outright physical possession. See security.

collusion Secret agreement or plan between two people to deceive another. Before the no-fault divorce, collusion was often used by spouses to fabricate grounds for divorce, such as adultery.

commingling The mixing together of community property and separate property to the extent that the properties cannot be traced back to their original status. In community property states, commingled property becomes community property.

common law marriage A marriage that takes place without a ceremony but solely because the parties live together as husband and wife for a certain amount of time, representing themselves as a married couple and intending to be legally married. The following states recognize common law marriage (sometimes only if entered into by a certain date, or for inheritance purposes only): Alabama, Colorado, District of Columbia, Georgia, Idaho, Iowa, Kansas, Montana, New Hampshire, Ohio, Oklahoma, Pennsylvania, Rhode Island, South Carolina, Texas and Utah.

community property Property owned jointly by a husband and wife. In some states, all property acquired and the responsibility for debts incurred during marriage. Generally, if community property principles are followed, all earnings during marriage and all property acquired with those earnings are considered community property, and all debts incurred during marriage are community property debts. At the death of one spouse, that spouse's half of the community property will go to the surviving spouse unless a will directs otherwise. If the couple divorces, community property and community debts are generally divided equally between the spouses. These states have community property laws: Arizona, California, Idaho, Nevada, New Mexico, Texas, Washington and Wisconsin. Compare equitable distribution and separate property.

community property with right of survivorship A community property law that allows one spouse's half-interest in community property to pass to the surviving spouse without probate: available in Arizona, California, Nevada, Texas and Wisconsin.

comparable rectitude A doctrine that grants a divorce to the spouse deemed to be less at fault when both spouses have shown grounds for divorce. It arose from a traditional common law principle that prevented a divorce when both spouses were at fault.

complaint A civil complaint is a document filed by the plaintiff with the court and served on the defendant (as a summons) to inform her or him of the facts constituting an alleged cause of action. In a divorce and in some other types of legal action (and in some states), complaints are called petitions and the person who files is called the petitioner. Having been served with the complaint, the defendant has the chance to respond by filing an answer. Pre-drafted complaints are available in form books used by lawyers.

composition of creditors Voluntary agreement of creditors with a debtor under which debts are reduced in amount and additional time may be allowed for repayment. The alternative may be bankruptcy, which usually involves greater loss for the creditors.

confidentiality Requirement that the privacy of certain relationships (e.g., lawyer-client, doctor-patient, priest-confessor, spouses) receive legal protection. Communications between these individuals cannot be disclosed in court unless the protected party waives (i.e., intentionally relinquishes) the protection. The intention that the communication be confidential is central, so that if the communication in question takes place in public in such a way that others are aware of it, it will not be considered confidential and can be admitted at a trial. Also known as privileged communication.

conservator An individual appointed by a court to oversee the affairs of someone who is incapacitated. A "conservator of the estate" is appointed to manage financial affairs. A "conservator of the person" is appointed to manage personal affairs (health care or living arrangements). The same individual may be appointed to manage all these tasks. Also known as a guardian, committee or curator.

consideration An inducement to and the basis of a contract: that which is bargained for and that which is given by one party in exchange for a promise by the other party. Consideration is often a promise to perform a certain act (e.g., paint a house) in exchange for another promise (e.g., to be paid a certain amount of money), but it can also be a promise to refrain from doing something (e.g., making an unsightly addition to a house).

consignment The turning over of goods to another for transportation or sale. Title is retained by the consignor.

Consumer Credit Counseling Service (CCCS) A national nonprofit agency that, free of charge, helps debtors plan budgets and debt repayments. Individual CCCS offices are funded mainly by voluntary donations from the creditors that receive payments from debtors who use that office to repay their debts; however, the CCCS does provide clients with useful and detailed advice.

Consumer Leasing Act A federal law stating that lease agreements must include certain terms: a listing of the number and amount of lease payments as well as a statement of penalties for late payments and any lump sums due at the end of the agreement. See balloon payment.

contingency A provision in a contract by which some or all of the terms will be altered or voided should a particular event occur. For example, in a contract to buy a house, a contingency might state that if the buyer does not approve the inspection report of the physical condition of the house, the buyer does not have to go through with the purchase.

contract A legally enforceable agreement, not contrary to any law, to do or not to do something. A contract involves two or more people or businesses; it sets forth what they will or will not do, and can be either oral or written (though real estate and larger commercial contracts must be in writing to be enforceable). A contract involves competent parties—usually adults of sound mind or business entities—agreeing to provide each other some benefit (called consideration), such as a promise to pay money in return for a promise to deliver, or the actual delivery of, particular goods or services.

co-signer A person who signs his or her name to a loan document, lease or application for credit when another person is the primary signatory. If the primary debtor does not make the agreed payments, the co-signer is fully responsible for the debt. Co-signers are often required on a person's credit card application and landlords may require a co-signer for rentals to students.

costs The expenses of the successful party in a court action ordered to be paid by the losing party. See court costs.

cotenants Two or more tenants who rent the same property under the same lease or rental agreement. Each of the cotenants is 100 percent responsible for abiding by the agreement, which includes paying the full rent and full damage charges, even if the other tenant defaults.

court calendar A list (by day, week, or month) of the cases and hearings to be held by a court. Also know as a docket, trial schedule or trial list.

court costs The fees charged by the court to cover some of the administrative costs of processing the paperwork connected with litigation. These fees include the initial filing fee; fees for serving the summons, complaint and other court papers; fees to pay a court reporter to transcribe depositions and in-court testimony; copying costs; and, in a jury trial, the stipends of the jurors. In general, court costs must be paid by both parties during the progress of the case, but the losing party will eventually be responsible for both parties' costs.

credit bureau A profit-making company that gathers information on the credit-worthiness of individuals and companies, and distributes this information to those providing credit facilities. Typical clients include banks, mortgage lenders and credit card companies that use the information to screen applicants. The major credit bureaus, Equifax, Experian and TransUnion, are regulated by the federal Fair Credit Reporting Act.

credit insurance Insurance against the risk of nonpayment of a commercial debt. Lenders often require this insurance. If the borrower dies or becomes disabled, or, in the case of a business, becomes insolvent, before paying off the loan, the policy will pay the remaining balance. Consumer protection laws require lenders to inform borrowers of the terms and costs of taking out such insurance.

credit report An individual's credit history, prepared by a credit bureau. Such a report contains not only details about how much individuals owe and to whom, and their record for on-time paying, but also personal material such as employment records, past addresses and past court appearances.

custody Of a child: Legal custody is the authority to make decisions affecting a child's interests; physical custody is the responsibility of taking care of the child. When parents separate or divorce, a decision must be made as to which parent will have custody. Generally, one parent has both legal and physical custody and the other parent has visitation rights. Sometimes both parents share legal custody and one parent has physical custody. Very infrequently, both parents share both legal and physical custody.

damages Money awarded by a court to a plaintiff for injury or loss caused by the defendant. Types of damages include compensatory damages intended to make good or replace the loss suffered; consequential damages when there is a breach of a sales contract by a seller, and a buyer suffers losses from unfulfilled requirements that the seller knew of or should have known of, when the contract was agreed; general damages, a type of compensatory damages related to nonmonetary losses, covering pain and suffering, shortened life expectancy, loss of companionship and loss of reputation (in libel and slander actions); incidental damages when there is a breach of a sales contract by a seller (the expenses incurred by the buyer to, for example, return the goods to the seller); nominal damages, an insignificant amount awarded when a defendant has violated the rights of the plaintiff, but no monetary loss has been suffered or can be proved (also known as token damages); punitive damages awarded in addition to compensatory damages to the victim of willful or malicious misconduct (also known as exemplary damages); special damages awarded to cover the winning party's out-of-pocket costs (e.g., medical expenses, loss of wages, repair fees, car rental costs if a car has been damaged); statutory damages required by statutory law; and treble damages, the actual damages determined by a judge or jury, multiplied by three—to punish the wrongdoer and to serve as an example.

default A failure to perform a legal duty, such as to keep a contractual agreement or to file an answer to a complaint. For example, one can default on a mortgage or a loan by failing to make the repayments on time or to maintain.

defined benefit plan A type of occupational pension in which the pension provision is defined (i.e., a fixed monthly amount for each year of service) and guaranteed (the employer has to make up the difference if the scheme fails to perform as well as expected). Also known as a final salary pension scheme, in which the benefit is calculated as a percentage of the final salary.

defined contribution plan A type of occupational pension that has a fixed contribution rate but does not guarantee any particular pension amount on retirement. The employer pays into the pension fund a certain amount every month or every year for each employee—usually a fixed percentage of an employee's wages or salary, though sometimes it may be a percentage of the company's profits. The plan is based on these contributions rather than on the final salary immediately before retirement. At retirement, the pension fund is used to purchase an annuity, the value of which depends on the level of contributions to the fund made on behalf of the employee, the investment returns received by the fund as a whole, and annuity rates at the time.

dependent A person who is supported by another.

deposition A statement (as transcribed by a court reporter, and now often videotaped), given under oath, usually outside of a court, for use in court. Depositions are the principal type of pretrial discovery procedure, when one party (or their attorney) questions the other party or a witness in a case. The deponent (the person making the deposition) may be represented by an attorney.

desertion The abandonment of one spouse by the other, without the abandoned spouse's consent. Desertion usually involves a spouse leaving the marital home for a specified length of time; it is grounds for divorce in states with fault divorce.

discharge In relation to debts: A court's erasure of the debts of a person or business that has filed for bankruptcy. Of a probate administrator: A court order that releases the administrator or executor from further duties in connection with the probate of an estate. This usually occurs when the duties have been fulfilled, but may also happen sooner if the individual concerned wishes to withdraw or is dismissed.

dischargeable debts Debts that can be erased via bankruptcy; this includes most debts incurred before an individual or business declares bankruptcy. Compare nondischargeable debts.

discovery The methods used under court order during the period between the filing of a lawsuit and the date of the trial to learn facts about the dispute through the exchange of information among the parties. Discovery allows parties to question each other and sometimes to question witnesses, and to insist that opposing parties produce requested documents or other physical evidence. Common types of discovery are interrogatories (written questions the other party must answer under penalty of perjury) and depositions (in-person sessions at which one party can ask oral questions of the other party or that party's witnesses under oath and on record). Parties may also be asked to confirm or deny key facts in the case. The discovery process is a way of assessing the strength or weakness of an opponent's case, and may lead to settlement talks. In discovery in criminal cases, a prosecutor must turn over to the defense any witness statements and any other evidence that might tend to exonerate the defendant.

divorce Termination of a marriage by court order; called dissolution in some states. A spouse is required to cite a legal reason for requesting a divorce when that spouse files the divorce papers with the court. Such reasons are grounds for divorce.

divorce agreement A written agreement made by a divorcing couple covering the division of property, custody and visitation rights concerning children, and alimony or child support payments. This must be signed by the parties and accepted by the court. It is used as part of the divorce decree and eliminates the need for a trial on the issues that the agreement deals with. Also known as a marital settlement agreement, marital termination agreement or settlement agreement.

durable power of attorney A power of attorney that remains in effect if the principal becomes incapacitated. If a power of attorney is not specifically made durable, it automatically expires if the principal becomes incapacitated. If it comes into effect only at incapacitation, it is called a springing power of attorney.

durable power of attorney for health care A legal document that gives someone authority to make medical decisions for a person if that person is unable to make those decisions herself or himself. The named representative is called an attorney-in-fact.

duty to disclose The responsibility of a seller to state or indicate material facts about a product being sold that the buyer could not be expected to discover from a reasonable investigation.

Electronic Fund Transfer Act A federal law that authorizes financial institutions to transfer funds through accounts without the use of paper instruments (i.e., checks or drafts). The same law grants consumers certain rights in the event that mistakes occur on their automated teller machine (ATM) or bank statements, or their ATM cards are lost or stolen. In general, the cardholder must report the mistake or lost card as soon as possible. If the bank is notified promptly, it must rectify the mistake or not charge the cardholder for withdrawals made by someone else. If a cardholder delays in reporting the card lost or stolen, he or she will be liable for some or all of the losses.

Employee Retirement Income Security Act (ERISA) A federal law regulating private pension plans that supplement Social Security. The Act sets minimum standards for such plans, provides workers some protection if a plan cannot pay the benefits to which they are entitled, and requires employers to provide full information about their employees' pension rights and to ensure that the administration of their pension funds is transparent.

estate The total of all the property of someone who has died.

estate planning The systematic analysis of the financial assets and liabilities of an individual (or married couple) to maximize the benefits from property and income during life (especially after retirement) and after death (especially by passing on property with the minimum of delay and expense). This can involve making a will, living trust, health care directive, durable power of attorney for finances or other documents.

estate taxes A tax imposed by the federal and some state governments on the giving of property to other persons or institutions after the death of the donor. All property, whatever the form of ownership, and whether or not it goes through probate after a person's death, is subject to federal estate tax. At present, federal estate tax is due only if a person's property is worth at least $1 million when that person dies. Property that is left to a surviving spouse (if he or she is a U.S. citizen) or to a tax-exempt charity is exempt from federal estate taxes. A few states also impose estate taxes, which are generally known as inheritance taxes.

exempt property In a bankruptcy proceeding, the possessions that one is allowed to keep (i.e., protect against seizure) if one loses a lawsuit to a creditor or files for Chapter 7 bankruptcy. In general, one can keep such basic items as clothing, household furnishings, a car worth $2500 or less and Social Security payments. In a few states, one can keep one's house.

Fair Credit Billing Act (FCBA) A federal law that permits users of credit cards to challenge, without penalty, the correctness of charges. The credit card company must be notified of the mistake within 60 days after the bill was mailed to the cardholder. The company must acknowledge receipt of the letter within 30 days, and must correct the error within 90 days or explain why it believes the charge on the statement was correct.

Fair Credit Reporting Act (FCRA) A federal law that allows consumers to check and correct credit information about themselves in the files of credit bureaus. These bureaus are required to adopt reasonable procedures for gathering, maintaining and disseminating information. In addition, they may not report negative information that is older than 7 years, except a bankruptcy, which may be reported for 10 years. If a credit bureau is notified of an error in a credit report, the FCRA requires the bureau to investigate the possible error within 30 days, review all information they are provided, remove inaccurate and unverified information, and take steps to keep the information from reappearing. The law also requires creditors to refrain from reporting incorrect information to credit bureaus.

fault divorce A type of divorce in which one spouse must prove that the other spouse has been legally at fault, at which point the "innocent" spouse is granted a divorce from the at-fault spouse. Most states still allow a spouse to claim fault in a divorce case. The most common fault grounds are adultery, cruelty, desertion, confinement in prison, physical incapacity and incurable insanity, which are collectively referred to as marital misconduct.

FCBA see Fair Credit Billing Act.

FCRA see Fair Credit Reporting Act.

FDIC see Federal Deposit Insurance Corporation.

Federal Deposit Insurance Corporation (FDIC) A body organized by the federal government to ensure the repayment of deposits in member banks that fail.

filing fee A fee charged by a public official to accept a document (e.g., a court plea, a deed) for administering.

foreclosure The forced sale of real estate to raise money to satisfy the creditor's claim for the unpaid balance of a loan that is in default. The shutting out of a person who has taken out a mortgage from the mortgaged property.

forum shopping The process by which a plaintiff chooses among two or more courts.

401(k) plan A savings plan with deferred compensation in which employees invest part of their wages (sometimes with employers also contributing) as a way of saving on taxes. The contributions are invested, usually as the employee chooses, in various instruments, including savings accounts, money market funds, stocks, bonds and mutual funds. Income taxes on the investments are not due in the year earned but when the employee withdraws money from the fund, usually at retirement when his or her tax liability will be lower. This plan, and others, is described in section 401 of the Tax Code.

fraud Deliberate misrepresentation made knowingly to mislead another and causing that person to suffer a loss. Also known as deceit.

garnishment A legal proceeding in which a creditor (or other plaintiff) gets a court order compelling a third party (i.e., the employer of a debtor or other defendant) to pay money earned by the defendant to the plaintiff. Up to a quarter of a debtor's wages can be deducted in this way. Garnishment is an example of attachment.

general power of attorney See power of attorney.

good faith *(Latin: bona fide)* A general obligation imposed by the Uniform Commercial Code on both buyers and sellers to practice honesty in conduct and in making contracts.

grounds for divorce The legal reasons for seeking a divorce. A spouse who files for divorce must declare the grounds, the court, and whether she or he is seeking a fault divorce or a no-fault divorce.

group life or group health insurance A single policy (usually term insurance) that covers all members of a designated group, such as employees of a company and their dependents.

guarantor One who makes a legally binding secondary promise to pay the debts of another or to perform another person's duty if that person fails to perform it. See guaranty.

guaranty As a verb, to promise to pay another person's debt or to fulfill their obligation should they fail to do so. As a noun, the written document stating these promises. For example, the co-signer of a loan has made a guaranty and will be legally responsible for the debt if the borrower fails to repay the money as promised. Also known as a guarantee or warranty. See guarantor.

guardian A person who has legal custody and control of another who is judged to be incapable of taking care of her or himself, such as a minor or incapacitated person. A "guardian of the estate" looks after a child's property. A "guardian of the person" is authorized to make personal decisions for the child concerning the child's physical, medical and educational needs. Someone appointed by a court to look after an incapacitated adult may also be known as a guardian, but is more frequently called a conservator.

head of household A person who supports and maintains, in a single household, one or more people who are closely related to her or him by blood, marriage or adoption. Heads of household receive favorable tax treatment only if they are unmarried and maintain a household that is the main home of dependent children or other relatives (e.g., a single woman supporting her children or a single man supporting his mother). Many states also consider a single person supporting only her or himself to be a head of household. In bankruptcy laws, the term householder is used.

hearing A formal legal proceeding in which issues are tried before a judge, although a hearing is not a full-scale trial. In a hearing, evidence and arguments are presented in an effort to resolve a disputed factual or legal issue. Hearings often take place before a trial when a party has asked the judge to decide, at least on an interim basis, a particular issue, such as awarding temporary child custody or child support.

holographic will A will that has been entirely handwritten, dated and signed by the will-maker him or herself. Such wills are normally not witnessed, and although they are legal in many states, making a holographic will is not recommended.

incapacity Legal, physical or mental inability to do something. Minority is an example of incapacity to make a contract; mental illness is an example of incapacity to understand one's actions and therefore to make a will.

incompatibility A personality conflict rendering a married couple's life together impossible. Incompatibility is a generally accepted grounds for a no-fault divorce. Compare irreconcilable differences; irremediable breakdown.

Individual Retirement Account (IRA) Private pension plan authorized by the federal government that supplements Social Security, under which qualified employees contribute a percentage of their income, tax-free, to a retirement account until their retirement. The money is then normally distributed in installments, beginning by April 1 after the year the employee reaches the age of 70 years and 6 months, when it is subject to personal income tax.

inherit To receive property from someone who has died. The traditional meaning applied only to property received from a relative who died without a will (intestate). Now the word is used in all cases in which someone receives property from the estate of a deceased person.

injunction A court order forbidding an action that is considered injurious, unlike most court decisions, which are intended to remedy harms that have already occurred. Injunctions are often orders that certain actions be stopped (e.g., ordering an abusive husband to stay away from his wife). Temporary injunctions (interlocutory decrees or preliminary injunctions) can be made on an interim basis, with a view that a future trial will consider and resolve the issues. Most injunctions order that something not be done; "mandatory injunctions" order a positive act (e.g., returning stolen property).

injunctive relief The granting of an injunction telling a party to stop doing something or to perform a particular action. Injunctive relief is usually granted after a court hearing at which testimony has been presented.

intangible property Personal property recognized by law even though it has no physical existence, such as stocks, bonds, debts, warranty rights, bank notes, easements, business goodwill, trade secrets and copyrights. Compare tangible property.

integrated pension plan A pension plan that is integrated with Social Security retirement benefits. The retiree's pension benefit is reduced by all, or some percentage of, his or her Social Security payments. The current law requires that the plan leave at least half of the pension amount.

interest A commission paid by borrowers to creditors for use of money belonging to the latter. An interest rate is the annual percentage that is added to the borrower's balance. If interest is compounded daily, the balance on an annual rate of seven percent will rise by 1/365th of seven percent each day; if compounded monthly, the balance will rise 1/12th of seven percent on the first day of each month.

intestate succession The statutory method (according to state law) for distributing inure. To take effect or to benefit. In property law, the term means to vest: to have rights or a vested interest in.

inventory A complete listing of all property owned by a deceased person at the time of death; this is filed with the court during probate. The estate's executor or administrator is responsible for making the inventory and seeing that it is properly filed.

IRA See Individual Retirement Account.

joint custody Responsibility taken on by both parents after a divorce, annulment or separation to share the upbringing of a child. The arrangement can be joint legal custody (in which both parents have a say in decisions affecting the child) or, less frequently, joint physical custody (in which the child spends a significant amount of time with both parents), but rarely both.

joint tenancy A method of co-ownership of property by two or more persons. Upon the death of any co-owner, his or her percentage interest goes to the surviving joint tenant(s) regardless of the decedent's will. This right of survivorship is the defining aspect of ownership by joint tenancy, and means that no probate is necessary.

judgment The final ruling by a court in a proceeding, determining the rights and obligations of the opposing parties.

jurisdiction The right of a court to exercise its power over a particular person ("personal jurisdiction") or type of case ("subject matter jurisdiction"). Also the geographic area in which a court has authority and the types of cases it can hear. State and federal courts have different subject matter jurisdictions, and no court can hear a case unless the parties agree to be there or have contacts that make it fair for them to answer to that court. Jurisdiction also defines the amount of money a court has the power to award. For example, small claims courts have jurisdiction to hear cases only up to a relatively low monetary amount—depending on the state, usually less than $10,000.

legal papers Documents (e.g., wills, deeds, leases, titles, birth certificates, contracts) that state or demonstrate legal status, identity, authority, ownership rights or obligations. Also documents (e.g., a complaint or summons) used in pursuit of a legal action.

liability A legal responsibility for an act, an omission, an obligation or a debt.

liability insurance coverage An insurance policy that covers the cost of paying compensation and court costs if negligence or other fault by the policyholder results in injury to someone or damage to property. Liability policies may cover damage caused by the policyholder in a car, at home, or in the course of business. Sometimes called third-party policies.

lien A legal claim by a creditor against property arising from some obligation of the property owner, usually a debt. Security interests are liens that an individual agrees to, such as mortgages, home and car loans, and personal loans for which property is pledged to guarantee repayment. Nonconsensual liens are made without a person's consent and include judgment liens (from a creditor who has sued and obtained a judgment), tax liens, and mechanic's liens (from an unpaid contractor or worker).

life beneficiary Someone who receives benefits, under a trust or by a will, for his or her lifetime.

life insurance An insurance policy for which the policyholder (i.e., the person whose life is insured) pays a premium, and when the policyholder dies, payment is made to the beneficiary (usually family members or business partners). Insurance proceeds are not subject to probate, though they are liable for federal estate taxes. Life insurance comes in several forms, with varying degrees of benefits, premiums, investment risks and tax implications.

litigation A lawsuit. Litigating is the process of pursuing a lawsuit.

loan consolidation Combining a number of loans into a single new loan. Doing this extends the repayment period and reduces the monthly payments, but significantly increases the amount of interest paid over the life of the loan.

loan value The sum that can be borrowed against an ordinary life insurance policy, up to the full cash surrender value.

Mail or Telephone Order Rule A Federal Trade Commission rule requiring a seller to ship goods ordered by mail, telephone, computer or fax to the buyer within the time promised or, if no time has been stated, within 30 days. If the seller cannot ship within that period, the seller must send the buyer notification of a new shipping date and give the buyer the option of canceling the order and getting a refund.

marital property The property, with some exceptions, accumulated by spouses during their marriage; in some states called community property. Some states include all property and earnings during the marriage, whereas others exclude gifts and inheritances.

Marital Settlement Agreement See divorce agreement.

Marital Termination Agreement See divorce agreement.

market value The price a house or other property would bring if offered for sale in a fair market (not at auction or in a forced sale) without either buyer or seller being under compulsion. Also known as fair market value.

marriage The legal union of a couple. The laws of the state in which the couple lives determine their specific rights and responsibilities toward one another concerning property and support. Marriages are terminated only when a court grants a divorce, dissolution or annulment. No state yet recognizes same-sex marriages, and some states have passed laws specifically barring them. Compare common law marriage.

med-arb A method of alternative dispute resolution (ADR) that combines mediation and arbitration. A neutral party is appointed to mediate the dispute. If that is unsuccessful, the neutral party is authorized to resolve the dispute by binding arbitration.

mediation The use of a neutral third party (the mediator) to assist in the resolution of disputes, without going to court. The mediator has no power to impose a solution and so differs from a judge or someone conducting binding arbitration. There are no formal rules of evidence in mediation. See alternative dispute resolution.

mediator See mediation.

Medicaid A program partly financed by the federal government and administered by the states that is designed for those who are unable to pay for regular medical services, especially those that Medicare does not cover. Financial need is defined by the Medicaid program of the state where the applicant lives.

Medicare A federal program that helps older and some disabled people in paying their medical costs. The program is divided into two parts. Part A is hospital insurance: this covers most of the costs of a hospital stay and some follow-up costs. Part B is medical insurance: this pays some of the cost of doctors and outpatient medical care.

minor A person younger than the age of legal competence; for most purposes and in most states, this is any person younger than 18 years of age. Minors must be under the care of an adult (parent or guardian) unless they have undergone emancipation (by joining the military, getting married or living independently with court permission). Property left to a minor must be handled by an adult guardian of the estate until the minor becomes an adult (a major) under the relevant state laws.

misrepresentation A false statement made intentionally, knowing it is not true, or a failure to disclose crucial information, with the intent to deceive. A misrepresentation before marriage (e.g., failing to mention that one is incapable of having children) can provide grounds for an annulment.

mortgage A contract in which a borrower puts up the title to real estate as security (collateral) for a loan, often borrowed to purchase the property serving as collateral. If the borrower fails to repay the debt as promised, the lender can foreclose on the real estate and force its sale as a way of paying off the loan.

net estate The value of all property owned at death (the gross estate) minus liabilities or debts.

net worth The difference between the total assets and the total liabilities of a person or organization (if liabilities exceed assets, the difference is a "deficit").

no-fault divorce A divorce granted by a court without either spouse having to prove fault in the other. Until this form of divorce became accepted in the 1970s, divorces were granted only to an "innocent" spouse, who had to prove that the other spouse was guilty of some misconduct, such as adultery, cruelty or desertion. Grounds for a no-fault divorce include incompatibility, irreconcilable differences, irretrievable or irremediable breakdown of the marriage, and, in some states, incurable insanity. Compare fault divorce.

nondischargeable debts Debts that are not erased by filing for bankruptcy. In Chapter 7 bankruptcy, such debts will remain when the case is over; in Chapter 13 bankruptcy, such debts will have to be paid in full as part of the payment plan or remain as a balance at the end of the case. Nondischargeable debts include alimony and child support, most income tax debts, many student loans, and debts for personal injury. Compare dischargeable debts.

nonexempt property Property that is at risk of being lost to creditors when a person files for Chapter 7 bankruptcy or when a creditor sues and wins a judgment against a debtor. Such property includes valuable clothing (furs) and electronic equipment, an expensive car that has been paid for, and most of the equity in the debtor's house. Compare exempt property.

notarized Signed in the presence of a person licensed by a state to perform identification services, such as a notary public. Most real estate documents (e.g., deeds, deeds of trust, mortgages, and easements) must be notarized, as must other legal documents (e.g., powers of attorney).

Older Workers Benefit Protection Act A federal law making it illegal for an employer to use an employee's age as the basis for discrimination in benefits or to target older workers for layoffs. The law also requires employers to give employees at least 21 days to consider waivers not to sue offered by an employer in return for early retirement benefits.

ordinance A written law enacted by a city or county, such as a zoning ordinance governing the use of land, or noise and garbage removal regulations. Such laws may not conflict with state or federal laws.

palimony A nonlegal term for the division of property or alimony-like support given works assisting lawyers and under their supervision. Independent paralegals work directly with the public—not for lawyers—assisting their customers by providing forms, helping people fill them out, and filing them with the proper authority.

party A person of a particular class, occupation, or relation (i.e., child, creditor or heir), or a person whose participation is either directly or indirectly necessary in a legal action before a court. Often the plaintiff or petitioner who files a lawsuit, or the defendant or respondent who defends against one. Also the signatory to a contract.

payee A person designated on a negotiable instrument as the person to whom payment is to be made, and in whose favor a check, draft or promissory note is drawn.

payor A person who makes a payment or who is designated on a negotiable instrument as the person by whom payment is to be made.

PBGC See Pension Benefit Guaranty Corporation.

pension A regular payment, made weekly, monthly or annually, after an employee retires from full-time employment, generally for the rest of the pensioner's life. Nongovernmental pensions come from an employee retirement fund paid for or contributed to by the employer as part of the employee's compensation.

Pension Benefit Guaranty Corporation (PBGC) A public nonprofit insurance fund created under the Employee Retirement Security Act to assure the financial soundness of specified private pension plans. The PBGC offers some limited coverage against bankrupt pension funds. In addition, should a pension fund be unable to pay all its obligations to its retirees, the PBGC may pay some of them.

perjury Willful lying under oath.

personal property All property that is not real estate (i.e., all property other than land and the fixtures permanently attached to it). Cars, bank accounts, wages, a small business, furniture, insurance policies, jewelry and patents are examples of personal property. Also known as personal effects, movable property, goods and chattels, and personalty.

plaintiff A person, corporation or other legal entity that brings a suit or complaint against another. In some states and for some types of lawsuits, the term petitioner is used.

power of attorney A document authorizing another person to act as one's agent. The person creating such a document is known as the principal and the person who is given the authority is called the attorney-in-fact. A "general" power of attorney gives the attorney-in-fact considerable powers over the principal's affairs (basically to do all acts not prohibited by law). A "limited" or "special" power of attorney gives the attorney-in-fact permission to handle a specific task or situation. A durable power of attorney remains in effect even if the principal becomes incapacitated. See durable power of attorney; durable power of attorney for health care.

premarital agreement An agreement between a couple before marriage that generally concerns property and support rights, personal rights and responsibilities, and custody and support obligations to any children born of the marriage. Courts usually uphold premarital agreements unless one party demonstrates that the agreement was likely to promote divorce or was entered into unfairly. Also known as an antenuptial or prenuptial agreement.

prenuptial agreement See premarital agreement.

principal A person who is responsible for the acts done for his or her benefit by another person appointed by him or her (an agent), or a person who creates a power of attorney or other legal document that appoints an attorney-in-fact. Another meaning of principal, in the law of trusts, is the property of the trust itself, as opposed to the income generated by it. This is also known as the trust corpus (Latin: body).

promissory note A negotiable instrument through which one person promises to pay money to another on demand or at a specified time in the future; it may contain terms of the loan, such as repayment schedule and interest rate. To be negotiable, it must comply with the Uniform Commercial Code.

real estate Land and the structures or fixtures permanently attached to it, including buildings, houses, stationary mobile homes, fences and trees. Also known as real property or realty.

receivership The placing of property into the hands of a court-appointed custodian (receiver) to ensure that it is managed properly.

recording Filing a copy of a **deed** or other document pertaining to **real estate** with the appropriate records office of the county in which the land is located. Recording creates a historical record, available to the public, of changes in ownership of all property in the county.

recovery The amount that a plaintiff is awarded on winning a lawsuit. See damages.

remainder An interest in property that takes effect only on the expiration of the interest previously in effect; a remainderman has a remainder interest.

replevin A type of legal action giving the right to the owner to recover property unlawfully taken or retained. Commonly used in **disputes** between buyers and sellers when the buyer has failed to pay for goods.

repossession A seller of goods (as creditor) taking them back because the buyer has breached the contract, usually by failing to make one or more payments on time, and has not attempted to work with the creditor to resolve the problem.

respondent The person against whom an action is taken; the party who is sued and must respond. In some states, the term is used instead of **defendant** or appellee (i.e., person against whom an appeal is filed), especially in **divorce** and other family law **cases**.

retainer A sum paid to a lawyer in advance as a down payment on an hourly or per-job fee. The lawyer in exchange agrees to be available to represent the client.

retirement benefits Under the Social Security system, a sum of money available to a person who has reached the age of 62 years; the money is equivalent to a small percentage of the total earnings during the person's working life. These benefits increase on an annual cost-of-living basis, and the amount of the benefit is higher if the person waits longer to claim it, up to the age of 70 years.

right of survivorship The right of a surviving joint tenant to take ownership of a deceased joint tenant's share of the property. A will is not required to transfer the property and probate is unnecessary. See **joint tenancy**.

ruling Any decision made by a judge during the course of a lawsuit or trial.

sale on approval Conditional sale in which the buyer gets possession and the right to use goods before deciding to buy.

secured loan Money borrowed in exchange for a pledge by the borrower of specific property (known as collateral or security) that may be forfeited if repayment is not made as promised. The pledge gives the creditor a lien, allowing the creditor to pursue **foreclosure** or **repossession** of the property identified by the lien if the borrower defaults. Compare unsecured loan.

security Collateral for a loan that is available to the creditor should the debtor default. In a home loan, or mortgage, the home itself is the security for the repayment.

separate property Property (whether real estate or personal property) owned entirely by one spouse in a marriage, that either was brought by the spouse into the marriage at the outset or was acquired by the spouse during the marriage through gift or inheritance, together with the profits directly attributable to the property (e.g., funds from the sale of an item of separate property, such as jewelry). The concept is relevant only in states that recognize community property. At **divorce**, separate property is retained by the spouse who owns it and is not subject to the state's property division laws.

settle To reach an agreement about the disposition of a pending suit or other claim without going to court.

small-claims court A state court that has jurisdiction over civil cases that do not exceed a certain sum (almost always less than $10,000) and provides a brief and inexpensive proceeding. Adversaries usually represent themselves (in some states, lawyers may not be used). The rules of evidence that apply in regular trials are not followed. Judgments have the same force as do those of other courts, so that judgments that are not paid voluntarily can be collected by **liens** and other means of enforcement.

Social Security A number of related government programs that provide benefits to retired or disabled workers and to the dependents or surviving family members of workers. The benefits are based on the average wage, salary or self-employment income (in work covered by Social Security) of the individual worker concerned. Social Security aims to provide workers and their families with some monthly income when their normal flow of income shrinks because of the retirement, disability or death of the earner. See survivors benefits.

solvent Being able to pay one's debts as they come due.

spousal support See alimony.

statute of limitations The legally prescribed time limit in which a lawsuit must be filed. Such statutes differ by state and by type of legal claim. Statute of limitations rules apply to cases filed in all courts, including federal court.

stepped-up basis A value that is used to determine profit or loss when property is sold. If a person inherits property that increased in value after the deceased person first acquired it, the tax basis of the new owner is "stepped-up" to the market value of the property at the time of death. Thus, when the new owner eventually sells the property, there will be less taxable gain.

subpoena (modern spelling: subpena) An order directing a person to appear at a certain time and place (usually a court) to give testimony as a witness.

substitution of parties A replacement of one of the sides in a lawsuit because the original party can no longer continue with the trial (e.g., because he or she has become ill or died).

summons In a civil suit, an official notification, issued by a court at the request of a plaintiff to a defendant, notifying of the complaint against him or her and ordering him or her to file a response with the court within a given period or to appear in court at a specified time. The actual presentation of the summons is known as "service of process" and the person who presents it is a "process server."

surrender value The sum a life insurance company refunds if an ordinary policy is canceled (i.e., sold back to the insurance company). See avails.

surviving spouse A widow or widower.

surviving spouse's trust Under an AB trust, after the death of the first spouse, this is the revocable living trust of the surviving spouse.

survivors benefits The money available to the surviving spouse and minors or disabled children of a deceased worker who qualified for Social Security retirement benefits or disability benefits.

tangible personal property Personal property that can be felt or touched, including furniture, cars, jewelry and works of art. Cash and bank accounts are not tangible personal property. Compare intangible property.

tenancy in common A form of co-ownership of property by two or more persons. Upon the death of any co-owner, his or her percentage interest passes not to the other owners but, by intestate succession or by will, to the co-owner's chosen beneficiary. Unlike joint tenancy, there is no right of survivorship by co-owners. Also unlike joint tenancy, the ownership shares need not be equal. In most states, each tenant in common may encumber only his or her share of the property, so that the other share is debt-free. In some states, two people are presumed to own property as tenants in common unless there is a written agreement stating otherwise.

testify To give oral evidence under oath at a trial or deposition.

title Evidence of the ownership of real estate or other property.

UI See unemployment insurance.

unemployment insurance (UI) A joint federal and state program that provides monetary benefits for a specified time (usually 26 weeks) after a worker has been laid off from a job. The amount of the unemployment check will be less than the worker's former pay. UI covers employees who worked at least six months during the year before they lost the job and who earned the minimum amount stipulated by the program. Also known as unemployment compensation.

unjust enrichment Improper or unfair gain (of property or money), which the recipient is required to return to the rightful owner, even if the property was not obtained illegally.

unsecured loan Money borrowed on the general credit of the borrower with no pledge of specific assets that may be forfeited to the creditor if repayment is not made as promised. The only remedy available to a creditor is to sue and get a judgment. Compare secured loan.

waiver An intentional relinquishment of a right or privilege.

with prejudice A binding decision by a judge on a legal matter. This means that the same matter cannot be pursued again in any court.

witness A person who testifies under oath at a deposition or trial as to what she or he has observed, providing firsthand or expert evidence. Also a person who has observed a transaction or watches another person sign a document and then adds her or his name to confirm ("attest") that the signature is genuine.

workout A plan devised by a debtor to pay off a debt or to have a loan forgiven. Such plans are ways to avoid bankruptcy or foreclosures.

Index

2-year rule 69
240-day rule 69
3-year rule 69
341 meeting 78, 85
8-year rule 70

A

absolute discharge 139, 203
accumulated debt 11
add a consumer statement 156, 159
advance fee loans 224
alimony payments 30, 120
allocating exemptions 47
amendment cover sheet 91
application and order to pay filing fee in
        installments 82, 114
automatic stay 23, 25, 26, 27, 28, 29, 30,
        31, 68, 70, 78, 82, 89, 94, 110, 113,
        125, 133, 135, 136, 137, 141

B

bankrate.com 168
bankruptcy 3, 4, 5, 6, 7, 9, 10, 11, 12, 13,
        15, 16, 17, 18, 19, 25, 26, 27, 28, 29,
        30, 31, 33, 34, 35, 36, 37, 39, 40, 42,
        43, 44, 45, 46, 48, 49, 50, 53, 54, 55,
        56, 59, 60, 61, 62, 63, 64, 65, 67, 68,
        69, 70, 71, 72, 73, 77, 78, 79, 80, 81,
        82, 83, 84, 85, 86, 87, 88, 89, 90, 91,
        93, 94, 95, 96, 97, 98, 101, 103, 105,
        106, 108, 109, 110, 111, 112, 113,
        114, 115, 116, 117, 118, 121, 123,
        124, 125, 126, 128, 129, 130, 133,
        134, 135, 136, 137, 138, 139, 140,
        141, 142, 143, 144, 145, 147, 152,
        153, 154, 155, 156, 157, 158, 160,
        165, 166, 167, 168, 171, 172, 173,
        175, 176, 196, 202, 203, 206, 208,
        211, 212, 225, 233, 234, 235, 236,
        237, 239, 240, 241, 244, 248
bankruptcy act 175
bankruptcy discharge 18, 69, 70, 81, 111
bankruptcy estate 23, 33, 34, 35, 36, 37,
        39, 53, 59, 61, 64, 78, 90, 97, 101,
        134
bankruptcy petition 10, 45, 82, 113
bankruptcy petition preparer 82, 113
bankruptcy sale 64, 65
bankruptcy trustee 35, 36, 39, 43, 44, 49,
        61, 62, 63, 64, 65, 79, 84, 88, 94, 96,
        97, 111, 117, 125, 129, 134, 135,
        141, 143
bank setoff 20
BIA 13, 68, 94, 139
BPP 82, 113, 114
budget analysis 171
bureau of labor statistics 176

C

Canada 4, 10, 11, 13, 33, 37, 40, 50, 58,
        64, 65, 67, 68, 69, 71, 73, 77, 78, 79,
        80, 93, 94, 109, 110, 133, 134, 137,
        143, 144, 149, 153, 171
Canadian association of insolvency and
        restructuring professionals 135
Canadian bankruptcy and insolvency act

N-O

P-Q

R

S

T

tax attributes 35
tax debt 69, 98, 121
tax lien 121
tax refunds 19, 30, 35, 87, 227
third parties 20, 215, 233
title 11 10, 67
transaction fees 183
trustee 27, 33, 35, 36, 39, 43, 44, 49, 61,
     62, 63, 64, 65, 69, 78, 79, 80, 84,
     85, 86, 87, 88, 89, 94, 96, 97, 104,
     110, 111, 114, 117, 118, 119, 120,
     124, 125, 126, 127, 129, 134, 135,
     136, 137, 138, 139, 141, 143
trust fund 35
truth in lending law 58

U-V-W

U.S. census 68
U.S. department of housing 55
unencumbered equity 60
unlimited homestead exemption 43, 60
unsecured credit card 168, 185, 187
voluntary petition 80, 82, 112, 113
wage garnishing 143, 144
white goods 17
willful evasion 69

SOCRATES
KNOW HOW TO DO MORE AND SAVE

BANKRUPTCY:
An Action Plan for Renewal

SPECIAL OFFER FOR BOOK BUYERS—
SAVE 15% ON THESE ESSENTIAL PRODUCTS AT
Socrates.com/books/bankruptcy-renewal.aspx

Socrates.com offers essential business, personal and real estate do-it-yourself products that can help you:

- Sell or lease a property
- Write a will or trust
- Start a business
- Get a divorce

- Hire a contractor
- Manage employees
- And much more

Bankruptcy Kit (K300)
NEWLY UPDATED WITH OCTOBER 2005 LAW CHANGES.
INCLUDES INSTRUCTION MANUAL AND 28 FORMS.

Obtain relief from debt and save on costly legal fees by preparing in advance for your bankruptcy proceedings. This comprehensive kit contains the legal forms and know-how you need to do it yourself.

Credit Repair Kit (K303)
INCLUDES INSTRUCTION MANUAL AND 14 TEMPLATE LETTERS.

Take control and turn your credit around with this easy-to-use kit. It provides all you need to determine your credit status and repair your credit rating without incurring costly legal fees.

Buying/Selling Your Home Kit (K311)
INCLUDES INSTRUCTION MANUAL AND 31 FORMS.

Ensure the process of buying or selling a home goes smoothly from beginning to end with the help of this kit's comprehensive information—on everything from financing to classifieds to open houses.

Last Will & Testament Kit (K307)

INCLUDES INSTRUCTION MANUAL AND 17 FORMS.

Protect your loved ones, make your wishes known and award your assets as you desire. Contains the forms and instructions you need to plan your estate responsibly and affordably.

Living Will & Power of Attorney for Health Care Kit (K306)

INCLUDES INSTRUCTION MANUAL AND 14 FORMS.

Express your choice of when to discontinue treatment and life support and who should make that decision for you if you're permanently incapacitated. Free state-specific forms at Socrates.com.

Divorce Kit (K302)

INCLUDES INSTRUCTION MANUAL AND 13 FORMS.

Save time and costly legal fees by preparing yourself for a simple, uncontested divorce. This convenient Divorce Kit helps you and your partner come to an agreement early in the process.